T0155539

Firmware Development

A Guide to Specialized Systemic Knowledge

Subrata Banik
Vincent Zimmer

Apress®

Firmware Development: A Guide to Specialized Systemic Knowledge

Subrata Banik
Bangalore, Karnataka, India

Vincent Zimmer
Issaquah, WA, USA

ISBN-13 (pbk): 978-1-4842-7973-1
https://doi.org/10.1007/978-1-4842-7974-8

ISBN-13 (electronic): 978-1-4842-7974-8

Managing Director, Apress Media LLC: Welmoed Spahr
Acquisitions Editor: Susan McDermott
Development Editor: Laura Berendson
Coordinating Editor: Jessica Vakili
Copyeditor: Kim Wimpsett

Distributed to the book trade worldwide by Springer Science+Business Media New York, 1 NY Plaza, New York, NY 10004. Phone 1-800-SPRINGER, fax (201) 348-4505, e-mail orders-ny@ springer-sbm.com, or visit www.springeronline.com. Apress Media, LLC is a California LLC and the sole member (owner) is Springer Science + Business Media Finance Inc (SSBM Finance Inc). SSBM Finance Inc is a **Delaware** corporation.

For information on translations, please e-mail booktranslations@springernature.com; for reprint, paperback, or audio rights, please e-mail bookpermissions@springernature.com.

Apress titles may be purchased in bulk for academic, corporate, or promotional use. eBook versions and licenses are also available for most titles. For more information, reference our Print and eBook Bulk Sales web page at http://www.apress.com/bulk-sales.

Any source code or other supplementary material referenced by the author in this book is available to readers on the Github repository: https://github.com/Apress/Firmware-Development. For more detailed information, please visit http://www.apress.com/source-code.

Printed on acid-free paper

Table of Contents

About the Authors

Subrata Banik is a firmware engineer with more than a decade of experience in the computer industry, with hands-on experience in system firmware design, development, and debugging across various firmware architectures like UEFI, coreboot, Slim bootloader, etc., for the x86 and ARM platforms. Subrata has extensive experience on platform enablement, which led to working for all the leading PC makers' products. Subrata is an active member of open source firmware (OSF) development across different projects like coreboot, oreboot, flashrom, EDKII, etc., where he is one of the leading contributors in open firmware (coreboot) development. Subrata holds multiple U.S. patents and is passionate about learning new technology and sharing knowledge with enthusiast engineers. Subrata has presented his technical talks at industry events such as the Open Source Firmware Conference, Institute for Security and Technology, Intel Developer Forum, and more.

When not writing or working, he enjoys watching sports (especially football) and spending time with his daughter. A fun fact about Subrata is that he is a strong believer in the existence of time travel.

You can chat with Subrata on Twitter (@abarjodi) or at https://www.linkedin.com/in/subrata-banik-268b3317/.

ABOUT THE AUTHORS

Vincent Zimmer has been working on embedded firmware for the last 30 years. Vincent has contributed to or created firmware spanning various firmware initiatives, including the Extensible Firmware Interface, where Vincent presently leads the Security subteam in the UEFI Forum. Vincent has also co-authored various papers and books, along with being a named co-inventor on more than 450 U.S. patents.

About the Technical Reviewer

 **Ron Minnich** is a software engineer at Google. He has been writing firmware for 40 years, starting with the z80 and 6800. He's also a long-time contributor in the Unix, BSD, Plan 9, and Linux communities. He started the LinuxBIOS project in 1999, which was renamed to coreboot in 2008 and is now used in tens of millions of Chromebooks. His most recent effort, LinuxBoot, is now part of the Linux Foundation and aims to bring the benefits of a full Linux kernel to several firmware environments, including coreboot, u-boot, and UEFI.

About the Foreword Author

 **Christian Walter** is a firmware engineer who started working with open source firmware five years ago. Christian is passionate about open source and is heavily involved in various open source firmware projects like coreboot, LinuxBoot, and EDKII for different architectures.

Christian is the cofounder of the Open Source Firmware Foundation and is actively involved in defining specifications around open source firmware. He is part of 9elements, which is one of the main contributors within the open source firmware ecosystem driving the community into an open world.

Christian has been involved in multiple technical talks around open source firmware and its development model for the industry, and he has held multiple talks around testing and building an ecosystem for open source firmware.

You can connect with him on Twitter (@nablahero).

Foreword by Christian Walter

Nowadays, firmware is one of the most critical parts within every device and every security concept. Typically, x86 firmware is hidden from the user, and little to no interaction is needed. Firmware has been closed source for the last 20 years. Whereas there are some exceptions to the general rule, the core parts of firmware are and will most likely remain closed source in the near future. From an outside perspective, this is not logical. Today, most of the software stack running on x86 platforms can be open sourced, beginning from the bootloader through the operating system up to the application level. Large hyperscalers make open source a requirement for some parts, and consumers love the freedom that open source software provides to them. Firmware is the last bastion that has not fallen. However, in recent years, the open source firmware community has leaped forward; thus, the industry is changing. Hyperscalers adopt open source firmware as the de facto firmware standard, and customers can buy open source firmware-enabled products off the shelf.

The idea of open source is not to open up the existing code base. It is rather about giving the community the ability to develop and maintain the code themselves. Two things are needed to reach this goal: sharing knowledge and providing the technical documentation. Obviously, both influence each other. Technical documentation is something that hardware vendors, OEMs, and ODMs can provide and are responsible for. This documentation enables developers to write the actual code and thus produce and maintain open source firmware. It is impossible, or at least extremely complicated, to write proper firmware code without technical documentation. Technical documentation is not about opening up the intellectual property but rather providing a path to bring up and configure the hardware components.

In addition, the community needs knowledge and experienced people who share this knowledge. Sharing knowledge enables others to become firmware developers, to understand the concepts, and ultimately to grow the community. Firmware and its development are among the most complex software systems a developer can dive into. Even though most of the components themselves are not complicated, the interaction between them makes it complex. Keeping this technical documentation closed source makes the components (unnecessarily) complicated.

This book shares some of the missing pieces in system firmware development and guides the reader through various topics. We are engineers who are passionate about open source and driving this effort forward.

Preface

Firmware is the first piece of code that runs on the target hardware after the end user has turned on a device. Depending on the types of target hardware, the operations being performed by the firmware may differ, but the fundamental operations of firmware remain the same across the target hardware: performing the bare minimal hardware initialization and either waiting for host-centric communication to initiate or handing off control to the high-level system software that allows the end-user interaction. Based on the target market segment, an OS can have multiple virtual machines, and/or various types of applications are installed that satisfy the end-user needs. Although the control goes to the OS, an instance of the firmware is still alive and available to manage a few critical tasks that for OS-based applications or drivers cannot perform.

Over time, CPU architectures have gotten more complicated, and platform requirements have evolved. This has pushed the firmware boundary and caused firmware to extend its services too.

Back in the 1950s, the only possible way to instruct a computer system to perform some operation was using *assembly language*. The processors were simple enough, and hence the expectations from the firmware were also minimal. Porting to different kinds of CPUs involved redundant effort. In the 1970s, with the evolution of microprocessors, which demanded the enhancement of firmware features, all firmware development started migrating to the low-level system programming language C. Later C became the *de facto* standard for firmware development as it's easily ported from one generation to the next. Since then, a different flavor of a C-based proprietary technology or framework evolved that made the hardware programming easier and created an abstraction such that it's easy for programmers to contribute to the system programming without a deep understanding of the hardware. When technology evolves in an enclosed environment like this, it actually limits the spread of specialized knowledge and positively affects the entire ecosystem.

In the 2010s, access to the Internet became cheaper, and hence demands for personal computing devices were booming. With new sets of devices becoming popular, the ecosystem was changing. Statistics suggest that between 2000 and 2019 in the United States the number of Internet users tripled. Having more computing devices meant demand for advanced user experiences. For example, an instant system response refers to less device latency, trillions of data transfers in seconds requires secure systems, and more users means the backend server capacity needs to be enhanced. These are all the driving forces for the industry to look beyond the traditional system development model and demand more transparent development of the system, be it hardware, firmware, or software. With the openness in the firmware development approach, many product differentiating ideas are evolving and intercepting in firmware which are enough to challenge the existence of traditional System Firmware development approach. This demands a revamp of the firmware development model. We wrote this book to be a bridge from the present firmware development model to the future and make sure the readers are well equipped with such knowledge that makes them ready for such a migration in future.

In other words, we wrote this book for people who want to learn about the future of firmware and prepare themselves with all required knowledge to excel. This book covers the essential knowledge that is required for a firmware developer, debug engineer, testing or validation engineer or even someone is working in a project as a DevOps engineer. Chapters 2 to 4 cover the specialized systematic knowledge needed for firmware development. Chapter 6 illustrates the concepts that are relevant for future development and can be learned by analyzing end-user use-case scenarios. The concepts presented as part of this book are based on practical results, and the data illustrates why we believe those ideas will definitely merge into the product line in the future. We present a large number of examples that are aligned to system firmware development as many developers have visibility into this area compared to other firmware developments.

Acknowledgments

Understanding firmware development is key before venturing into low-level hardware-centric projects. The topic requires subject-matter experts to share their journey with new engineers. This book involved contributions from talented industry experts who we were honored to work with, and they deserve acknowledgement.

We would like to thank Kumar N. Dwarakanath for his significant contribution in preparing Chapter 5. Understanding firmware security is essential knowledge, and we know our audience will benefit from his contributions.

Subrata thanks Vincent Zimmer, Ronald G. Minnich, and Stefan Reinauer for their expertise and making this venture enjoyable and learnable. Above all, Subrata is thankful to his family, especially his wife, Barnali, and daughter, Samriddhi, who were patient with many nights and weekends consumed by this effort, and his parents, who influenced him to translate his technical curiosity into a book.

Vincent thanks Subrata for the great collaboration on this project and in other endeavors. Along with Subrata, he would also like to thank collaborators across different communities, standards groups, and his employer.

Introduction

"Learning never exhausts the mind."

—Leonardo da Vinci

The era that we are currently living in is famous for its continuous evolution; things around us are changing quite rapidly, legacy technologies are fading over time, and modern development ideas are mature enough to fill the void. The only constant in this volatile world is continuous learning. Albert Einstein said it best: "Once you stop learning, you start dying."

A study suggests that people who are actively involved in continuous learning and have passion toward learning something new are able to connect well with an industry that is migrating toward newer technology, compared with other who rely on a narrow set of skills and experiences. There are lots of materials available on the Internet that motivate people to start engaging in development activity without even paying attention to the details of the technology such as its architecture, intrinsic operations, and interfaces that are used while communicating with other components to define a complete system.

Focusing on depth while learning will help to expand the scope of learning. For example, understanding system firmware in depth will help to understand the working operational model of an operating system due to its interface with underlying firmware, realize different hardware components while initializing, and recognize the value of the compiler, toolchains, and so many other components that are an extrinsic part of firmware being operational. It also helps to level up and look beyond the traditional boundary of existing offerings to discover something that is more applicable for future needs. The value of in-depth knowledge is something that can easily be described as *the deeper the roots, the greater the fruits*. Like a gardener who nurtures a sapling and creates a tree for tomorrow, we have prepared the soil for harvesting using our previous book, *System Firmware: An Essential Guide to Open Source and Embedded Solutions*. The purpose of *Firmware Development: A Guide to Specialized Systemic Knowledge* is to cultivate on that foundation and anchor the developers' journey into the firmware world.

Firmware Development is not intended to teach any particular programming language (except for the appendix that highlights the evolution of system programming languages) or method that can be used for developing firmware. Rather, this book explains the operational model of different technologies or frameworks being used for developing various types of firmware. Firmware is an essential entity that is used to bring all forms of hardware to life. Additionally, the book will prepare its readers to be ready for a future of possible architecture migration and understand the need to adopt a different framework or technology over the conventional approach that best meets the product's need.

Over time, device manufacturers and consumers have started realizing the power of developing a transparent product development ecosystem where components that are combined to create a computing system are visible enough. It helps to remove the dependency from a limited group of people and make the scope wider where things can be taken care of differently. For example, over the years firmware layers are preferred for making awful workarounds due to limited or even no visibility into the operating system and its driver operational model. This might induce unwanted latency while the device transitions between different system states. Traditionally, computing devices were developed with proprietary firmware, which limits innovation and restricts the essential knowledge of the system. Firmware is the closest possible entity to the hardware, and the best way to learn system knowledge is by exploring the hardware and firmware communications. Unless the firmware development is open, it will always remain under the influence of a specific group that decides what goes into certain hardware.

Let's take a real-world example of Baseboard Management Controller (BMC) firmware development. For several years, the BMC firmware was developed using proprietary source code, and its innovation was also limited until 2014 when Facebook created a prototype open source BMC stack named OpenBMC. In 2018, OpenBMC became a Linux Foundation project. The introduction of OpenBMC on the server platform also influenced the industry and gave birth to u-bmc (u-bmc is a open source firmware for baseboard management controllers, or BMCs) and RunBMC (RunBMC is a smarter, simpler, open approach to out-of-band management for servers). The key highlight that we would like to emphasize here is the evolving nature of firmware. You should start preparing yourself to gain the required knowledge that makes you ready for any such architecture migration.

Firmware Development is based on two firmware engineers' real-world experiences, and the book captures the specialized systemic knowledge that typically a firmware engineer needs to possess after the base foundation is created. In a software project development cycle, development is one of the key pillars that is being highlighted, but there are other essential components that remain cloaked, and without them, the project development might not be productive. A software project cost evaluation model suggests that the cost of debugging, integration, testing, and verification is estimated at 50 to 75 percent of the total budget. This book includes those components as part of specific chapters and stresses the value of having specialized knowledge.

Additionally, this book simplifies the need to enforce firmware security as firmware is the most privileged entity of the system stack. Modern systems on chip (SoC) are getting complicated, and typically a computing system has multiple firmware to manage during boot, implements a robust upgrade methodology to ensure the system never goes out of maintenance, and has the provision to comprehend any bug fixes through firmware updates. Hence, it's important to build the security principles for the platform, and it's essential that all firmware ingredients adhere to the principles without failure to define a sustainable security solution.

This introduction gives an overview of the firmware development model and expectations for future firmware and also describes what readers can expect in the remainder of this book.

Identifying a Better Firmware Development Model

Firmware development is considered essential knowledge that can bring hardware to life. While the user presses the power button or connects the power supply to the computing system (be it consumer, industrial, and/or data centers), an autonomous entity called *firmware* starts its execution and performs the essential hardware initialization prior to handing over power to the higher-level software like the operating system. In a computing system, there are various types of firmware that exist; one can assume that almost each independent hardware block that belongs to the computing system contains firmware. Depending on the complexity of the operation that the hardware block performs, it contains a *Boot ROM* (which is typically nonupdatable in-field) and/or a *updatable firmware* if the hardware block has its dedicated nonvolatile storage or shares it with the other components on the motherboard. Being the device manufacturer or system integrator or owner of the device, it's the fundamental right to know what is running on the device. It's also a prevailing reason to have visibility into firmware development as firmware is running at the utmost privileged layer, and several vulnerabilities have been reported in past years due to compromised firmware.

The minimal expectation for future firmware is to have visibility into its operational model and empower firmware wizards to build and boot their target hardware with it. The objective is to be able to configure all possible hardware knobs using the open source system firmware. It's important to ensure that in case the silicon firmware block is not instantly available in the open source to meet the primary objective but still the open source firmware development effort is unblocked by adhering to a standard specification that defines the interfacing requirement between various firmwares and documents its basic operational model.

The future of firmware development can be predicted as it might not only be limited to the low-level firmware programming language and its technique rather it might start migrating towards the advanced or high-level programming languages. Also, future firmware may have a smaller firmware boundary and extended trusted boundary beyond firmware to use the powerful kernel as a replacement of the advanced firmware stage that maximizes the code reusability across platform components (i.e., low-level firmware and high-level software), running more validated code on top of the hardware with confidence. For example, the OpenBMC image contains a bootloader (u-boot), a Linux kernel, open source and board-specific packages. oreboot is another open source firmware, written in Rust, that has support for booting an ASpeed AST2500 ARM BMC. Many internet devices have adapted to open source device firmware as well. For example, the TP-Link and Xiaomi router firmwares are derived from OpenWrt, an open source firewall/router distribution based on the Linux kernel.

Motivation for This Book

This book provides the specialized knowledge that an engineer needs to have while working on a low-level hardware project. It's presumed that a person working on a overall system development or on firmware development, validation, and/or integration should equipped with essential knowledge of the computer architecture; several hardware blocks like memory, I/Os, bus, etc.; and specific firmware interface knowledge such as ACPI, SMBUS, Device Tree, etc., to be able to communicate with the operating system. *System Firmware: An Essential Guide to Open Source and Embedded Solutions,* from the same authors, creates that foundation. The current book in your hands covers the specific knowledge that engineers might encounter while working on day-to-day tasks such as the following:

> *Firmware development*: Having architecture knowledge is essential, but outcomes from that knowledge are also expected. An engineer needs to understand what it takes to create the firmware that can boot on the target hardware. Hence, understanding different technologies is important.

> *Build tools*: Writing a firmware module wouldn't be enough to solve a problem unless developers understand what it takes to convert this piece of source code into executables that runs on the device while it's powering on.

> *Configuration*: Having a solid testing and verification infrastructure is crucial for a product to meet its quality milestones and claim to be a best-in-class product that has negligible user-visible defects. In hardware-driven project development, a lot depends on validation to ensure all possible hardware interfaces are operational to meet the wider user requirements. Hence, every firmware is expected to provide a possible configuration

option during product development that allows configuration of all possible hardware interfaces.

Source control management (SCM): In an organization that has more than one developer working on the project or that wants to maintain the source code in a more structured way, one needs to understand the value of source code management. As the majority of future firmware development models are expected to adapt the open source model, it's kind of inevitable to avoid the need to have SCM for firmware development.

Developing the open source mindset: In the future, the majority of firmware product development will be breaking its internal-only development model and starting to adapt to the culture of upstreaming (a term typically used in open source development, which suggests that downstream forks of the project are also contributing into the source). Based on our personal experience, this requires a change in mindset. Working on open source projects demands persistence toward solving a problem, which is entirely different than working on proprietary source code where no one has visibility into what the developers check in at the end of the day. Statistical data shows that people working or learning in open environments have a wider and more diverse social circle. Open source firmware development helps to network with industry leaders (by attending various conferences throughout the year or listening them weekly basis during open forum that discuss the scope for firmware improvement) who are providing the vision as technologies are evolving rapidly. This book highlights the best-known practices that one should have while working on an open source project.

Knowledge of debugging: According to a CVP survey, a programmer typically spends 49.9 percent of their time debugging. Debugging is an art that can come only with an in-depth understanding of the domain and technology. Most of the time, engineers are short of ideas about what it takes to start debugging a defect. A skillful debug engineer always keeps their arsenal full of key tools (which can be hardware and/or software depending on the nature of the defaults). Also, there is no rule of thumb for debugging, and the debug methodology is also widely varied among different architectures. Chapter 4 covers the different debug techniques that can be used while debugging system firmware defects, describes the architecture of different hardware-based debugging tools applicable across architectures, and illustrates certain real-world scenarios where developers can apply those tools.

The purpose of the book is to give engineers the more specialized knowledge that is required to build their own system firmware for target embedded systems. As specified, the book includes knowledge that is specific for firmware development like understanding the firmware build procedure that involves compilers and toolchain knowledge, understanding the need for product-specific utilities, integrating the several pieces of the firmware and allowing configuration, updating the firmware, creating a development infrastructure for allowing multiparty collaboration in firmware development, and debugging advanced system firmware. This book covers such advanced knowledge to ensure readers assume better control while developing their own firmware and interacting with native hardware while debugging. Additionally, it provides guidance for developing secured system firmware for the target hardware.

After reading this book, you will be ready for the future with this specialized systemic knowledge as well as understand key principles for developing future firmware using newer technology.

Who Is This Book For?

This book is related to embedded system and firmware programming models. Readers are expected to be comfortable with low-level programming languages such as assembly and C. A few topics require specific knowledge on UEFI technology and an understanding of modern programming languages like Rust and Go.

As this book will focus on advanced firmware development, the expectation from its audience is to have an essential understanding of system firmware, its architecture, and basic hardware. If you don't already understand these topics, read *System Firmware: An Essential Guide to Open Source and Embedded Solutions* from the same authors.

Firmware development is a unique art, and the wider the audience, the better the scope of evolution in technology; hence, the target audience of this book ranges from students interested in STEM topics to recent college graduates working on developing skill sets as per the market needs to embedded firmware/software engineers wanting to improve their skill sets to be ready for any architecture migrations in the future.

Also, it would be benefitting for engineers currently working in open source firmware development.

The book will do the following:

- Describe different types of firmware that a computing system is typically equipped with, such as system firmware (running on the host CPU), device firmware (firmware running on peripherals attached with motherboard), and manageability firmware (the firmware part of special hardware that allows out-of-band access into the computing system).

- Explain the current working model of the different firmware types and analyze the scalable firmware development model in the future that provides the required visibility into the most privileged stack running on computing systems.

- Describe the infrastructure required for creating your own firmware for targeted hardware. This book explains the build procedure of different technologies being used while creating system firmware.

- Highlight the importance of proper infrastructure for seamless firmware development where multiple parties can collaborate.

- Debugging is a fine art. The expectation from this book is that you will be able to understand the different debug tools used across architectures and learn the different debugging methodologies used during various phases of firmware product development. It will help engineers to develop their skills to easily distinguish a defect between various components of a system and prepare a debug environment for the root cause of the defects.

- Understand the definition of platform security and how much of it is actually dependent on underlying firmware. Firmware is the initial code block that runs immediately after power-on; hence, defining the trust in firmware is the minimal requirement for calling a system secure.

- Set up key expectations for future firmware, including thinner firmware footprints and faster execution time, easier configuration, and increased transparent security.

Overview of the Book

In general, this book assumes readers are reading the chapters in sequence, where each chapter builds on a knowledge block gained from earlier chapters. As the book progresses, we will look at the application of that knowledge.

Chapters can be divided into two categories: concepts and application. In the concept chapters, readers will learn about various aspects such as understanding the different types of firmware, using various types of tools required for firmware projects, building project infrastructure, and realizing the need for firmware security to ensure a secured system. In the application chapters, we'll build a few applications using the knowledge learned from the concept chapters.

Spotlight on Future Firmware: Chapter 1 covers a subset of the total number of firmwares that exist on a typical computing system. (*System Firmware: An Essential Guide to Open Source and Embedded Solutions* provides the specific details on the boot firmware and payload.) Chapter 1 is like a spotlight on the other firmwares such as device and manageability firmware along with system firmware. It explains the different technologies being used in modern firmware development and highlights that several firmware development models are transitioning from closed source to open source in the future.

Tools: Chapter 2 focuses on the details on various types of tools that a user should be equipped with while creating their own firmware. It includes the following:

- *Build tool*: Developing source code and converting it into the final binary that can be flashed on the SPINOR involves several intermediated steps and involves various tools.

- *Configuration tool*: The need for configuration tools becomes inevitable when firmware development follows the hybrid work model as explained in Chapter 1. The need for configuration tools increases when the ability to modify the source code is limited during product development.

- *Flashing/update tool:* There might be several instances where product integrators or users would like to update the preflash boot firmware without the hardware-based utilities.

Infrastructure for Building System Firmware: Chapter 3 provides an infrastructure overview required for open source firmware development. In this process of firmware migration, knowing the correct infrastructure and setting it up is required for efficient communication during the firmware development process. Additionally, defining the correct standards for open source firmware development is important to support seamless architecture migration without any additional cost (in terms of effort and time).

System Firmware Debugging: Chapter 4 explains the different debugging methodologies used in boot firmware such as legacy methods, advanced software-based debugging, hardware-based debugging, source code debugging, etc.

Security at Its Core: Chapter 5 covers that firmware is closed to hardware and explains how abstracting the operating system from the underlying hardware provides another reason to ensure the communication channel is secure. This chapter focuses on designing the boot firmware, keeping security in mind.

The Future of System Firmware: Chapter 6 shares knowledge for creating firmware based on the market need. This chapter will discuss a few futuristic proposals and their implementation details to reduce the firmware boundary by adopting these principles: performance, simplicity, security, and open source.

The **appendixes** support the claim that firmware development in the future is looking into the possibility of high-level system programming language adaptation.

The **glossary** and **index** are applicable for connecting back to the main topics.

CHAPTER 1

Spotlight on Future Firmware

"In real open source, you have the right to control your own destiny."

—Linus Torvalds

When purchasing a computing device, users are concerned with the hardware configuration of the device and whether it has the latest versions of the software and applications. Most computer and consumer electronics device users don't realize that there are several layers of programs that run between the user pressing the power button of the device and when the operating system starts running. These programs are called *firmware*.

Firmware is responsible for bringing the device into its operational state and remains active while the OS is running, even when the device is in low-power mode. A computing system, irrespective of consumer, server, or IoT type, contains many different types of firmware. Firmware that runs on the host CPU is known as *system firmware*, and firmware that is specific to devices is called *device firmware*. In addition, there are other microcontrollers being used to manage the device, and firmware running on those controllers is called *manageability firmware*. The firmware code that runs on these devices has certain responsibilities prior to handing over control to the higher-level

The original version of this chapter was revised. A correction to this chapter is available at https://doi.org/10.1007/978-1-4842-7974-8_7

© Subrata Banik and Vincent Zimmer 2022, corrected publication 2023
S. Banik and V. Zimmer, *Firmware Development*,
https://doi.org/10.1007/978-1-4842-7974-8_1

system software. For example, the system firmware upon platform reset is the main interface for initializing CPUs, configuring the physical memory, communicating with peripheral devices, and finally picking the OS loader to boot an operating system. Every computing device is equipped with peripherals such as input and output devices, block devices, and connectivity devices. While system firmware is focusing on the host CPU and its associated interface initialization, device firmware has started its execution either by executing a self-start program or by waiting for an initiation command from the system firmware to become operational. Figure 1-1 shows an overview of typical computing system (consumer or server) firmware.

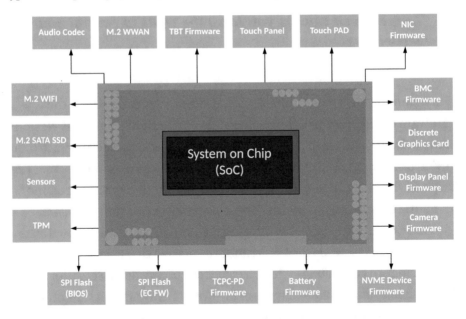

Figure 1-1. *Typical computing system firmware inventory*

Recent research from the LinuxBoot project on the server platform claims that the underlying firmware is at least 2.5x times bigger than the kernel. Additionally, these firmware components are capable. For example, they support the entire network stack including the physical layer, data link layer, networking layer, and transportation layer; hence, firmware is complex as well. The situation becomes worse when the majority of the firmware is proprietary and remains unaudited. Along with end users, tech companies and cloud service providers (CSPs) may be at risk because firmware that is compromised is capable of doing a lot of harm that potentially remains unnoticed by users due to its privileged operational level. For example, exploits in Base Management Controller (BMC) firmware may create a backdoor entry into the server, so even if a server is reprovisioned, the attacker could still have access into the server. Besides these security concerns, there are substantial concerns regarding performance and flexibility with closed source firmware.

This chapter will provide an overview of the future of the firmware industry, which is committed to overcoming such limitations by migrating to open source firmware. Open source firmware can bring trust to computing by ensuring more visibility into the source code that is running at the Ring 0 privilege level while the system is booting. The firmware discussed in this chapter is not a complete list of possible firmware available on a computing systems, rather just a spotlight on future firmware so you understand how different types of firmware could shape the future. Future firmware will make device owners aware of what is running on their hardware, provide more flexibility, and make users feel more in control of the system than ever.

Migrating to Open Source Firmware

Firmware is the most critical piece of software that runs on the platform hardware after boot, and it has direct access to hardware registers and system memory. Firmware is responsible for bringing the system into a state where higher-level software can take control of the system and the end user can make use of the peripheral devices. Prior to that, the user doesn't have any control of the system while the system is booting. A misconfiguration in firmware might make the system unusable or create security loopholes. Hence, it's important to know what is running at the lowest level of the platform hardware. Figure 1-2 shows the privilege level of software programs running on a computing system. Typically, computer users are more familiar with the system protection rings between Ring 0 and Ring 3, where Ring 0 is considered as the most privileged level where the kernel is operating and Ring 3 is considered as the least privileged for running applications or programs. Interestingly, underneath the kernel's Ring 0 layer, there is firmware space running, which provides a more privileged mode of operations compared to the kernel. In this chapter, these layers running beneath Ring 0 are referred to as Ring -1 to Ring -3.

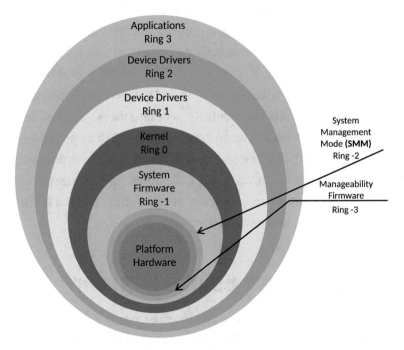

Figure 1-2. *System protection rings*

Let's take a look into these "minus" rings in more detail.

Ring -1: System Firmware

System firmware is a piece of code that resides inside the system boot device, i.e., SPI Flash in most of the embedded systems, and is fetched by the host CPU upon release from reset. Depending on the underlying SoC architecture, there might be higher-privileged firmware that initiates the CPU reset (refer to the book *System Firmware: An Essential Guide to Open Source and Embedded Solutions* for more details).

Operations performed by system firmware are typically known as *booting*, a process that involves initializing the CPU and the chipsets part of systems on chip (SoCs), enabling the physical memory (dynamic RAM, or DRAM) interface, and preparing the block devices or network devices to finally boot to an operating system. During this booting process, the firmware drivers can have access to direct hardware registers, memory, and I/O resources without any restrictions. Typically, services managed by system firmware are of two types: *boot services*, used for firmware drivers' internal communication and vanished upon system firmware being booted to the OS; and *runtime services*, which provide access to system firmware resources to communicate with the underlying hardware. System firmware runtime services are still available after control has transferred to the OS, although there are ways to track this kind of call coming from the OS layer to the lower-level firmware layer at runtime.

System firmware belonging to the SPI Flash updatable region qualifies for in-field firmware update, and also supports firmware rollback protection to overcome vulnerabilities.

Ring -2: System Management Mode

System Management Mode (SMM) is the highest privileged mode of operations on x86-based platforms. There are two widely used ways to allow the system to enter into SMM:

- *Hardware-based method*: This triggers a system management interrupt (SMI), a dedicated port 0xb2 with the unique SMI vector number.

- *Software-based method*: This uses a general-purpose interrupt through the Advanced Programmable Interrupt Controller (APIC).

During initialization of the system firmware, a code block (program) can get registered with an SMI vector, which will get executed while entering into SMM. All other processors on the system are suspended, and the processor states are saved. The program that is getting executed when in SMM has access to the entire system, i.e., processor, memory, and all peripherals. Upon exiting from SMM, the processor state is restored and resumes its operations as if no interruption had occurred. Other higher-level software doesn't have visibility about this mode of operation.

SMM exploits are common attacks on computer systems, where hackers use SMI to elevate the privilege level, access the SPI control registers to disable the SPI write protection, and finally write BIOS rootkits into the SPI Flash.

The major concern with SMM is that it's completely undetectable, so one doesn't know what kind of operation is running in SMM.

Ring -3: Manageability Firmware

Ring -3 firmware consists of the separate microcontrollers running its firmware and later booted to a real-time operating system (RTOS). This firmware always remains on and is capable of accessing all the hardware resources; it's meant to perform the manageability operations without which one might need to access these devices physically. For example, it allows the remote administration of the enterprise laptops and servers by IT admins, such as powering on or off the device, reprovisioning the hardware by installing the operating system, taking the serial log to analyze the failure, emulating the special keys to trigger recovery, performing active thermal management like controlling the system fans, and handling the critical hardware device failure like a bad charger, failure of storage device, etc.

Although this firmware has access to system resources (access to the host CPU, unlimited access to the host system memory and peripherals) of the host CPU (based on how it is being interfaced with the host CPU), the operations performed by these processors are "invisible" to the host processor. The code that is running on these processors is not publicly available. Moreover, these codes are provided and maintained by the silicon vendors; hence, they are assumed to be trusted without verifying through any additional security layer like a verified boot or secure boot.

The fact to consider here is that all these software codes are developed by humans and reviewed by other sets of humans. It's possible to have some bugs exist irrespective of which layer of ring it's getting executed in, and the concern is that the more privileged layer that gets executed, the more opportunity there is for hackers to exploit the system.

As per the National Vulnerability Database (NVD), there are several vulnerabilities being reported or detected by security researchers on production systems every year. Among those security defects there are many that exist within the "minus" rings. For example, CVE-2017-3197, CLVA-2016-12-001, CLVA-2016-12-002, CVE-2017-3192, CVE-2015-3192, CVE-2012-4251, etc., are vulnerabilities reported in firmware from the NVD.

Most of the firmware being discussed was developed using *closed source*, which means the documentation and code source to understand what's really running on a machine is not publicly available. When a firmware update is available, you may be worried about clicking the accept button because you don't have any clue whether this update is supposed to run on your machine. The user has a right to know what's really running on their device. The problem with the current firmware development model is not the *security*; a study done on 17 open source and closed source software showed that the number of vulnerabilities existing in a piece of software is not affected by the source availability model that it uses. The problem is *lack of transparency.*

Transparency is what is missing in closed source firmware if we park the argument about the code quality due to internal versus external code review. All these arguments will point back to the need to have visibility into what is really running on the device that is being used. Having the source code available to the public might help to get rid of the problem of running several "minus" rings.

Running the most vulnerable code as part of the highest privileged level makes the entire system vulnerable; by contrast, running that code as part of a lesser privileged level helps to meet the platform initialization requirement as well as mitigates the security concern. It might also help to reduce the attack surface.

Additionally, performance and flexibility are other concerns that can be improved with transparency. For example, typically closed source firmware development focuses on short-term problems such as fixing the bugs with code development without being bothered about redundancy if any. A case study presented at the Open Source Firmware Conference 2019 claimed that a system is still functional and meets the booting criteria even after 214 out of 424 firmware drivers and associated libraries were removed, which is about a 50 percent reduction. Having more maintainers of the code helps to create a better code sharing model that overcomes such redundancy and results in instant boot. Finally, coming to the security concerns, having a transparent system is more secure than a supposed secure system that hides those potential bugs in closed firmware.

This is a summary of the problems with the current firmware:

- Firmware is the most critical piece of code running on the bare hardware with a privileged level that might allure attackers.

- A compromised firmware is not only dangerous for the present hardware but all systems that are attached to it, even over a network.

- Lower-level firmware operations are not visible to upper-level system software; hence, attacks remain unnoticed even if the operating system and drivers are freshly installed.

- Modern firmware and its development models are less transparent, which leads to multiple "minus" rings.

- Having a transparency firmware development model helps to restore trust in firmware as device owners are aware of what is running on the hardware. In addition, better design helps to reduce the "minus" rings, represents less vulnerability, and provides better maintenance with improved code size and higher performance.

Open source firmware (OSF) is the solution to overcome all of these problems. The OSF project performs a bare-minimum platform initialization and provides flexibility to choose the correct OS loader based on the targeted operating system. Hence, it brings efficiency, flexibility, and improved performance. Allowing more eyes to review the code while firmware is getting developed using an open source model provides a better chance to identify the feature detects, find security flaws, and improve the system security state by accommodating the community feedback. For example, all cryptographic algorithms are available in GitHub publicly. Finally, to accommodate the code quality question, a study conducted by Coverity Inc. finds open source code to be of better quality. All these rationales are adequate to conclude why migrating to OSF is inevitable. Future firmware creators are definitely looking into an opportunity to collaborate more using open source firmware development models.

This chapter will emphasize the future firmware development models of different firmware types such as system firmware, device firmware, and manageability firmware using open source firmware.

Open Source System Firmware Development

Most modern system firmware is built with proprietary firmware where the producer of the source code has restricted the code access; hence, it allows private modification only, internal code reviews, and the generation of new firmware images for updates. This process might not work with a future firmware development strategy where proprietary firmware is unreliable, or the functionality is limited in cases where device manufacturers relied on a group of firmware engineers who know only what is running on the device and therefore are capable of implementing only the required features. Due to the heavy maintenance demands of closed source firmware, often device manufacturers defer regular firmware updates even for critical fixes. Typically, OEMs are committed to providing system firmware updates two times during the entire life of the product, once at the launch and another six months later in response to an operating system update. System firmware development with an open source model in the future would provide more flexibility to users to ensure that the device always has the latest configuration. For that to happen, future system firmware must adhere to the open source firmware development principle. The open source firmware model is built upon the principle of having universal access to source code with an open source or free license that encourages the community to collaborate in the project development process.

This book provides the system architecture of several open source system firmware types including the bootloader and payload. Most open source bootloaders have strict resistance about using any closed source firmware binary such as binary large objects (BLOBs) along with open source firmware. Typically, any undocumented blobs are dangerous for system integration as they could be rootkits and might leave the system in a compromised state. But, the industry recognizes that in order to work on the latest processors and chipsets from the silicon vendors, the crucial piece of the information is the silicon initialization sequence. In the majority of cases, this is considered as restricted information prior to product launch due to innovation and business reasons and may be available under only certain legal agreements (like NDAs). Hence, to unblock the open source product development using latest SoCs, silicon vendors have come up with a proposal for a binary distribution. Under this binary distribution model, the essential silicon initialization code is available as a binary, which eventually unblocks platform initialization using open source bootloaders and at the same time abstracts the complexities of the SoC programming and exposes a limited set of interfaces to allow the initialization of SoC components. This model is referred to in this book as the *hybrid work model.*

This section will highlight the future system firmware journey using following operational models:

- *Hybrid system firmware model*: The system firmware running on the host CPU might have at least one closed source binary as a blob integrated as part of the final ROM. Examples: coreboot, SBL on x86 platforms.

- *Open source system firmware model*: The system firmware code is free from running any closed source code and has all the native firmware drivers for silicon initialization. Example: coreboot on RISC-V platforms.

Hybrid System Firmware Model

As defined earlier, the hybrid system firmware model relies on a silicon-provided binary for processor and chipset initialization; hence, it needs the following components as part of the underlying system firmware:

- *Bootloader*: A boot firmware is responsible for generic platform initialization such as bus enumeration, device discoveries, and creating tables for industry-standard specifications like ACPI, SMBIOS, etc., and performing calls into silicon-provided APIs to allow silicon initialization.

- *Silicon reference code binary*: One or multiple binaries are responsible for performing the silicon initialization based on their execution order. On x86-platforms, Firmware Support Package (FSP) is the specification being used to let silicon initialization code perform the chipset and processor initialization. It allows dividing the monolithic blob into multiple sub-blocks so that it can get loaded into system memory as per the associated bootloader phase and provides multiple APIs to let the bootloader configure the input parameters. Typically, this mode of FSP operation is known as *API mode*. Unlike other blobs, the FSP has provided the documentation, which includes the specification and expectation from each API and platform integration guide. This documentation clearly calls out the expectations from the underlying bootloader, such as the bootloader stack requirement, heap size, meaning for each input parameter to configure FSP, etc.

Facts   Intel FSP Specification v2.1 introduces an optional FSP boot mode named *Dispatch mode* to increase the FSP adaptation toward PI spec bootloaders.

- *Payload*: An OS loader or payload firmware can be integrated as part of the bootloader or can be chosen separately, which provides the additional OS boot logic.

The book *System Firmware: An Essential Guide to Open Source and Embedded Solutions* provides the detailed system architecture of the bootloader and payload and defines the working principle with hybrid firmware as FSP. This section will focus on defining the work relationship between open source boot firmware with FSP.

- coreboot using FSP for booting the IA-Chrome platform

- EDKII Minimum Platform Firmware for Intel Platforms

coreboot Using Firmware Support Package

Firmware Support Package (FSP) provides key programming information for initializing the latest chipsets and processor and can be easily integrated with any standard bootloader. In essence, coreboot consumes FSP as a binary package that provides easy enabling of the latest chipsets, reduces time-to-market (TTM), and is economical to build as well.

FSP Integration

The FSP binary follows the UEFI Platform Initialization Firmware Volume Specification format. Hence, each firmware volume (FV) as part of FSP contains a phase initialization code. Typically, FSP is defined as a single firmware device (FD) binary, but because it contains several FVs and each FV represents a different initialization phase and runs at different noncontiguous addresses, a monolithic binary wouldn't work here. Since the FSP 2.0 specification, the FSP binary can be split into three blobs as *FSP-T*, called FSP for Temporary RAM Initialization; *FSP-M*, called FSP for Memory Initialization; and *FSP-S*, called for Silicon Initialization. Here are some required steps for the FSP integration:

- *Configuration*: The FSP provides configuration parameters that can be customized based on target hardware and/or operating system requirements by the bootloader. These are inputs for FSP to execute silicon initialization.

- *eXecute-in-place and relocation*: The FSP is not position independent code (PIC), and each FSP component has to be rebased if it needs to support the relocation, which is different from the preferred base address specified during the FSP build. The bootloader has support for both these modes where components need to be executed at the address where it's built, called eXecute-In-Place (XIP) components and marked as --xip, for example, FSP-M binary. Also, position-independent modules are modules that can be located anywhere in physical memory after relocation.

- *Interfacing*: The bootloader needs to add code to set up the execution environment for the FSP, which includes calling the FSP with correct sets of parameters as inputs and parsing the FSP output to retrieve the necessary information returned by the FSP and consumed by the bootloader code.

FSP Interfacing

Since its origin, FSP has tried to provide a flexible interface between the bootloader and FSP to have correct sets of parameters required to perform the silicon initialization. Although FSP has gone through significant specification changes since its first introduction, the basic input/output architecture remains unchanged between all these different FSP versions. For example, a data structure used to pass a configuration parameter from the bootloader to FSP works as input parameters, and hand-off blocks (HOBs), a standard mechanism to pass FSP information back to the bootloader, work as output parameters. Figure 1-3 shows the evolution of FSP interfaces along with its specification.

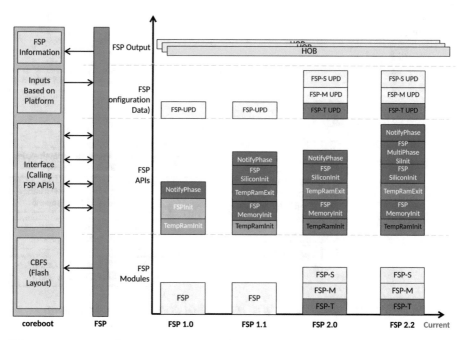

Figure 1-3. *Explaining FSP interfacing with coreboot boot-firmware*

coreboot supports FSP Specification version 2.x (the latest as of this writing is 2.2).

FSP Configuration Data

Each FSP module contains a configuration data structure called
the *updatable product data* (UPD), which is used by FSP for silicon
initialization. Typically, UPD contains the default parameters for FSP
initialization. The bootloader contains a separate UPD data structure
for each FSP module, which allows the bootloader to override any of
the default UPD parameters. As part of the FSP integration process,
the bootloader is also required to keep FSP UPD data structures in the
bootloader source code along with the corresponding FSP binary. See
Figure 1-4.

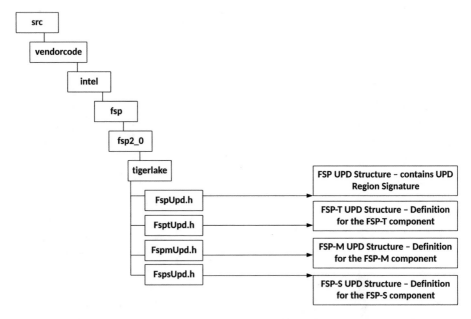

Figure 1-4. *UPD data structure as part of coreboot source code*

It is recommended that the bootloader copy the whole UPD structure
from the FSP component to memory, update the parameters, and initialize
the UPD pointer to the address of the updated UPD structure. The FSP
API will then use this updated data structure instead of the default

configuration region as part of the FSP binary blob while initializing the platform. In addition to the generic or architecture-specific data structure, each UPD data structure contains platform-specific parameters.

Open Source Challenges with FSP Configuration Data

FSP configuration data structures are crucial for the hybrid system firmware development model as it is used to configure the default built-in UPD configuration data, which might not be applicable for the current open source project to ensure the correct silicon initialization. Hence, while integrating the FSP blobs with the bootloader, it is recommended to ensure it has the same version of UPD structures as part of the bootloader source code. FSP is responsible for the entire silicon-related initialization process and feature enabling, and only inputs from the bootloader are in the UPD data structure. Hence, while calling the FSP APIs like `TempRamInit()`, `FspMemoryInit()`, and `FspSiliconInit()`, the bootloader needs to pass a pointer that provides the updated data structure. Figure 1-5 shows the bootloader code structure that ensures the initialization of the FSP configuration data for an open source firmware development project.

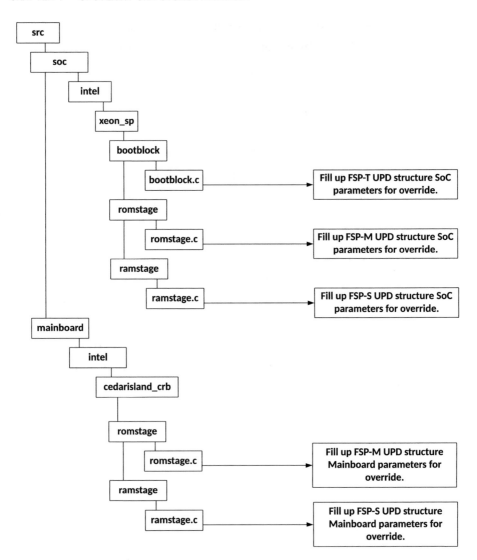

Figure 1-5. *coreboot code structure to override UPD data structures*

OSF development efforts expect the entire project source code is available for review and configuration, but due to business reasons like innovation and/or competition, the early open sourcing of the FSP configuration data structure is not feasible for non-production-release qualification (PRQ) products. It poses risk while developing an open source project using the latest SoC prior to PRQ. Consequences of this restriction would be incomplete SoC and mainboard source code per platform initialization requirements and incomplete feature enabling.

To overcome this problem, a solution is being developed that is open source friendly even for open project development using non-PRQ SoC, called *partial FSP configuration data structure* (also known as *partial header*). Here are the working principles of the partial FSP configuration data structure generation process:

- This structure consists only of platform UPDs required for a specific bootloader to override for the current project.

- The rest of the UPDs are renamed as *reserved*. For any project, reserved fields are not meant for bootloader overrides.

- Embargoed UPD parameters' names and descriptions are being abstracted.

Partial headers are generated using a Python-based tool. This tool will generate the partial headers for those bootloaders that do not need the full list of UPD data structures. It takes two arguments for the header generation process.

- *First argument*: This is the path for the complete FSP-generated UPD data structure. The tool will run on this header itself to filter out only the required UPD parameters as per the second argument.

- *Second argument*: This is a file that provides the lists of required UPD parameters for bootloader overrides.

This effort will ensure complete source code development on the bootloader side along with enabling new features without being bothered about the state of the silicon release. Post SoC PRQ, after the embargo is revoked, the complete FSP UPD data structure gets uploaded into FSP on GitHub, which replaces all reserved fields of the partial header with the proper naming.

coreboot and FSP Communications Using APIs

Since the FSP 2.1 specification, FSP supports two possible boot flows based on the implementation of the bootloader and its selection for the operational mode of FSP. The majority of the open source bootloaders are working with FSP and are using the API mode boot flow. Figure 1-6 shows the coreboot boot flow using FSP in API mode.

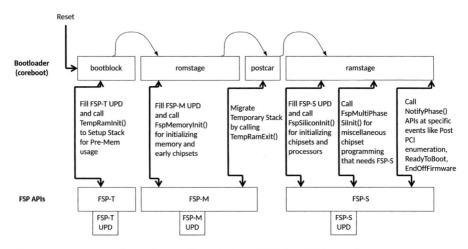

Figure 1-6. *coreboot boot flow using FSP in API mode*

Here is the detailed boot flow description:

1. coreboot owns the reset vector.

2. coreboot contains the real mode reset vector handler code.

3. Optionally, coreboot can call the FSP-T API (`TempRamInit()`) for temporary memory setup using (CAR) and create a stack.

4. coreboot fills in the UPD parameters required for the FSP-M API, such as `FspMemoryInit()`, which is responsible for memory and early chipset initialization.

5. On exit of the FSP-M API, either coreboot tears down CAR using the `TempRamExit()` API, if the bootloader initialized the temporary memory in step 3 using the FSP-T API, or coreboot uses the native implementation in coreboot.

6. It fills up the UPD parameters required for silicon programming as part of the FSP-S API, FspSiliconInit. The bootloader finds FSP-S and calls into the API. Afterward, FSP returns from the `FspSiliconInit()` API.

7. If supported by the FSP, the bootloader enables multiphase silicon initialization by setting `FSPS_ARCH_UPD.EnableMultiPhaseSiliconInit` to a nonzero value.

8. On exit of FSP-S, coreboot performs PCI enumeration and resource allocation.

9. The bootloader calls the `FspMultiPhaseSiInit()` API with the `EnumMultiPhaseGetNumberOfPhases` parameter to discover the number of silicon initialization phases supported by the bootloader.

10. The bootloader must call the `FspMultiPhaseSiInit()` API with the `EnumMultiPhaseExecutePhase` parameter n times, where n is the number of phases returned previously. The bootloader may perform board-specific code in between each phase as needed.

11. The number of phases, what is done during each phase, and anything the bootloader may need to do in between phases, will be described in the integration guide.

12. coreboot continues the remaining device initialization. coreboot calls `NotifyPhase()` at the proper stage like `AfterPciEnumeration`, `ReadyToBoot`, and `EndOfFirmware` before handing control over to the payload.

Facts   If FSP returns the reset required status from any API, then the bootloader performs the reset as specified by the FSP return status return type.

FSP Drivers

The bootloader implements a corresponding version driver to support the calling convention of the FSP entry point. Ideally, the purpose of these drivers are as follows:

- Find the FSP header to locate the dedicated entry point, and verify the UPD region prior to calling.

- Copy the default value from the UPD area into the memory to allow the required override of UPD parameters based on the target platform using driver-provided callbacks into the SoC code, for example: before calling into memory `init` or before silicon `init`.

- Fill out any FSP architecture-specific UPDs that are generic like `NvsBufferPtr` for MRC cache verification.

- Finally, call the FSP-API entry point with an updated UPD structure to silicon initialization.

- On failure, handle any errors returned by FSP-API and take action; for example, manage the platform reset request to either generic libraries or SoC-specific code.

- On success, retrieve the FSP outputs in the form of hand-off blocks that provide platform initialization information. For example, FSP would like to notify the bootloader about a portion of system memory that is being reserved by FSP for its internal use, and coreboot will parse the resource descriptor HOBs produced by the FSP-M to create a system memory map. The bootloader FSP driver must have capabilities to consume the information passed through the HOB produced by the FSP.

Current coreboot code has drivers for the FSP 1.1 and FSP 2.0 specifications. The FSP 2.0 specification is not backward compatible but updated to support the latest specification as FSP 2.2.

Mitigate Open Source Challenges with FSP Driver

Typically, system firmware development using an open source model has expectations that all new silicon feature-related documentation should be available to the public to allow the development of the new feature. But in reality, with the latest processors and chipsets, the feature programming lists are growing and expected to grow even more in future. With more capable and complex SoC solutions in the future, there might be some cases where certain feature programming might be classified as restricted; hence, it is not feasible to implement using an open source bootloader. For example, the current coreboot is capable enough to handle the multiprocessor (MP) initialization on the x86-platform using the coreboot native cpu and mp drivers. The Boot Strap Processor (BSP) performs the MP initialization and typically involves two major operations.

- *Bringing-up process*: This enables application processors (APs) from a reset. It loads the latest microcode on all cores and syncs the latest Memory Type Range Register (MTRR) snapshot between BSP and APs.

- *Perform CPU feature programming*: Allow vendor-specific feature programming to run such as to ensure higher power and performance efficiency, enable overclocking, and support specific technologies like Trusted eXecution Technology (TXT), Software Guard Extensions, Processor Trace, etc.

Typically, the bringing-up process for APs is part of the open source documentation and generic in nature. But, the previously listed CPU feature programming lists are expected to grow in the future and be considered proprietary implementations. If the system firmware implementation with the open source bootloader isn't able to perform these recommended CPU features, programming might resist the latest hardware features. To overcome this limitation, the hybrid system firmware model needs to have an alternative proposal as part of the FSP driver.

Currently, coreboot is doing CPU multiprocessor initialization for the IA platform before calling FSP-S using its native driver implementation and having all possible information about the processor in terms of maximum number of cores, APIC IDs, stack size, etc. The solution offered here is a possible extension of coreboot support by implementing additional sets of APIs, which are used by FSP to perform CPU feature programming.

FSP uses the Pre-EFI Initialization (PEI) environment defined in the *PI Specification* and therefore relies on install/locate PPI (PEIM to PEIM Interface) to perform certain API calls. The purpose of creating a PPI service inside the bootloader is to allow accessing its resources while FSP is in operation. This feature is added into the FSP specification 2.1 onward where FSP is allowed to make use of external PPIs, published by boot firmware and able to execute by FSP, being the context master.

In this case, coreboot publishes a multiprocessor (MP) service PPI, `EFI_MP_SERVICES_PPI`, as per PI Specification Volume 1, section 2.3.9. coreboot implements APIs for the `EFI_MP_SERVICES_PPI` structure with its native functions as follows:

APIs as per the Specification	coreboot Implementation of APIs	APIs Description
`PeiGetNumberOf Processor`	`get_cpu_count()` to get processor count	Get the number of CPUs.
`PeiGetProcessorInfo`	Fill `ProcessorInfoBuffer`: - Processor ID: `apicid` - Location: `get_cpu_ topology_from_ apicid()`	Get information on a specific CPU.
`PeiStartupAllAps`	Calling the `mp_run_on_ all_aps()` function	Activate all the application processors.
`PeiStartupThisAps`	`mp_run_on_aps()` based on the argument `logical_cpu_number`	Activate a specific application processor.

(*continued*)

APIs as per the Specification	coreboot Implementation of APIs	APIs Description
PeiSwitchBSP	Currently not being implemented in coreboot due to scoping limitations	Switch the bootstrap processor.
PeiEnableDisableAP		Enable or disable an application processor.
PeiWhoAmI	Calling to activate the cpu_index() function	Identify the currently executing processor.
PeiStartupAllCpus Only available in EDKII_ PEI_MP_SERVICES2_PPI	mp_run_on_aps() based on MP_RUN_ON_ ALL_CPUS	Run the function on all CPU cores (BSP + APs).

Here is code flow between coreboot and FSP while running the restricted CPU feature programming:

1. coreboot selects either CONFIG_MP_SERVICES_ PPI_V1 or CONFIG_MP_SERVICES_PPI_V2 from the SoC directory as per the FSP recommendation to implement the MP Services PPI for FSP usage. coreboot does the multiprocessor initialization as part of ramstage early, before calling the FSP-S API. All possible APs are out of reset and ready to execute the restricted CPU feature programming.

2. coreboot creates the MP (MultiProcessor) Services APIs as per PI Specification Vol 1, section 2.3.9, and is assigned into the EFI_MP_SERVICES or EDKII_ PEI_MP_SERVICES2_PPI structure as per the MP specification revision.

3. FSP-S to install `EFI_MP_SERVICES` or `EDKII_PEI_MP_SERVICES2_PPI` based on the structure provided by coreboot as part of the CpuMpPpi UPD. At the later stage of FSP-S execution, locate the MP Services PPI and run the CPU feature programming on APs.

4. While FSP-S is executing multiprocessor initialization using Open Source EDKII UefiPkg, it invokes a coreboot-provided MP Services API and runs the "*restricted*" feature programming on APs.

Figure 1-7 shows the pictorial representation of the boot flow.

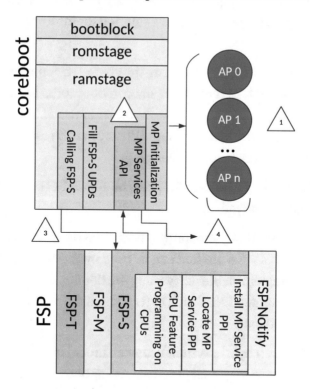

Figure 1-7. *coreboot-FSP multiprocessor init flow*

This design would allow running SoC vendor-recommended restricted CPU feature programming using the FSP module without any limitation while working on the latest SoC platform (even on non-PRQ SoC) in the hybrid system firmware model. The CPU feature programming inside FSP will be more transparent than before as it's using coreboot interfaces to execute those programming features. coreboot will have more control over running those programming features as the API optimization is handled by coreboot.

This solution is future-proof, because in the future this design of the PEIM-PEIM interface (PPI) can be expanded beyond just running the restricted CPU feature programming in a coreboot context. Here is a list of other opportunities to scale this solution for future hybrid system firmware:

- Today on the CrOS platform, the `cbmem -c` command is capable only of redirecting the coreboot serial log into the cbmem buffer using the bootloader driver. With this approach, the coreboot serial library may be used by FSP to populate serial debug logs.

- The same can be used for post code-based debug methods as well.

- Rather than implementing a dedicated timer library inside FSP, this method can be used by FSP to inject any programmable delay using the bootloader-implemented PPI, which natively uses the bootloader timer driver.

To summarize, a hybrid system firmware model in the future provides the ease of porting to a new silicon. It allows for bootloaders (coreboot, SBL, UEFI MinPlatform, etc.) to have an FSP interfacing infrastructure for finding and loading FSP binaries, configuring FSP UPDs as per platform need, and finally calling FSP APIs.

EDKII Minimum Platform Firmware

Since the introduction of the Unified Extensible Firmware Interface (UEFI) firmware in 2004, all Intel architecture platforms have migrated from legacy BIOS to UEFI firmware implementations. With a blistering speed, UEFI firmware has taken over the entire PC ecosystem to become the de-facto standard for system firmware. Historically, platforms that use UEFI firmware have been nourished and maintained by a closed group; hence, the source used in a platform that uses UEFI firmware remains closed source although the specifications are open standards. Details about the UEFI architecture and specification are part of *System Firmware: An Essential Guide to Open Source and Embedded Solutions*.

Over the years the platform enabling activity has evolved and demands more openness due to firmware security requirements, cloud workloads, business decisions for implementing solutions using more open standards, etc.

Minimum Platform Architecture

The Minimum Platform Architecture (MPA) provides the design guidelines for implementing platform initialization using the open source EDKII standard to meet the industry expectations from the UEFI firmware. Figure 1-8 shows the high-level firmware stack used in the MPA.

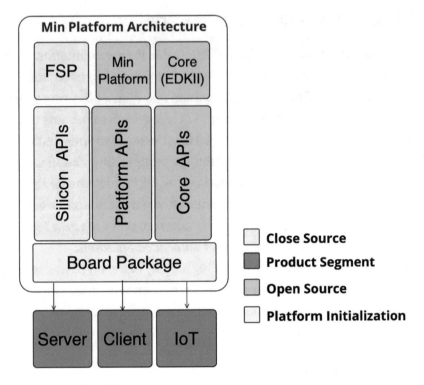

Figure 1-8. *MPA diagram*

The MPA firmware stack demonstrates the hybrid-firmware development work model where it combines the several closed and open source components for platform initialization.

Core

Tianocore is an open source representation of the UEFI. EDKII is the modern implementation of UEFI and Platform Initialization (PI) specifications. Typically, the EDKII source code consists of standard drivers based on the various industry specifications such as PCI, USB, TCG, etc.

Silicon

A closed source binary model was developed and released by silicon vendors (example: Intel, AMD, Qualcomm etc.) with an intention to abstract the silicon initialization from the bootloader.

Prior to the MPA architecture, the FSP API boot mode was the de facto standard for silicon initialization when the bootloader needs to implement a 32-bit entry point for calling into the APIs as per the specification. This limits the adaptation of SoC vendor-released silicon binaries aka FSP toward a bootloader that adheres to the UEFI PI firmware specification. Traditionally, the UEFI specification deals with firmware modules responsible for platform initialization and dispatched by the dispatcher (Pre-EFI Initialization aka PEI and Driver eXecution Environment aka DXE core). To solve this adaptation problem in the UEFI firmware platform enabling model, a new FSP boot mode has been designed with the FSP External Architecture Specification v2.1 known as *dispatch mode.*

Dispatch Mode

FSP API boot mode requires bootloaders to perform a call into the FSP entry points like FSP-M (for Memory Init) and FSP-S (for Silicon Init) for initiating the silicon initialization. The dispatch mode is more aligned with the UEFI specification where FSP-M and FSP-S are containers that expose firmware volumes (FVs) that can be directly used by a UEFI PI–compliant bootloader. For example, the UEFI bootloader known as an FSP wrapper uses FSP the same way as any other firmware file system partition. The PEIM in these FVs are executed as is in the PEI environment with the bootloader being the context master. All the FSP entry points introduced as part of API boot mode (i.e., `FspMemoryInit()`, `FspSiliconInit()`, and `NotifyPhase()`) are not in use. Figure 1-9 shows the work relationship between a UEFI PI bootloader and FSP in dispatch mode.

- The UEFI PI bootloader adhering to the MPA is equipped with a PCD database to pass the configuration information between bootloaders to FSP. This includes hardware interface configuration (typically, configured using UPD in API mode) and boot stage selection. Refer to the "Min-Tree" section to understand the working principle and MPA stage approach for incremental platform development.

- PEI Core as part of Silicon Reference code blob aka FSP is used to execute the modules residing into the firmware volumes (FVs) directly.

- The PEIMs belonging to these FVs are communicating with each other using PPI as per the PI specification.

- The hand-off-blocks are being used to pass the information gathered in the silicon initialization phase with the UEFI PI bootloader.

- The UEFI bootloader doesn't use NotifyPhase APIs; instead, FSP-S contains a DXE driver that implements an equivalent implementation using a DXE native driver that is getting invoked at `NotifyPhase()` events.

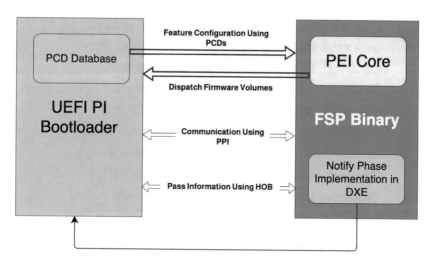

Figure 1-9. *FSP work model in dispatch mode with UEFI bootloader*

UEFI Bootloader and FSP Communications Using Dispatch Mode

The communication interface designed between the UEFI bootloader and FSP in dispatch mode is intended to remain as close as possible to the standard UEFI boot flow. Unlike API mode, where the communication between the bootloader and FSP takes place by passing configuration parameters known as UPD to the FSP entry points, in dispatch mode the Firmware File Systems (FFSs) that belong to FVs consist of Pre-EFI Initialization Modules (PEIMs) and get executed directly in the context of the PEI environment provided by the bootloader. This can also be referred to as the *firmware volume drop-in model.* In dispatch mode, the PPI database and HOB lists prepared by FSP are shared between the bootloader and FSP.

Here is the detailed boot flow description:

1. The bootloader owns the reset vector and SecMain as part of the bootloader getting executed upon the platform start executing from the reset vector.

2. SecMain is responsible for setting up the initial code environment for the bootloader to continue execution. Unlike the coreboot workflow with FSP in API mode, where coreboot does the temporary memory initialization using its native implementation on the x86 platform instead calling the FSP-T API, dispatch mode tries to maximize the usage of FSP and uses FSP-T for initializing temporary memory and setting up the stack.

3. The bootloader provides the boot firmware volume (BFV) to the FSP. The PEI core belonging to FSP uses the BFV to dispatch the PEIMs and initialize the PCD database.

4. In addition to the bootloader PEI modules, FSP dispatches the PEI module part of FSP-M to complete the main memory initialization.

5. The PEI core continues to execute the post-memory PEIMs provided by the bootloader. During the course of dispatch, the PEIM included within FSP-S FV is executed to complete the silicon-recommended chipset programming.

6. At the end of the PEI phase, all silicon-recommended chipset programming is done using the closed source FSP, and DXE begins its execution.

7. The DXE drivers belonging to the FSP-S firmware volume are dispatched. These drivers will register events to be notified at different points in the boot flow. For example, NotifyPhase will perform the callbacks to complete the remaining silicon-recommended security configurations such as disabling certain hardware

interfaces, locking the chipset register, and dropping the platform privilege level prior to handing control off to the payload or operating system.

8. The payload phase executes the OS bootloader and loads the OS kernel into the memory.

9. The OS loader signals the events to execute the callbacks, registered as part of the DXE drivers to ensure the pre-boot environment has secured the platform.

Platform

In the past, UEFI firmware development has used closed source for platform initialization, but with MPA, this limitation is diminished by creating a platform standard known as the EDKII Minimum Platform Specification. This approach allows the platform using UEFI firmware to open source and improves customer engagement, brings transparency to product development, establishes the trust in the community, and finally establishes the ecosystem that encourages the community to contribute toward platform implementation. The key innovation in this architecture is the layered approach called *stages*, which are based on the development phase and the functionality for specific use cases. Each stage builds upon its previous stage with extensibility to meet silicon, platform, or board requirements. The MPA tries to split the platform implementation into two parts.

- *Generic*: This part remains generic in nature by providing the required APIs to define the control flow. This generic control flow is being implemented inside MinPlatformPkg (`Edk2-Platforms/Platform/Intel/ MinPlatformPkg`), such that the tasks performed by the MinPlatformPkg can be reused by all other platforms (belonging to the board package) without any additional source modification.

- *Board package*: This part focuses on the actual hardware initialization source code aka board package. Typically, the contents of this package are limited to the scope of the platform requirements and the feature sets that board users would like to implement. As described in Figure 1-8, the board package code is also open source and represented as `Edk2-Platforms/Platform/Intel/<xyz>OpenBoardPkg`, where `xyz` represents the actual *board package* name. For example, TiogaPass, a board supported by Open Compute Project (OCP) based on Intel's Purley chipset, uses the `PurleyOpenBoardPkg` board package.

Facts   A closed source representation of the `OpenBoardPkg` is just `BoardPkg`, which still directly uses the `MinPlatformPkg` from EDKII platforms.

The board package consists of a standard EDKII package along with the following items and must implement the guidelines:

- A *board package* may consist of one or more supported boards. These boards are sharing the common resources from the board package.

- Board-specific source code must belong to the board directory and name after the supported board. For the previous example, the board directory for `TiogaPass` is named as `BoardTiogaPass`.

- All the board-relevant information is made available to the `MinPlatformPkg` using board-defined APIs.

To summarize MPA, it consists of a closed source FSP package for silicon initialization, and the rest of the source code is potentially open source where `MinPlatformPkg` and a board package are combined together to call the *platform*.

Min-Tree

MPA is built around the principle of a structural development model. This structural development model can be referred to as a *min-tree*, where the source code tree is started with a minimalistic approach and enriched based on the required functionality getting included over time as the platform is getting matured. To make this model structural, the design principle relied on dividing the flow, interfaces, communication, etc., into a *stage-based architecture* (refer to "Minimum Platform Stage Approach" section).

Figure 1-10 shows the min-tree development model over the product life cycle. Typically, in the product development cycle, the early phase is always focusing on creating the bare-minimum source code. The target is to make sure the early silicon-based simulation or emulation platform is able to perform the basic boot to an operating system. To meet this goal, the platform development starts by leveraging the source code of the previous generation platform (typically referred to as *n-1* where *n* is the current generation platform) and existing feature sets. This often includes creating the new sets of silicon and platform code on top of the prior platform after analyzing the basic differences between the new target platform from its prior generation. Hence, at the start of the product development cycle, the min-tree just consists of silicon and platform-related changes that are applicable for the present platform and leverages existing features from the prior generation platform.

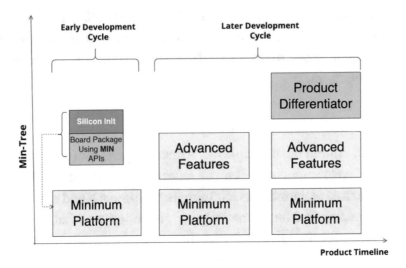

Figure 1-10. *Min-tree evolution over product timeline*

The later product development stages are targeted more toward meeting the product milestone releases; hence, it focuses on the code completion that includes development of the full feature sets applicable for this platform. Next is platform development, which focuses on the enablement of the product differentiator features, which is important for product scaling. Finally, the platform needs to be committed to sustenance, maintenance, and derivative activities. The staged platform approach is a more granular representation form of the min-tree where based on product requirement, timeline, security, feature sets, etc., one can decide the level of the tree to design the minimum platform architecture. For example, product-distinguishing features are not part of the essential or minimum platform or advanced feature list, and the board package is free to exclude such features using boot stage PCD (gMinPlatformPkgTokenSpaceGuid.PcdBootStage). This may be used to meet a particular use case based on the platform requirement. For example, a board may disable all advanced features by setting the board stage PCD value to 4 instead of 6 to improve the boot time. Decrementing the additional stages might also be used for SPINOR size reduction as the final bootloader executable binary size is expected to get reduced.

Minimum Platform Stage Approach

The MPA staged approach describes the minimal code block and binary components required while creating system firmware. The flexible architecture allows modifying the FD image to make it applicable for the target platform. In this architecture, each stage will have its own requirement and functionality based on the specific uses. For example, Stage III, Boot to UI, is focused on interfacing with console I/Os and other various hardware controllers using the command-line interface. Additionally, decrementing a stage might also translate to reducing the platform feature set. For example, a Stage III bootloader won't need to publish ACPI tables as this feature is not useful for the platform.

Figure 1-11 describes the stage architecture, including the expectations from the stage itself. Each stage is built upon the prior stage with extensibility to meet the silicon, platform, or board requirements.

Stage I: Minimal Debug

Stage I (Minimal Debug) is the base foundation block for the later stages supported by this architecture to add more complexity by introducing advanced functionality.

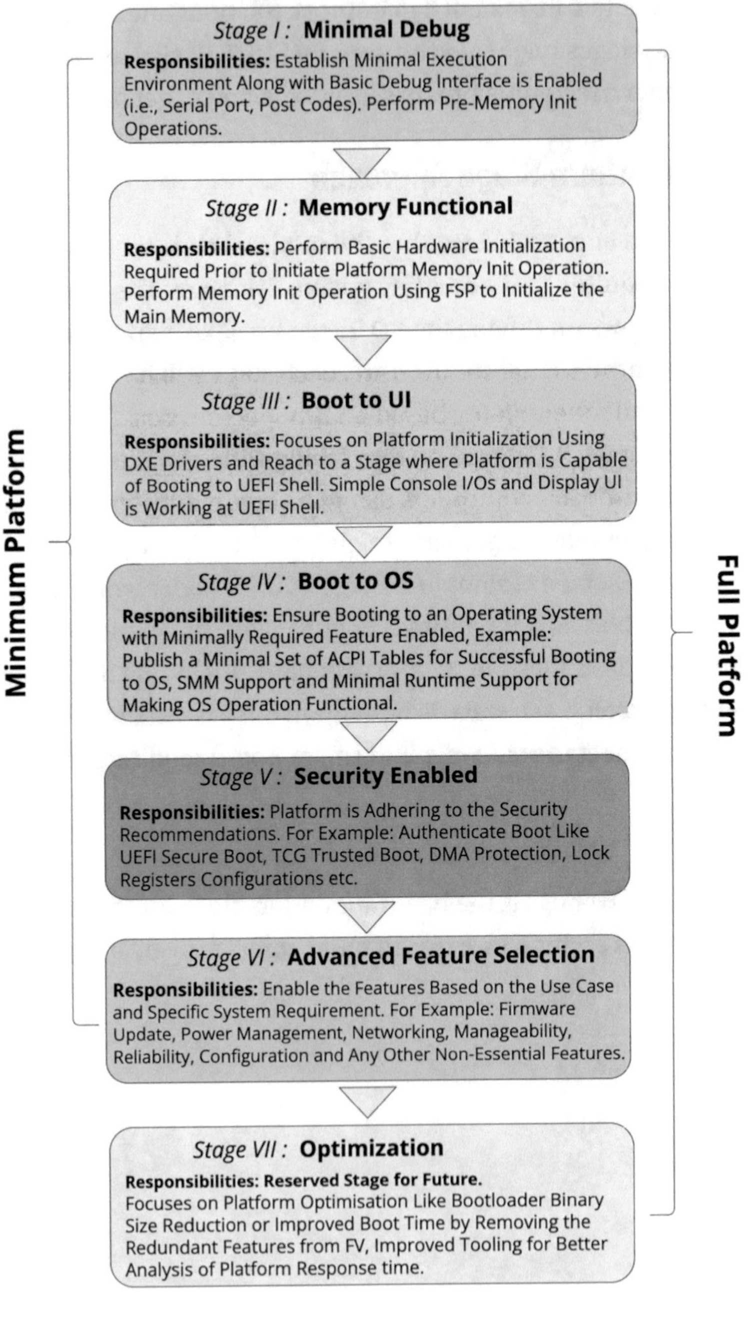

Minimum Platform

Full Platform

Stage I : **Minimal Debug**

Responsibilities: Establish Minimal Execution Environment Along with Basic Debug Interface is Enabled (i.e., Serial Port, Post Codes). Perform Pre-Memory Init Operations.

Stage II : **Memory Functional**

Responsibilities: Perform Basic Hardware Initialization Required Prior to Initiate Platform Memory Init Operation. Perform Memory Init Operation Using FSP to Initialize the Main Memory.

Stage III : **Boot to UI**

Responsibilities: Focuses on Platform Initialization Using DXE Drivers and Reach to a Stage where Platform is Capable of Booting to UEFI Shell. Simple Console I/Os and Display UI is Working at UEFI Shell.

Stage IV : **Boot to OS**

Responsibilities: Ensure Booting to an Operating System with Minimally Required Feature Enabled, Example: Publish a Minimal Set of ACPI Tables for Successful Booting to OS, SMM Support and Minimal Runtime Support for Making OS Operation Functional.

Stage V : **Security Enabled**

Responsibilities: Platform is Adhering to the Security Recommendations. For Example: Authenticate Boot Like UEFI Secure Boot, TCG Trusted Boot, DMA Protection, Lock Registers Configurations etc.

Stage VI : **Advanced Feature Selection**

Responsibilities: Enable the Features Based on the Use Case and Specific System Requirement. For Example: Firmware Update, Power Management, Networking, Manageability, Reliability, Configuration and Any Other Non-Essential Features.

Stage VII : **Optimization**

Responsibilities: Reserved Stage for Future.
Focuses on Platform Optimisation Like Bootloader Binary Size Reduction or Improved Boot Time by Removing the Redundant Features from FV, Improved Tooling for Better Analysis of Platform Response time.

Figure 1-11. *Minimum platform stage architecture*

Stage I is contained within the SEC and PEI phases; hence, it should get packed and uncompressed inside the firmware volume. The minimal expectation from this stage is to implement board-specific routines that enable the platform debug capability like serial output and/or postcode to see the sign of life.

The major responsibilities of Stage I are as follows:

- This is similar to all other bootloaders that come up on a memory-restricted environment like x86. Perform initialization of temporary memory and set up the code environment.

- Perform pre-memory board specific initialization (if any).

- Detect the platform by reading the board ID after performing the board-specific implementation.

- Perform early GPIO configuration for the serial port and other hardware controllers that are supposed to be used early in the boot flow.

- Enable the early debug interface, typically, serial port initialization over legacy I/O or modern PCH-based UARTs.

The functional exit criteria of Stage I is when temporary memory is available and the debug interface is initialized where the platform has written a message to indicate that Stage I is now getting terminated.

Stage II: Memory Functional

Stage II (Memory Functional) is primarily responsible for ensuring the code path that executes the memory initialization code for enabling the platform permanent memory. This stage extends the operations on top of Stage I and performs the additional/mandatory silicon initializations required prior to memory initialization. Because of the memory-restricted nature of platform boot, this stage is also packed uncompressed. Stage II is more relying on the FSP-M firmware volume in terms of finding the PEI core and dispatching the PEIMs.

The following of the major responsibilities of Stage II:

- Perform pre-memory recommended silicon policy initialization.

- Execute memory initialization module and ensure the basic memory test.

- Switch the program stack from temporary memory to permanent memory.

The functional exit criteria of Stage II are that early hardware devices like GPIOs are being programmed, main memory is initiated, temporary memory is disabled, memory type range registers (MTRRs) are programmed with main memory ranges, and the resource description HOB is built to pass that initialization information to the bootloader.

Stage III: Boot to UI

The primary objective of Stage III (Boot to UI) is to be able to successfully boot to the UEFI Shell with a basic UI enabled. The success criteria of this stage is not to demonstrate that every minimum platform architecture should be equipped with the UEFI Shell, but rather more focuses on the generic DXE driver execution on top of the underlying stages like Stages I and II (mainly targeted for silicon and board). The bare-minimal UI capability required for Stage III is a serial console.

Stage III is contained with the Driver Execution Environment (DXE) and Boot Device Selection (BDS) for booting to the UEFI Shell. The major responsibilities of Stage III are as follows:

- Bring generic UEFI-specific interfaces like DXE Initial Program Load (IPL), DXE Core, and dispatch DXE modules. This includes installing the DXE architectural protocols.

- Perform post-memory silicon-recommended initialization.

- Have a provision to access the nonvolatile media such as SPINOR using UEFI variables. Additionally, capabilities that can be enabled as part (but not only limited to this lists) of this phase allow various input and output device driver access such as USB, graphics, storage, etc.

The functional exit criteria of Stage III is to ensure all generic device drivers are not operational and the platform has reached the BDS phase, meaning the bootloader is able to implement minimal boot expectations for the platform.

Stage IV: Boot to OS

Leveraging on the previous stage, Stage IV (Boot to OS) is to enable a minimal boot path to successfully boot to an operating system (OS). The minimal boot path is the delta requirement over Stage III that ensures booting to an OS.

The minimal boot path for Stage IV includes the following:

- Add minimum ACPI tables required for booting an ACPI-compliant operating system. Examples are ACPI tables, namely, RSDT (XSDT), FACP, FACS, MADT, DSDT, HPET, etc.

- Based on the operating system expectation, it might additionally publish DeviceTree to allow the operating system to be loaded.

- Trigger the boot event that further executes the callbacks being registered by the FSP-S PEIMs to ensure locking down the chipset configuration register and dropping the platform privilege prior to launching the application outside trusted boundaries.

- This phase will also utilize the runtime services being implemented by the UEFI bootloader for communication like Timer and nonvolatile region access from the OS layer.

After the platform is able to successfully boot to a UEFI-compliant OS with a minimal ACPI table being published, it is enough to qualify Stage IV to call its termination. Additionally, this stage implements SMM support for x86–based platforms where runtime communication can get established based on software triggering SMI.

Stage V: Security Enable

The basic objective of Stage V (Security Enable) is to include security modules/foundations incrementally over Stage IV. Adhering to the basic/ essential security features is the minimal requirement for the modern computing systems. Chapter 5 is intended to highlight the scenarios to understand the security threat models and what it means for the platform to ensure security all around even in the firmware.

The major responsibilities of Stage V are as follows:

- Ensure that the lower-level chipset-specific security recommendation such as lockdown configuration is implemented.

- Hardware-based root of trust is being initialized and used to ensure that each boot phase is authenticated and verified prior to loading into the memory and executing it as a chain throughout the boot process.

- Protect the platform from various memory-related attacks if they implement the security advisory well.

- At the end of this phase, it will allow running any trusted and authenticated application including the operating system.

Stage VI: Advanced Feature Selection

Advanced features are the nonessential block in this min-tree structural development approach. All the essential and mandatory features required for a platform to reach an operating system are developed using stages I to V. The advanced feature selection is focused on developing firmware modules based on a few key principles such as modularization, reducing interdependencies over other features, etc. It helps these modules to get integrated with min-tree as per the user requirements, product use cases, and even the later product development cycle.

The design principles behind Stage VI are as follows:

- Platform development models become incremental where more essential features are integrated and developed at an early phase. Otherwise, the complex but generic advanced features can be developed without being bottlenecked on the current silicon and board but can be readily shared across platforms.

- Advanced feature modules necessarily do not contain functionality that is unrelated to the targeted feature.

- Each feature module should be self-content in nature, meaning it minimizes the dependencies to the other feature.

- The feature should expose a well-defined software interface that allows easy integration and configuration. For example, all modules should adhere to EDKII configuration options such as PCD to configure the feature.

Stage VII: Optimization

In the scope of current architecture, Stage VII (Optimization) is a proposed architectural stage reserved for future improvements. The objective of this stage is to provide an option for the platform to ensure optimization that focuses on the target platform. For example, on a scaling design without Thunderbolt ports, there should be a provision using PCD that disables dispatching of Thunderbolt drivers (including host, bus, and device). This is known as a *configurable* setting.

Additionally, there could be compilation-time configuration attached to the PCD that strips unused components from the defined FV. For example, FSP modules are used for API boot mode. It is intended that such optimization/tuning can be intercepted in the product even at a later stage without impacting the product milestone aka schedules.

These are just examples that demonstrate the architecture freedom to improve the platform boot time and SPINOR size reduction at the later stage.

To summarize, a hybrid system firmware development using EDKII MPA is intended to improve the relationship between open source and closed source components. An MPA design brings transparency to platform development even with EDKII platform code. The min-tree design serves as a basic enablement vehicle for the hardware power-on and allows cross-functional teams to get started on feature enablement. The feature enablement benefits from its modular design that is simple to maintain.

Open Source System Firmware Model

The ideal philosophy of open source system firmware is to make sure that all pieces of the firmware are open source, specifically, the ones required for the boot process post CPU reset. This effort of achieving the system firmware code is 100 percent open source and has significant dependency over the underlying platform hardware design. Typically, due to the unavailability of the detailed hardware interface document and programming sequence for boot-critical IPs like memory controller, system firmware projects should choose the hybrid system firmware model over complete open source system firmware. RISC-V is a good example of an open standard hardware specification that allows pure open source system firmware development on RISC-V-based embedded systems, personal computers, etc. The word *pure* being used here intentionally to differentiate a firmware project that supports closed source blobs for platform pre-reset flow from the transparent system reset flow (pre and post CPU reset) with all possible open source firmware.

There are several open source system firmware projects available, and this section is about having a detailed overview about expectations from the future open source system firmware. Hence, future system firmware will focus not only on getting rid of proprietary firmware blobs but also on adopting a modern programming language for developing system firmware. *oreboot* is an aspiring open source system firmware project that is slowly gaining momentum by migrating its supports from evaluation boards to real hardware platforms. oreboot has a vision of *pure* open systems, meaning firmware without binary blobs. But to add the latest x86-based platforms, it had made an exception to include only boot-critical blobs (for example, manageability firmware, AMD AGESA, FSP for performing specific silicon initialization), where feature implemented by blobs during boot is not possible to implement in oreboot.

This section will provide an architecture overview of oreboot and its internals, which will be valuable for developers to learn for preparing themselves for system firmware architecture migration into a more efficient and safe programming language. It's like a recurrence of events that happened a few decades back that had migrated the present system firmware programming language to C from assembly.

oreboot = Coreboot - C + Much More

At a high level, it's easy to define oreboot as downstream of the coreboot project, which is developed without the C programming language. The oreboot system firmware project has zero C code, very minimal code written in assembly to just set up the programming environment, and remaining code in the Rust language. With the introduction of the Rust code for system firmware development, it offers better security and reliability. The oreboot image is licensed under the GPL, version 2. Here are the design principles of oreboot, which make it different from the other boot firmware used on embedded systems:

- oreboot is focused on reducing the firmware boundary to ensure instant system boot. The goal for oreboot is to have fewer than one boot on embedded devices.

- It improves the system firmware security, which typically remains unnoticed by the platform security standards with a modern, safe programming language. Refer to Appendix A for details about the usefulness of Rust in system firmware programming, which deals with direct memory access and even operations that run on multithreaded environments.

- It removes dedicated *ramstage* usage from the boot flow and defines a stage named Payloader Stage. This will help to remove the redundant firmware drivers and utilities from LinuxBoot as payload.

- It jumps to the kernel as quickly as possible during boot. Firmware shouldn't contain the high-level device drivers such as network stack, disk drivers, etc., and it can leverage the most from LinuxBoot.

Currently, oreboot has support for all the latest CPU architecture, and adding support for the newer SoC and mainboards are a work in progress. Currently the RISC-V porting being done using oreboot is fully open sourced. In addition, it's able to boot an ASpeed AST2500 ARM-based server management processor as well as a RISC-V OpenTitan "earlgrey" embedded hardware.

oreboot Code Structure

The source code organization of an oreboot project is similar to coreboot with a more simplified build infrastructure. The makefile parts of oreboot directories are much simpler; unlike coreboot, they don't contain the control flow. The .toml-based configuration file is used to define and configure sets of tasks to run as part of control flow. A task is Rust code that needs to be executed. Tasks can have dependencies that are also tasks that will be executed before the current task itself. The following table describes the oreboot code structure:

Directory	Description
src/arch	Lists of supported CPU architecture, for example: armv7, armv2, risc-v, x86, etc.
src/drivers	Supported firmware drivers, written in Rust, that follow oreboot unique driver model, for example: clock, uart, spi, timer, etc.
src/lib	Generic libraries like devicetree, util, etc.

(*continued*)

Directory	Description
src/mainboard	Lists of supported mainboards as part of the oreboot project. This list contains emulation environments like qemu, engineering board such as upsquared based on x86, and HiFive the RISC-V based development board, BMC platform ast2500, etc.

Each mainboard directory contains a makefile and `Cargo.toml` file to define the build dependencies, which will allow it to build all boards in parallel.

Example of `Cargo.toml`:

```
[dependencies]
cpu = { path = "../../../cpu/armltd/cortex-a9"}
arch = { path = "../../../arch/arm/armv7"}
payloads = { path = "../../../../payloads"}
device_tree = { path = "../../../lib/device_
tree" }
soc = { path = "../../../soc/aspeed/ast2500" }

[dependencies.uart]
path = "../../../drivers/uart"
features = ["ns16550"]
```

Include source files written in Rust (`.rs`) and assembly (`.S`) as per the boot phase requirements.

Two special files reside in the mainboard directory as `fixed-dtfs.dts` to create the flash layout and describe system hardware configuration as `mainboard.dts`. `mainboard.dtb` is the binary encoding of the device tree structure.

(continued)

Directory	Description
src/soc	Source code for SoC that includes clock programming, early processor initialization, setting up code environment, DRAM initialization sequence, chipset registers programming, etc. Each SoC directory also contains Cargo.toml that defines the dependent drivers and library required for SoC-related operations.
payloads/	Library for payload-related operations like loading into memory and executing.
tools/	Tools directory that contains useful utilities like layoutflash to create an image from binary blobs, as described in the layout specified using device tree, bin2vmem to convert binary to Verilog VMEM format, etc.
README.md	Describes the prerequisites to getting started with oreboot, cloning source code, compilation, etc., useful for the first-time developer.
Makefile.inc	This makefile is included by the project mainboard directory makefile.

oreboot Internals

This section will guide developers through the various key concepts of oreboot that are required to understand its architecture. Without understanding these architectural details, it would be difficult to contribute to a project. Also, these are the key differentiating features for oreboot, compared to the coreboot project.

Flash Layout

Flash layout specifies how different binaries as part of oreboot are getting stitched together to create the final firmware image (ROM) for flashing into the SPI Flash. This file is named fixed-dtfs.dts, belonging to each mainboard directory.

oreboot has replaced the coreboot file system (CBFS) with the Device Tree File System (DTFS). It is easy to expose the layout of the flash chip without any extra OS interface. DTFS provides an easy method to describe the different binary blobs.

Here is sample code to describe the different regions belonging to the flash layout (see Figure 1-12):

```
area@x {
    description = "Boot Blob";
    offset = <0xff0000>;
    size = <0x20000>; // 512KiB
    file = "$(TARGET_DIR)/bootblob.bin";
};
```

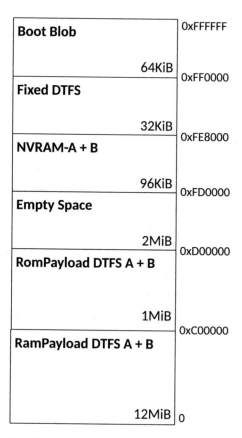

Figure 1-12. *32MiB flash layout*

The *description* field defines the type of binary, *offset* is the base address of the region, the *size* field specifies the region limit, and the *file* field is used to mention the path of the binary. *x* is the region number inside the flash layout, for example: boot blob, rampayload, NVRAM, etc. With reduced boot phases, the oreboot architecture allows ample headroom in flash.

Build Infrastructure

coreboot uses make menuconfig to allow configuration, but oreboot doesn't have such a provision; hence, it relies on conditional compilation. An oreboot build starts when the developer executes the make command from a specific mainboard directory. The code inside src/mainboard/*/*/ src/main.rs starts with assembly instruction first, which performs the minimal amount of initialization that is required to call into the Rust program. Compared to other C-based firmware modules, which have predefined entry points such as main(), here main.rs has the pub extern "C" fn 'entry_func_name' method that is being called from the assembly to start the program. The code written in Rust does the platform initialization and prepares the system to load and run the payload. The mainboard code uses only the core library, which means no heap allocated structures and that arrays should be with statically allocated size. See Figure 1-13.

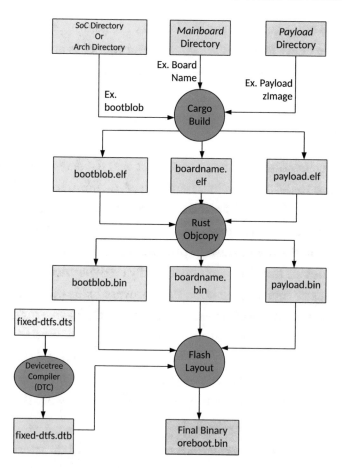

Figure 1-13.   *oreboot build flow*

The binary generation process is a two-step approach.

- Create an executable and linking format (ELF) binary from source code using the cargo build command.

- Convert the .elf file to binary format (.bin) with the rust objcopy command.

The output binary (.bin) belongs to a region specified using the *file field* as part of the flash layout file. Now these binaries need to construct an image that will be flashed into the device. The tool name layoutflash is (source code belongs to the `tools` directory as mentioned earlier) used to construct the final binary (.ROM). It takes arguments as an oreboot device tree to specify the image layout and compiled binary files generated by the compilation process.

Device Tree

The DTS specification specifies a construct called a *device tree*, which is typically used to describe system hardware. A device tree is a tree data structure with nodes that describe the device present in the system. Each node has a value that describes the characteristics of the device. At compilation, the boot firmware prepares the device information in the form of device tree that can't necessarily be dynamically detected during boot, and then during boot, the firmware loads the device tree into the system memory and passes a pointer to the device for the OS to understand the system hardware layout. Unlike coreboot, the device tree structure prepared by oreboot is more scalable and can be parsed by existing OSs without any modification.

In oreboot, the device tree is mainly used to serve two different purposes.

- *Hardware device tree*: Part of the mainboard directory, this is used to describe the system hardware that the system firmware is currently running. This is typically named after the mainboard; for example, a device tree name for RISC-V processor–based development board HiFive is `hifive.dts`.

- *oreboot device tree*: This is the device tree used to define the layout of the image that is flashed into the device.

The `device_tree` library inside the `src/lib` source code is used to operate on the device tree data structure. *Device Tree Syntax* (DTS) is a human-friendly text representation of the device tree, which is used by the *Device Tree Compiler* (DTC) to convert into either *Device Tree Blob* (DTB) format or *Flattened Device Tree* (FDT) format, a binary encoding of the device tree structure. Figure 1-14 shows an example representation of a simple hardware device tree that represents the HiFive board. Device nodes are shown with properties and values inside each node.

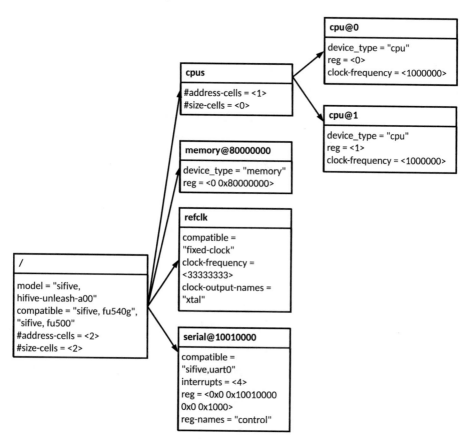

Figure 1-14. *Device tree example from oreboot HiFive mainboard*

In the previous example, *cpus, memory, refclk,* and *serial* are node names, and *root node* is identified by a forward slash (*/*). @ is used to specify the *unit-address* to the bus type on which the node sits.

Driver Model

oreboot defines an unique driver model that creates a driver trait, an interface that implements four functions: `init()`, `read()`, `write()`, and `shutdown()`. The details of these functions are as follows:

Driver Functions	Description
`init()`	Initializes the device.
`pread()`	Positional read. It takes two arguments:
	- *First argument:* A mutable buffer that will get filled data from the driver.
	- *Second argument:* The position that one would like to read from.
	The function returns the result; the type of the result could be either a number, defined the number of bytes being read, or an error. If there are no more bytes to read, it returns an end-of-file (EOF) error.
`pwrite()`	Positional writing. It takes two arguments:
	- *First argument:* A buffer that contains data is used by the driver to write on the hardware.
	- *Second argument:* The position that one would like to write into.
	The function returns the number of bytes written.
`shutdown()`	Shuts down the device.

This model is useful for different types of devices like block devices and character devices since the driver could ignore the position like the offsets while operating on hardware devices. Here are some examples of different driver types that oreboot supports:

- *Physical device drivers*: The drivers that are used to operate on real hardware devices like memory drivers are capable of performing reads/writes to physical memory addresses, serial drivers used to read/writes to serial devices, clock drivers to initialize the clock controller present on the hardware, and DDR drivers to perform DRAM-based device initialization.

- *Virtual drivers*: Drivers that are not associated with any real hardware device but rather used to create the interface for accessing the hardware device. For example, the union driver is capable of stream input or output to multiple device drivers; refer to the following example of mainboard, which implements the union driver for a serial device; and section reader, which reads a section from another device window specified using offset and size and returns EOF when the end of the window is reached.

The following is an example of a mainboard implementing more than one UART. The system firmware would like to use all of them and hence implements the union driver as shown. The oreboot mainboard code creates an array of these drivers, and the union driver uses this array. Meanwhile, the console calls the init() function, initializes all these UART controllers, and then writes a string using the pwrite() function to write into all these UARTs.

```
let mut uarts = [
    &mut PL011::new(0x1E72_3000, 115200) as &mut dyn Driver,
    // UART 1
    &mut PL011::new(0x1E72_D000, 115200) as &mut dyn Driver,
    // UART 2
    &mut PL011::new(0x1E72_E000, 115200) as &mut dyn Driver,
    // UART 3
```

```
    &mut PL011::new(0x1E72_F000, 115200) as &mut dyn Driver,
    // UART 4
];
let console = &mut Union::new(&mut uarts[..]);
console.init();
console.pwrite(b"Welcome to oreboot\r\n", 0).unwrap();
```

oreboot Boot Flow

The boot flow defined by oreboot is similar to coreboot, except for the fact that oreboot has accepted that a firmware boundary has to be reduced, so it makes sense to leverage more from the powerful payload offerings as LinuxBoot with a more mature Linux kernel driver. oreboot replaces the need to have a dedicated stage like ramstage, which is meant to perform an operation that can be replaced by a powerful payload and load a payload. The oreboot boot flow provides an option to load the Linux kernel as part of the flash image as the payload from the payloader stage.

Facts   Some of the work done in a coreboot project is separating the payload loading and running operations from a dedicated stage like ramstage and having a flexible design where the bootloader is free to decide which stage can be used to load the payload. This work is known as Rampayload or coreboot-Lite, which influences the design of oreboot having an independent stage for payload operations and being called from prior stages as per the platform requirements.

The following sections explain the oreboot boot flow in detail with a hardware porting guide. The oreboot boot process is divided into three stages.

- *Bootblob*: This is the first stage post CPU reset, which is executed from the boot device. It holds the first instruction being executed by the CPU. This stage is similar to coreboot's first stage called *bootblock*.

- *Romstage*: This is functionally similar to the coreboot romstage boot phase, which is intended to perform the main memory initialization.

- *Payloader stage*: This is only intended to load and run the payload. This is a feature differentiator from the coreboot, where the ramstage boot state machine has tasks to load and run payload at the end of hardware initialization.

Here is a more detailed description of each stage operations based on the real hardware. The hardware used for this demonstration of the oreboot boot flow is the open source HiFive Unleashed Board based on the SiFive FU540 processor. Figure 1-15 shows the hardware block diagram.

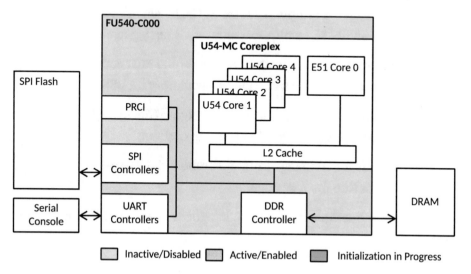

Figure 1-15. *Hardware block diagram of SiFive-HiFive Unleashed*

In this example, RISC-V SoC has four pins (0001, MSEL0 is 1 and MSEL1-3 are set to 0) called MSEL to choose where the bootloader is, and Zeroth Stage Boot Loader (ZBL) is stored in the ROM of the SoC. ZBL loads oreboot from the SPI Flash, and control reaches the bootblob.

Bootblob

In the oreboot boot flow architecture, bootblob is the first stage, which gets control upon the CPU coming out from the reset. In a multiprocessor boot environment, it's getting executed by the Boot Strap Processor (BSP) using temporary memory. Operations performed by the bootblock phase include the following:

- The early piece of the code in bootblob is written in assembly, which is executed by the CPU immediately after release from power-on reset. It performs the processor-specific initialization as per the CPU architecture.

- It sets up the temporary RAM as Cache as RAM, aka CAR or SRAM, as physical memory is not yet available.

- It prepares the environment for running Rust code like setting up the stack and clearing memory for BSS.

- It initializes UART(s) to show the sign-of life using the debug print message "Welcome to oreboot."

- It finds the romstage from the oreboot device tree and jumps into the romstage.

Here is some sample bootblob code written in assembly belonging to the SoC directory:

soc/sifive/fu540/src/bootblock.S

```
/* Early initialization code for RISC-V */
.globl _boot
_boot:
    # The previous boot stage passes these variables:
    #    a0: hartid
    #    a1: ROM FDT
    # a0 is redundant with the mhartid register. a1 might not
      be valid on
    # some hardware configurations, but is always set in QEMU.
    csrr a0, mhartid

setup_nonboot_hart_stack:
    # sp <- 0x02021000 + (0x1000 * mhartid) - 2
    li sp, (0x02021000 - 2)
    slli t0, a0, 12
    add sp, sp, t0

    # 0xDEADBEEF is used to check stack underflow.
    li t0, 0xDEADBEEF
    sw t0, 0(sp)
      # Jump into Rust code
    call _start_nonboot_hart
```

Figure 1-16 represents the operations performed by the bootblob stage pictorially.

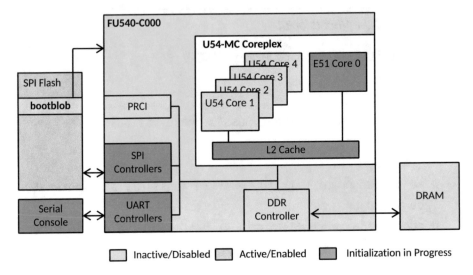

Figure 1-16. *Operational diagram of bootblob stage*

Romstage

The romstage is the stage invoked right after the bootblob in the boot flow. This stage gets executed from the SPI Flash and performs DRAM initialization. The responsibilities of the romstage are as follows:

- Perform early device initialization, for example configuring memory-mapped control and status register for controlling component power states, resets, clock selection and low-level interrupts, etc.

- Initiate the DRAM initialization. Configure memory controllers as part of the SoC hardware block. This process involves running SoC vendor-specific routines that train the physical memory or implementing memory reference code in Rust (basically a direct porting from C to Rust). For the HiFive Unleashed platform, oreboot has implemented DDR initialization

code in Rust belonging to `soc/sifive/fu540/`
`src/ddr*.rs` by referring to open source FSBL
implementation.

Here is some sample romstage code written in Rust that
initializes clocks:

```
// Peripheral clocks get their dividers updated when the PLL
initializes.
let mut clks = [spi0 as &mut dyn ClockNode, spi1 as &mut dyn
ClockNode, spi2 as &mut dyn ClockNode, uart0 as &mut dyn
ClockNode];
let mut clk = Clock::new(&mut clks);
clk.pwrite(b"on", 0).unwrap();
```

Figure 1-17 represents the operations performed by the romstage
pictorially.

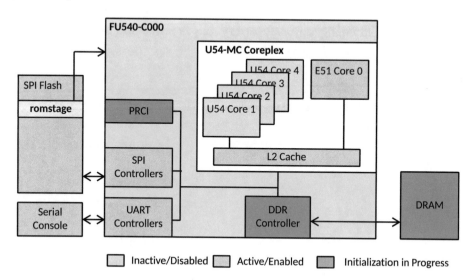

Figure 1-17. *Operational diagram of romstage*

Payloader Stage

The Payloader stage is the first stage on the RISC-V platform running from the DRAM after physical memory is available. Unlike coreboot, where the ramstage boot phase has many other tasks along with loading and running the payload at the end of the ramstage, in oreboot, the payloader stage has only one job: find, load, and run a payload. The payloader stage doesn't have any high-level firmware device drivers like storage device, audio device, etc. This helps to reduce the complexity and save the SPI footprint compared to other system firmware. Here is a sample payloader stage code written in Rust that loads a payload file by the path specified in the oreboot device tree and jumps into it:

```
use payloads::external::zimage::PAYLOAD;
let p = PAYLOAD;
writeln!(w, "Loading payload\r").unwrap();
p.load();
writeln!(w, "Running payload entry 0x{:x} dtb 0x{:x}\r",
p.entry, p.dtb).unwrap();
p.run();
```

Figure 1-18 represents the operations performed by the payloader stage pictorially.

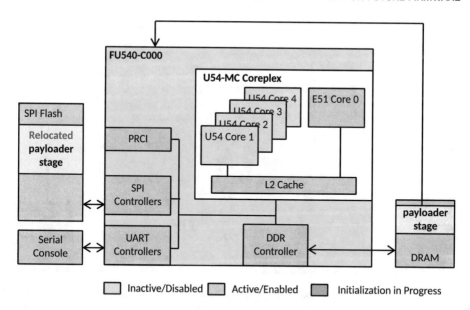

Figure 1-18. Operational diagram of payloader stage

Payload

An oreboot project by default uses LinuxBoot as a payload, which allows it to load the Linux kernel from the SPI Flash into DRAM. The Linux kernel is expected to initialize the remaining devices using kernel drivers that include block devices and/or network devices etc. Finally, locate and load the target operating system using kexec. LinuxBoot uses u-root as initramfs, which is the root filesystem that the system has access to upon booting to the Linux kernel. *systemboot* is an OS loader as part of u-root to perform an iterative operation to attempt boot from a network or local boot device.

Figure 1-19 represents the operations performed by the payload (LinuxBoot) pictorially.

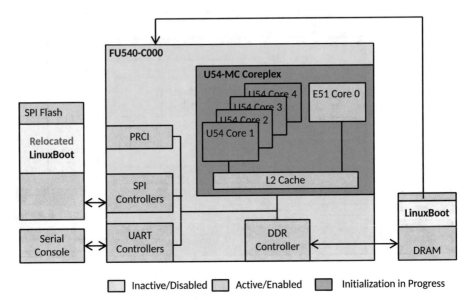

Figure 1-19. *Operational diagram of payload stage*

The payload operation is expected to end when the Linux kernel part of LinuxBoot calls into the kernel image from the block device or network and executes the first instruction. Figure 1-20 shows the final system hardware component initialization state while it reaches an operating system.

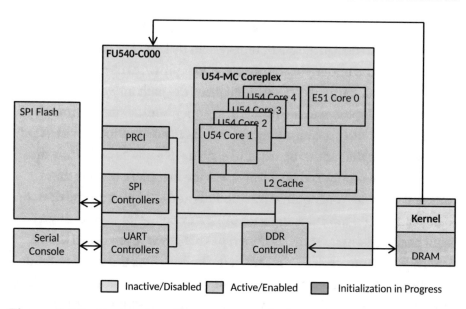

Figure 1-20. *System hardware state at the kernel*

To summarize, the complete open source system firmware model using oreboot like the bootloader is not only meant to provide freedom from running proprietary firmware blobs on hardware. Additionally, it's developed using safe system programming languages like Rust. The payloader userland is written in Go and advocates the architectural migration of the system firmware development using a high-level language in the future. Finally, a reduced boot phase allows ample free space in the flash layout, which will provide an opportunity to reduce the hardware bill of materials (BoM) cost with instant boot experience.

Open Source Device Firmware Development

System firmware is the firmware that is running on the host CPU after it comes out from the reset. In traditional computing systems, system firmware is owned by independent BIOS vendors (IBVs), and adopting the open source firmware model will help to get visibility into their code. This will help to design a transparent system by knowing the program is running on the underlying hardware, and it provides more control over the system. Earlier sections highlighted the path forward for system firmware development in the future using open source system firmware as much as possible. In a computing system, there are multiple devices that are attached to the motherboard, and each device has its own firmware. When a device is powered on, firmware is the first piece of code that runs and provides the required instructions and guidance for the device to be ready for communicating with other devices or for performing a set of basic tasks as intended. These types of firmware are called *device firmware*. Without device firmware being operational, the device wouldn't be able to function. Based on the type of the devices, a complexity in the firmware is introduced. For example, if a device is a simple keyboard device, then it has only a limited goal and no need to worry about regular updates, whereas more complex ones, like graphics cards, need to define an interface that allows it to interact with the system firmware and/or an operating system to achieve a common goal, which is to enable the display.

The majority of device firmware present on consumer products is running proprietary firmware that might lead to a security risk. For example, at the 2014 Black Hat conference, security researchers first exposed a vulnerability in USB firmware that leads to a BadUSB attack, a USB flash device, which is repurposed to spoof various other device types to take control of a computer, pull data, and spy on the user. A potential solution to this problem is that device firmware should be developed using open source so that the code can be reviewed and maintained by others rather than only the independent hardware vendors (IHVs).

This section will describe the evolution in device firmware development for discrete devices that has a firmware burned into its SPINOR.

Legacy Device Firmware/Option ROM

An option ROM (OpROM) is a piece of firmware that resides either in the system firmware code as a binary blob or on an expansion card, which needs to be copied into system memory and executed using legacy interrupts by system firmware during the platform initialization phase. It acts as an interface between the system firmware and underlying specific hardware device. The BIOS Boot Specification (BBS) was developed to standardize the initialization sequence of OpROM. Figure 1-21 shows a sample discrete graphics where VBIOS is located inside a dedicated chip.

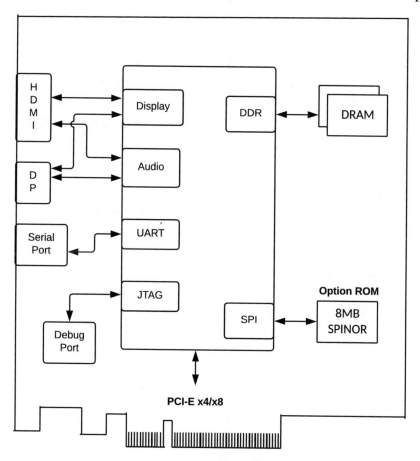

Figure 1-21. *Discrete graphics card hardware block diagram*

A common example of OpROM is the Video BIOS (VBIOS), which can be used to program either on-board graphics or discrete graphics cards and is specific to the device manufacturer. In this section, VBIOS is referred to and used to initialize the discrete graphics card after the device is powered on. It also implements an INT 10h interrupt (interrupt vector in an x86-based system) and VESA BIOS Extensions (VBE) (to define a standardized software interface to display and audio devices) for both the pre-boot application and system software to use.

A video services BIOS interrupt sets up a real mode interrupt handler; meaning, to get this interrupt serviced, the system needs to enter into real address mode. As real mode is limited to 20-bit addressing, it provides a limited space for OpROMs. A total 122KB (between 0xc0000 to 0xdffff, sometimes if it's extended and then stored at 0xe0000–0xeffff, and so on) is shared by all option ROMs. An OpROM typically compacts itself by getting rid of some initialization code (leaving behind a smaller runtime code). During the power-on self-test (POST), the BBS specifies that the BIOS will detect and shadow VBIOS into 0xc0000, and it will traverse the PCI configuration space to check the Expansion ROM base address (PCI config space header type 00 and 20 devices only have an expansion ROM base address to support an add-on ROM) and copy the discrete card OpROM from MMIO space to the predefined OpROM region. The system firmware then scans the region and detects if the OpROM has a PnP option ROM header. The following table describes the PnP OpROM header structure:

Offset	Length	Value	Description
0x00	0x02	0xAA55	Signature
0x02	0x01	Varies	Option ROM length
0x03	0x4	Varies	Initialization vector
0x07	0x13	Varies	Reserved
0x12h	0x02	Varies	Offset to PCI data structure
0x1A	0x02	Varies	Offset to PnP expansion Header structure

- *Signature*: All ISA expansion ROMs are currently required to identify themselves with a signature word of AA55h at offset 0. This signature is used by the system firmware as well as other software to identify that an option ROM is present at a given address.

- *Length*: The length of the option ROM in 512 byte increments.

- *Initialization vector*: The system BIOS will execute a far call to this location to initialize the option ROM. The field is four bytes wide even though most implementations adhere to the custom of defining a simple three-byte NEAR JMP. The definition of the fourth byte may be OEM specific.

- *Reserved*: This area is used by various vendors and contains OEM-specific data and copyright strings.

- *Offset to PCI data structure*: This location contains a pointer to a PCI data structure, which holds the vendor-specific information.

- *Offset to PnP expansion header*: This location contains a pointer to a linked list of option ROM expansion headers.

The system firmware performs a read operation to read the first two bytes of the PnP OpROM structure and verifies the signature as 0xAA55. If a valid option ROM header is present, then the system firmware reads the offset + 02h to get the length of the OpROM and then performs a far call to offset + 03h to initialize the device. After video OpROM has initialized the graphics controller, it provides lists of services like setting the video mode, character and string output, and other VBE functions to operate in graphics mode.

Here is a list of a few supported functions implemented by OpROM. The system BIOS needs to hook INT 10h to call these functions as per programming requirements.

General Video Service Functions (AH = 00 to FF, except 0x4F)

Operation	Function	Subfunction
Set Video Mode	AH=0x00	AL=Video Mode
Set Cursor Characteristics	AH=0x01	CH bits 0-4 = start line for cursor in character cell
		bits 5-6 = blink attribute (00=normal, 01=invisible, 10=slow, 11=fast)
		CL bits 0-4 = end line for cursor in character cell
Set Cursor Position	AH=0x02	DH,DL = row, column
		BH = page number (0 in graphics modes; 0–3 in modes 2 and 3; 0–7 in modes 0&1)
Write String (AT, VGA)	AH=0x13	AL = mode
		BL = attribute if AL bit 1 clear
		BH = display page number
		DH,DL = row,column of starting cursor position
		CX = length of string
		ES:BP -> start of string

VBE Functions (AH = 0x4F and AL = 0x00 to 0x15)

Return VBE Controller Information	AH=0x4F	AL = 0x00; ES:DI = Pointer to buffer in which to place VbeInfoBlock Structure.
Return VBE Mode Information	AH=0x4F	AL = 0x01; CX = Mode Number; ES:DI = Pointer to ModeInfoBlock Structure.
Set VBE Mode	AH=0x4F	AX = 02h
		BX = Desired Mode to set
		ES:DI = Pointer to CRTCInfoBlock structure

Figure 1-22 describes the communication between video OpROM and system firmware.

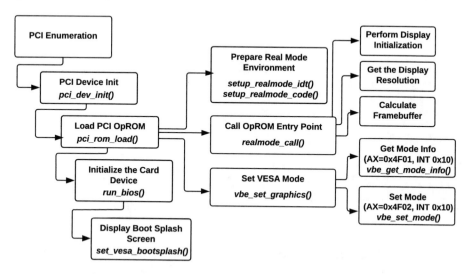

Figure 1-22. *Discrete graphics card hardware block diagram*

In this sample implementation, the system firmware calls video OpROM to initialize the graphics controller and uses video services to set the display to show the pre-OS display screen or OS splash screen during boot.

Figure 1-23 decodes the video OpROM from the system memory 0xc0000 location, and Figure 1-24 shows the OpROM initialization code in assembly.

```
C:\WINDOWS\system32\cmd.exe - debug                                        _ □ ×

C:\DOCUME~1\subratab>debug
-d c000:0000
C000:0000   55 AA 63 E9 0B BD 30 30-30 30 30 30 30 30 30 30   U.c....0000000000
C000:0010   30 30 A4 18 E9 BD 17 BB-40 00 B0 0A 30 30 49 42   00......@...00IB
C000:0020   4D 20 56 47 41 20 43 6F-6D 70 61 74 69 62 6C 65   M UGA Compatible
C000:0030   20 42 49 4F 53 2E 20 03-5A 00 6A 00 78 00 8B C0    BIOS. .Z.j.x....
C000:0040   50 43 49 52 52 86 80 02-2E-00 00 18 00 00 00 03   PCIR............
C000:0050   80 00 00 00 00 00 80 00-00-66 03 00 C0 00 00 00   .........f......
C000:0060   00 00 00 00 00 00 00 00-74 00 00 C0 00 00 00 00   ........t.......
C000:0070   00 00 00 00 1A 00 2F 03-00 C0 00 00 00 00 00 00   ....../.........
```

Figure 1-23. *Display video BIOS option ROM at address 0xC0000*

Offset + 03h specified the initialization vector, which will transfer the call into video OpROM initialization code for display initialization, which is referred as *jmp 0xbd11*.

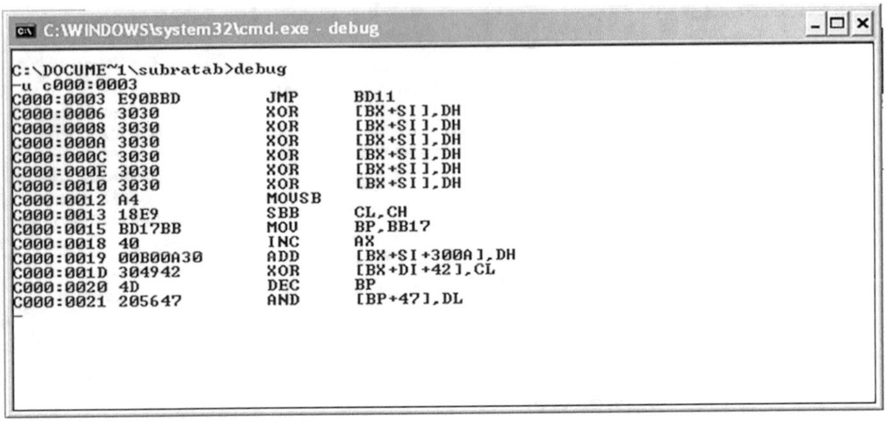

```
C:\WINDOWS\system32\cmd.exe - debug                                    _ □ ×

C:\DOCUME~1\subratab>debug
-u c000:0003
C000:0003 E90BBD        JMP     BD11
C000:0006 3030          XOR     [BX+SI],DH
C000:0008 3030          XOR     [BX+SI],DH
C000:000A 3030          XOR     [BX+SI],DH
C000:000C 3030          XOR     [BX+SI],DH
C000:000E 3030          XOR     [BX+SI],DH
C000:0010 3030          XOR     [BX+SI],DH
C000:0012 A4            MOVSB
C000:0013 18E9          SBB     CL,CH
C000:0015 BD17BB        MOV     BP,BB17
C000:0018 40            INC     AX
C000:0019 00B00A30      ADD     [BX+SI+300A],DH
C000:001D 304942        XOR     [BX+DI+42],CL
C000:0020 4D            DEC     BP
C000:0021 205647        AND     [BP+47],DL
```

Figure 1-24. Initialization vector address at address 0xC0003

This execution of OpROM for device initialization has several limitations while working with modern firmware solutions. Option ROM attacks can be considered an initial infection or ones to spread malicious firmware from one firmware component to another. Compromised OpROM firmware can be viewed as an initial method of infection that remains persistent even after modifying the system firmware. There is still a legacy implementation, where the system firmware and/or payload relies on the option ROM for device initialization and runtime services. Therefore, modern devices like discrete graphics cards and network cards still need to support legacy OpROMs.

UEFI OpROM

The Graphics Output Protocol replaces the legacy video BIOS and eliminatew the VGA hardware functionality from the discrete graphics card or on-board graphics controller. It's an UEFI implementation to create the generic GOP UEFI display driver image that can be either located on the device ROM or present inside system firmware. GOP has some unique advantages over legacy OpROM.

- It has a modern and well-defined interface, which is implemented using an industry-standard specification.

- All GPUs within a platform become "equal," and there's no more unique "VGA-enabled VGA."

- Code is written in C and doesn't need a legacy interrupt handler to communicate between the platform and GPU.

- Implementing UEFI graphics OpROM using EBC (EFI Byte Code) allows a single image to operate on multiple CPU architectures.

- There are clearer and portable solutions that allow new features to be implemented.

The services implemented by the GOP driver are available only until EFI Boot Time Services are available (prior to `ExitBootServices()`). However, the framebuffer populated by the GOP driver persists, meaning the OS graphics driver and applications can continue to use the framebuffer for graphics output. The implementation of the UEFI-compliant video option ROM starts with an implementation of the UEFI GOP driver. The GOP driver follows the UEFI driver model and hence installs a driver binding protocol at the entry point of the UEFI driver. The

GOP driver binding protocol implements functions such as `Supported()`, `Start()`, and `Stop()`.

- *Supported()*: The "Supported" method of the GOP driver binding protocol tests to see whether the given handle is a manageable adapter. Also, check that `EFI_DEVICE_PATH_PROTOCOL` and `EFI_PCI_IO_PROTOCOL` are present to ensure that the handle that is passed is a valid PCI device. The PCI I/O protocol gets the PCI configuration header from the device and verifies that the device is supported by the present GOP driver.

- *Start()*: The "Start" method of the GOP driver binding protocol tells the graphics driver to start managing the controller. The GOP driver uses the device-specific knowledge to perform the following operations:

  - Initialize the graphics adapter.

  - Initialize platform parameters like LID Present, Dock Supported, etc.

  - Initialize the display manager module that enumerates all the supported displays and checks its live status and EDID to detect the enabled display device.

  - Create child handles for each detected and enabled physical output device and install the `EFI_DEVICE_PATH_PROTOCOL`.

  - Get EDID information from each enabled physical output device and install `EFI_EDID_DISCOVERED_PROTOCOL` on the child handle.

- Create child handlers for each valid combination of two or more video output devices and install `EFI_DEVICE_PATH_PROTOCOL`.

- Set the initial mode, required to initialize the mode field of GOP.

- Install the `GRAPHICS_OUTPUT_PROTOCOL` on the selected device.

- *Stop()*: The Stop function performs the opposite operation of the Startfunction. In general, `Stop()` functions uninstall all protocols, close the protocol instances, release all resources, and disable the graphics adapter.

Figure 1-25 shows an example of GOP driver stack implementation.

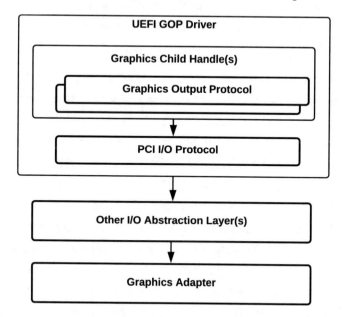

Figure 1-25. *GOP driver implementation*

Apart from initializing the graphics adapter, the GOP protocol publishes three functions: QueryMode(), SetMode(), and Blt(). They allow the system firmware to communicate with the device hardware to configure the display capabilities. These functions replace the legacy OpROM VBE functionality.

- The QueryMode() function is used to return extended information on one of the supported video modes. It's important that QueryMode() only return modes that can actually be displayed on the attached display device.

- The SetMode() function allows system firmware to select the specific mode based on the mode argument, between 0 and numModes.

- The Blt() function is used for transferring information to and from the video buffer. It allows graphics contents to be moved from one location of the video frame buffer to another location of the video frame buffer.

The GRAPHICS_OUTPUT_PROTOCOL.Mode pointer is populated when the graphics controller is initialized and gets updated with the SetMode() function call. The FrameBufferBase member of this object may be used by a UEFI OS loader or OS kernel to update the contents of the graphical display after ExitBootServices() is called and the Graphics Output Protocol services are no longer available. A UEFI OS may choose to use this method until a graphics driver can be installed and started.

The EDKII build infrastructure tools allows one to convert one or more UEFI drivers in PE/COFF image formats into a single PCI Option ROM image that can be included with a discrete add-in card. When a discrete add-in card, for example, a graphics card, is attached over a PCI slot into a target platform, the PCI Bus Driver detects the presence of PCI OpROM contents, and the UEFI driver is loaded into memory and executed automatically. See Figure 1-26.

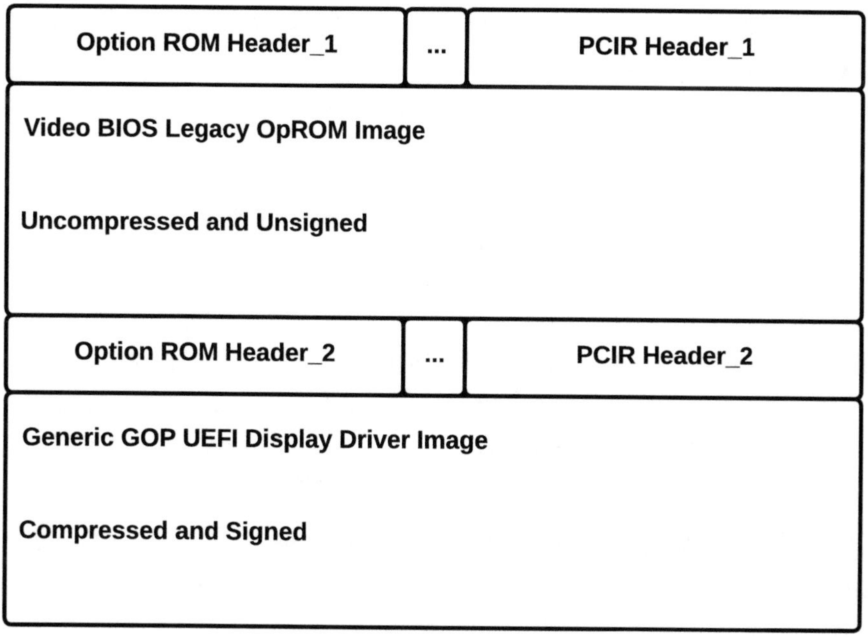

Option ROM Header_1	...	PCIR Header_1

Video BIOS Legacy OpROM Image

Uncompressed and Unsigned

Option ROM Header_2	...	PCIR Header_2

Generic GOP UEFI Display Driver Image

Compressed and Signed

Figure 1-26. *Hybrid ROM layout*

EfiRom is the utility located inside the EDKII source code at
BaseTools/Source/C/EfiRom and is used to build PCI OpROM images
containing UEFI drivers, Legacy OpROM, or both. It also allows UEFI
drivers to be compressed using the UEFI compression algorithm as per
the UEFI specification. The following command shows the method to
generate a single PCI OpROM image that combines one UEFI binary and
one legacy OpROM:

```
EfiRom -o FinalOpRom.rom -f <vendor_id>-i <device_id> -ec
File1.efi -b Legacy.bin
```

Figure 1-26 shows the layout of the hybrid OpROM image located on a graphics add-on card.

Here is a comparison of interfaces implemented by the UEFI graphics driver part of UEFI OpROM and Legacy VGA BIOS:

	Set a Display Mode	Retrieve EDID from a Display Device	Display Switch
GOP Driver	GRAPHICS_ OUTPUT_ PROTOCOL. SetMode()	Using EFI_EDID_ DISCOVERED_ PROTOCOL	Reentrant with different child handle in EFI_DRVER_BINDING. Start() followed by a SetMode()
Legacy VGA BIOS	Set VBE Mode using AX = 0x4F02 and other subfunctions	VBE DDC Extension AX = 0x4F15 and other subfunctions	Implement vendor-specific VGA BIOS extension

Currently, the majority of GPU vendors have migrated graphics device firmware to a GOP driver–based solution for add-on graphics cards or on-board GPU to be legacy-free. The GOP driver images that are part of the add-on graphics card can be signed and authenticated by the vendor and can be verified using Secure Boot. But for the hybrid image on an add-on graphics card, Secure Boot is unable to verify the legacy OpROM image as the legacy VGA BIOS doesn't support authentication and hence is considered to be a security threat.

Why Is Open Source Device Firmware Needed?

Typically, IHVs are developing firmware for the device that is flashed into the ROM, with an assumption that the device doesn't need periodic updates. But there might be cases where preflashed device firmware exposed some vulnerability while operating as part of the whole system and communicating with other devices and the host CPUs. Also, these devices have dedicated firmware storage for to keep the device firmware in, which is not accessible by the host CPU and hence unable to provide a patch over the runtime kernel or system firmware during boot. Here are several factors that highlight the need for an open source model while developing the device firmware:

- *Performance*: As most device firmware is not able to handle the runtime updates and becomes stale over the period of time, it may not be able to work with the latest processor and chipsets. Open source firmware development would provide an opportunity to update the device firmware code with the latest algorithm and research that would provide better performance compared to proprietary firmware.

- *Security*: Open source device firmware doesn't allow any hidden backdoor for snooping into the system. As device firmware would get regular maintenance, common vulnerabilities are expected to get fixed and updated without any delay.

- *Extensibility*: While vendor device firmware comes with fixed sets of capability, open source firmware would expose its capability beyond its fixed scope.

- *Community support*: The open source community provides more eyes and hands for maintaining the code.

- *Cost*: The product source code is available freely using a GPL license and hence doesn't require any subscription and licensing fees.

Many wireless routers are using open source device firmware. For example, TP-Link, which is Xiaomi router firmware, is derived from OpenWrt, an open source firewall/router distribution based on the Linux kernel.

Open Source Manageability Firmware Development

In computing, the system owner typically has access to control and manage all the required hardware and software services for the target device. To satisfy the need for hardware management, the system administrator might set up an *in-band management system* through Virtual Network Computing (VNC) and Secure Shell (SSH) that provides remote access for the device over the network or using serial ports. This mechanism to access the device is typically cost effective because software that is required for remote management is installed on the system itself and works only after the system has booted to an operating system. Hence, in-band management has limited scope, and when the system is off, it's not possible to be managed by in-band management. It also isn't capable of meeting the remote IT infrastructure management requirements, where an IT administrator would like to access system firmware settings, reinstall the operating system remotely, or provide a fix for when the system is unable to boot. Figure 1-27 shows the in-band management block diagram.

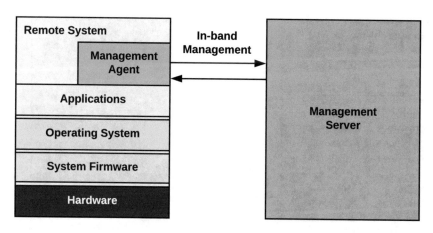

Figure 1-27. *High-level diagram of in-band remote management*

This mode of managing the remote systems doesn't have any dependency over the underlying firmware running on the remote system. When the network is down or the system is in an off state, one needs physical access to bring the system back into the network; it needs someone to travel near to the device, which might not be a feasible solution for data centers and remote sites. The Natick project from Microsoft is building the world's first underwater data center. Therefore, *out-of-band management* provides an alternative path for managing the remote system. Even when the system is not on a network, it is turned off, in sleep mode, hibernated, or inaccessible to any mode of in-band access. This mode of operation relies on the remote management hardware, which is completely independent of the main processor power supply and network connection and can even perform remote operations such as reboot, shutdown, and monitoring the hardware sensors (i.e., fan speed, power voltages, hard disk health, chassis intrusion, etc.). Figure 1-28 shows the out-of-band remote management hardware block diagram.

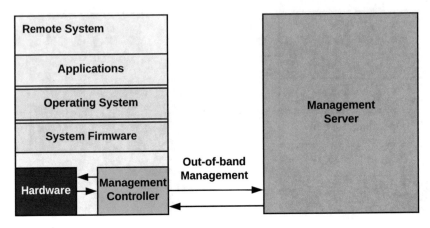

Figure 1-28. *High-level diagram of out-of-band remote management*

The modern server motherboards are the default coming with a built-in remote management controller. The out-of-band remote management can use either dedicated network interface controllers (NICs) or shared NICs for remote access. The shared NIC can be used for multiplexing the Ethernet connection between the host system operating system and the remote management controller so that while incoming traffic flows on the hardware, it is routed to the remote management controller before reaching the host system. It also has multiple interfaces like Enhanced Serial Peripheral Interface (LPC/eSPI), PCIe, SMBUS, USB, etc., to communicate with the host system.

Here are the operations that a remote admin can perform with out-of-band enabled:

- *Keyboard-video-mouse (KVM)*: Out-of-band management allows access to host CPU resources like the keyboard, video, and mouse, which provides broadcasting of video output to the remote terminals, and receiving the input from the remote keyboard and mouse can be used to configure the system firmware settings even prior to booting the OS.

- *Perform remote recovery*: An admin can also access remote system disk images from the local boot media or over a network and therefore can be used to recover the system in case the OS crashes and the system reaches an OS recovery.

- *Remote power on/off*: The remote administrator can schedule wake and update-like features to ensure the system is always updated with critical security patches. It also ensures the system's availability over the network 24/7 using resource preservation by keeping the device in low-power mode after an update.

- *Remote sessions*: It allows client-initiated remote sessions to monitor, manage, and troubleshoot any pre-OS and OS-related defects.

Out-of-band management requires seamless access of the system, and the remote management controller belongs to the platform hardware. The firmware that is running as part of the remote management controller is considered to be highly privileged components (Ring -3 as described earlier). This firmware remains active during the entire life of the system and can even control the system when it is powered off. Thus, any vulnerability that exists in the manageability firmware can easily remain hidden from the traditional security measures and put the entire system at risk where intruders can take over the system remote management and allow data exfiltration attacks.

This section will provide a brief overview of some manageability firmware that was developed using proprietary firmware and looking at the possibilities of migrating to the open source firmware.

Baseboard Management Controller

A baseboard management controller (BMC) is a special processor that sits on the server motherboard and is responsible for providing the server management. Other components like high-end switches and Just a Bunch of Disks (JBODs) and/or Just a Bunch of Flash (JBOFs) platforms also include BMCs for out-of-band management. The BMC is responsible for monitoring and managing the physical state of a computer, network server, or other sensor-based hardware and passing that information to the system administrator through an independent connection. The key parameters that BMC measures are temperatures and voltages, fan speeds, humidity, inventory data such as serial numbers or product names, and remote powering on/off of the main CPUs. It notifies the system administrator if any of these parameter values has drifted from its allowable known limit. It allows the system admin to take measures to avoid any anomalies in the server stability and reliability. Figure 1-29 shows the hardware block diagram of a server platform using an ASPEED BMC chip (AST2500).

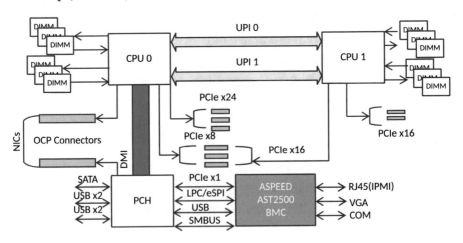

Figure 1-29. *Server motherboard hardware block diagram with BMC*

Figure 1-30 shows the AST2500 BMC chip, which is the leading BMC chip used on the server platform (the latest is AST2600 with ARM Cortex A7) using an ARM11-based SoC with these features:

- *Ethernet*: The Reduced Media-Independent Interface (RMII) and Reduced Gigabit Media-Independent interface (RGMII) are interfaces to connect an Ethernet MAC block to a PHY chip.

- *Flash memory*: This is the Serial Peripheral Interface (SPI) flash memory that contains the BMC firmware for booting the SoC.

- *Memory*: This is 800Mbps DDR3 or 1600Mbps DDR4 memory with 16-bit data bus width. Having more memory provides increased performance.

- *PCIe*: The on-chip PCIe 2D VGA provides a local display capability with resolution up to 1920×1200 without adding an extra VGA add-on card.

- *USB*: The USB 2.0 virtual hub controller allows up to five devices and a USB 1.1 HID device controller for keyboard and mouse support.

- *LPC/eSPI*: This is a Low Power Count (LPC) or Enhanced SPI (eSPI) bus for communicating with the host.

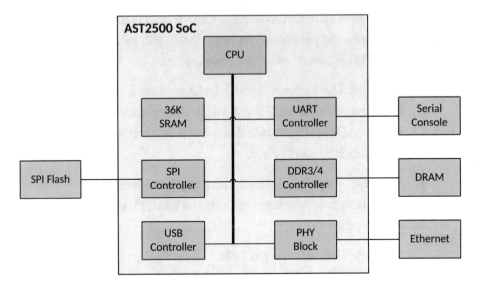

Figure 1-30. *AST2500 hardware block diagram*

BMC allows system administrators to make use of KVM functionality for remote redirection of the keyboard, video, and mouse to a remote network-attached management console. Hence, it allows the remote admin to perform the low-level tasks while the operating system is not yet available.

Intelligent Platform Management Interface

The Intelligent Platform Management Interface (IPMI) is an interface specification that allows manageability firmware to monitor or manage the host system independent of the host CPU, system firmware, and operating system. IPMI is a message-based, hardware-level interface specification that is used by the system admin for out-of-band management of computer systems. This specification, jointly developed by Intel, Hewlett Packard, Dell, and NEC, is intended to perform the following operations:

- *OS-independent scenarios*: Regular monitoring of platform-critical components like temperature. Various built-in sensors in the computer system and power supply voltage allow remote access to the system if the host system is powered off. It allows changing the BIOS settings for recovery boot and/or installing new operating systems into the block device.

- *While the OS is running*: It allows the admin to access the operating system login console remotely to manage services such as installing virtual drives, populating management data and structures to the system management software, etc.

IPMI supports the extension of platform management by connecting additional management controllers to the system. Figure 1-31 shows the IPMI subsystem block diagram, which consists of BMC as the *main controller* and other management controllers distributed among different system components that are referred to as *satellite controllers*. The BMC is the heart of the IPMI architecture that manages the interface between the system management software and the platform management hardware. It provides autonomous monitoring, event logging, and recovery control, and it works as the main channel between the system management software and the IPMB and ICMB. The *Intelligent Platform Management Bus/Bridge* (IPMB) is an I2C-based bus that provides a standardized interface between BMC and the satellite controllers within a chassis. It also serves as a standardized interface for auxiliary management add-in cards. The *Intelligent Chassis Management Bus* (ICMB) provides a standardized interface for connecting satellite controllers and/or the BMC in another chassis. By providing the standardized interface, a baseboard can be easily integrated into a variety of chassis that have different management features. The Field Replaceable Unit (FRU) information is used to provide the inventory information, such as vendor ID and manufacturer, etc., about the boards that the FRU information device is located on. A sensor data record (SDR) repository provides the properties of the individual sensors (i.e., temperature, fan speed, and voltage) present on the board. Physical interfaces to the BMC include SMBUSs, the RS-232 serial console, and IPMB, which enables the BMC to accept IPMI messages from other management controllers in the system.

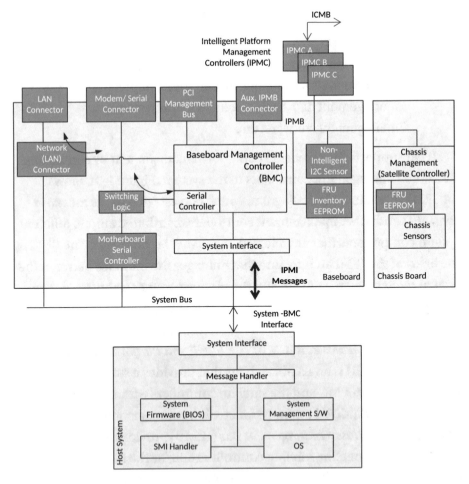

Figure 1-31. *IPMI subsystem block diagram*

There is a significant concern that the BMC is a closed infrastructure that allows administrators to have direct access to the host systems. A direct serial connection to the BMC is not encrypted, and the connection over the LAN may or may not use encryption and might raise the platform security risks. The following sections provide some serious security concerns with BMC and the reason for open source adaptation in the BMC project.

Figure 1-32 shows the typical server platform remote management that allows remote accesses with BMC implementing IPMI specifications.

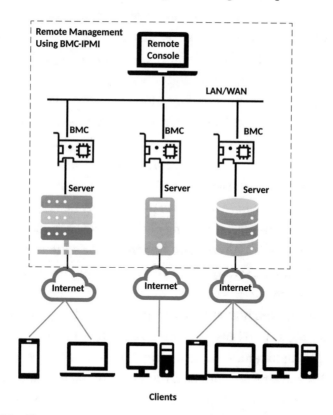

Figure 1-32. *Remote server management using BMC-IPMI*

The assumption was that the admins would be managing the computer systems over the trusted and controlled network, and the IPMI stack doesn't pay great attention to ensuring security. Many BMC firmware doesn't implement Secure Boot. The BMC is the ultimate security liability due to its privileged operations, and a compromised BMC would allow attackers to have access to a remote network connection, which had been in the realm of physical administrative access.

The BMC would allow the remote admin to access the OS console and mount the virtual media, typically used for recovering remotely or installing a custom OS image. A group of security researchers has found a severe BMC vulnerability on a server platform where the virtual media service allows plaintext authentication, allows unencrypted data over network, uses a weak encryption algorithm using a fixed key compiled into the BMC firmware, and possibly allows authentication bypass while authenticated to the virtual media service. These weaknesses would allow an attacker to gain unauthorized access to the virtual media. The BMC hardware allows the creation of virtual USB devices. Hence, upon authenticating using a well-known default username and password for the BMC, an attacker would be able to perform any of a USB-based attacks against the server remotely including data exfiltration, booting from untrusted OS images, or direct manipulation of the system using a virtual keyboard and mouse. A study also reveals that more than 47,000 BMCs from different countries are exposed to the Internet. Also, an attacker who compromises the host system could use it to attempt to compromise the BMC as well, as BMC always remains on without power-off. Hence, it would be difficult to remove such malware from the BMC. A BMC rootkit could provide the attacker with backdoor access that remains hidden from IPMI access logs and insusceptible to host OS reinstallation or password changes. In 2019, a vulnerability was detected on the BMC chip, where malware could be installed on the BMC from the local host via the PCIe or LPC interface. Because of the closed nature of the IPMI implementation, once attackers gain control of the BMC, it's difficult to know their presence and remove them from the system. Such requirements lead the data centers to adopt the BMC firmware that is getting developed using open source projects.

OpenBMC

The OpenBMC project is a Linux Foundation project, which is intended to replace the proprietary BMC firmware with a customizable, open source firmware implementation. OpenBMC is a Linux distribution for management controllers that is used in devices such as servers, rack switches, telecommunications, etc. In 2014, four Facebook engineers at Facebook's hackathon event created the first prototype of the open source BMC firmware, called OpenBMC for BMC inside the Wedge (a rack switch developed by Facebook) platform. In 2018, OpenBMC became a Linux Foundation project. OpenBMC uses the Yocto Project for creating the building and distribution framework. It uses D-Bus as an interprocess communication (IPC) method. OpenBMC includes a web application for interacting with the firmware stack. OpenBMC added Redfish support for hardware management.

Facts   Redfish is an open industry-standard specification used for hardware management. It is defined by the Distributed Management Task Force (DMTF). OpenBMC uses Redfish as a replacement for IPMI over LAN.

The features being implemented by the OpenBMC include the following:

- Host management: power on/off, cooling, LEDs, inventory, and events

- Compliant to the IPMI 2.0 specification

- Code update support for multiple BMC/BIOS images

- Provides web-based user interface

- REST management: BMCWeb Redfish, host management using REST APIs

- SSH-based SOL

- Remote KVM

- Virtual media, etc.

This section provides the implementation details of OpenBMC running on Wedge. As described earlier in Figure 1-26, BMC hardware is a reduced-feature computer system; hence, OpenBMC is designed as a complete Linux distribution so that it can extend the support for other BMC vendor SoCs and boards. The OpenBMC project includes a bootloader as u-bootb, a Linux kernel with a minimal rootfs that contains all the tools and binaries needed to run OpenBMC, and board-specific packages:

- Both the bootloader and the Linux kernel include various SoC-specific firmware and hardware drivers like I2C, USB, PWM, and SPI drivers, etc.

- The open source packages include common applications such as busybox, i2c tools, openssh, and Python.

- The board-specific package includes initialization scripts and tools that are specific to a board. Examples are a tool that dumps inventory from the EEPROM and a fan-controller daemon to control the fan speed based on environment readings.

Figure 1-33 illustrates the OpenBMC package running on the BMC inside the Wedge platform.

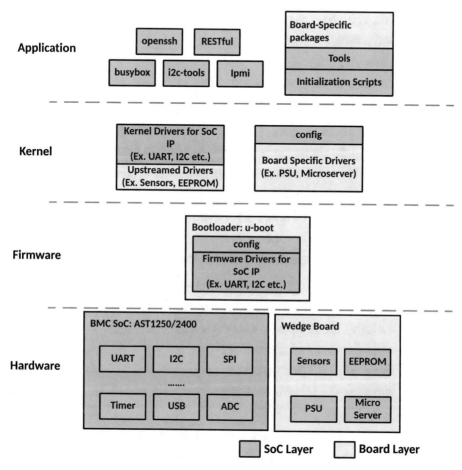

Figure 1-33. *OpenBMC Stack on the Wedge platform*

All packages in OpenBMC are grouped into three layers, as
shown here:

Common Layer	This layer includes packages that can be used across different SoCs and boards. For example:
	`common/recipes-rest`
	`common/recipes-connectivity`
	`common/recipes-utils`

SoC Layer	The SoC layer includes packages that are specific to BMC SoCs. Figure 1-29 shows the SoC layer is part of both the bootloader and Linux driver as it implements a specific driver to communicate with the Aspeed BMC chipset. For example:
	`meta-aspeed/recipes-bsp/u-boot`
	`meta-aspeed/recipes-core`
	`meta-aspeed/recipes-kernel/linux`

Board Layer	The packages being included in this layer are specific for the current board. Figure 1-29 shows the configuration, initialization scripts, and tools that are specific for Wedge. For example:
	`meta-aspeed/recipes-core`
	`meta-aspeed/recipes-kernel`
	`meta-aspeed/recipes-wedge`

Generating an OpenBMC image for a specific board requires these
three layers: the common layer, a SoC layer for the BMC SoC used in the
board, and a board-specific layer for the targeted BMC board.

u-bmc

u-bmc is a project that was developed almost at the same time as
OpenBMC. u-bmc is a Linux OS distribution for the BMC that was
developed using open source firmware. The goal of u-bmc is to ensure
that critical and highly privileged code like the BMC is easy to audit

and adheres to modern security. u-bmc was written in Go and replaces the industry-standard IPMI with gRPC to reduce the attack surface and provide improved security.

u-bmc uses u-root as a framework to create a minimal Linux distribution that gets loaded after bare-minimal initialization by the BMC bootloader. Figure 1-34 shows the u-bmc boot flow where it loads the Linux kernel after the basic platform initialization as part of u-bmc.

Facts   u-root incorporates four different projects as follows:

- Go versions for standard Linux tools, for example: ls, cp, etc.

- To compile many Go programs into a single binary

- To create a Go-based userland that works as initramfs for the Linux kernel

- Go bootloaders that use kexec to boot Linux kernels

```
U-Boot 2016.07-00036-g8b3fd4183a-dirty (Sep 22 2018 - 19:47:23 +0200)

DRAM:  120 MiB
WARNING: Caches not enabled
Flash: 32 MiB
Using default environment

In:    serial
Out:   serial
Err:   serial
Net:   aspeednic#0
Error: aspeednic#0 address not set.

Hit any key to stop autoboot:  1
ubi0: user volume: 2, internal volumes: 1, max. volumes count: 128
ubi0: max/mean erase counter: 2/0, WL threshold: 4096, image sequence number: 1921506432
ubi0: available PEBs: 16, total reserved PEBs: 488, PEBs reserved for bad PEB handling: 0
Loading file 'u-boot.boot.img' to addr 0x40000000...
Done
## Executing script at 40000000
Loading file 'u-boot.env' to addr 0x40000000...
Done
## Info: input data size = 31714 = 0x7BE2
Loading file 'quanta-f06-leopard-ddr3.dtb' to addr 0x40000000...
Done
Loading file 'zImage' to addr 0x40008000...
Done
Kernel image @ 0x40008000 [ 0x000000 - 0x24e350 ]
## Flattened Device Tree blob at 40000000
   Booting using the fdt blob at 0x40000000
   Loading Device Tree to 47387000, end 4738fa6e ... OK

Starting kernel ...
```

***Figure 1-34.** u-bmc firmware boot flow*

It's possible to ship the entire server firmware development using open source firmware where the system firmware is developed using coreboot, and u-bmc can be used for the BMC to boot the Linux distribution.

RunBMC

The benefit of open source is not only limited to firmware and software. Using open source projects has security advantages over closed source firmware software, where with more eyes and hands for review, testing and bug fixes provide improved code quality. Within Open Compute

Project (OCP), the community has started looking into designing open source hardware that provides more efficient, flexible, secure, and scalable design. RunBMC is an open source hardware specification that defines the interface between the BMC subsystem and OCP hardware platforms, such as network or computer motherboards. The BMC is built around a SoC that provides access to common functionality like RMII, and RGMII provides access to the Ethernet, PCIe, or LPC/eSPI interface to interact with the host system. Typically, the BMC chip is soldered onto the motherboard. The RunBMC design separates the BMC from the host motherboard by creating a RunBMC daughterboard card that interfaces with the host system through a 260-pin SODIMM DDR4 connector. Figure 1-35 shows an example of RunBMC daughterboard I/O connectivity. The RunBMC interface includes specifications such as RGMII, RMII, LPC/ESPI, PCIe, USB and various serial interfaces, and GPIOs for communication.

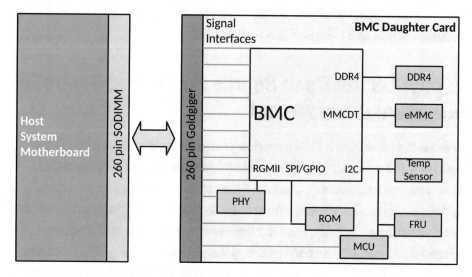

Figure 1-35. *RunBMC daughterboard card block diagram*

This design is more stable and secure because it modularizes the BMC subsystem, where the entire security effort is now shifted onto a single BMC card. It provides an opportunity to vendors for hardening the hardware security independently by adding security features like Titan, Cerberus, or TPM chips into the daughter card to implement a hardware-based root of trust. Also, a swappable BMC card is easy to replace if detected vulnerable or updated, without impacting the entire host system.

To summarize, out-of-band management for computing systems is an innovation that saves costs and minimizes the computer downtime on failure without physically visiting the data centers. But the availability of monitoring, accessing, and controlling the host system using BMC might increase the platform attack surface due to the closed source nature of BMC firmware and the higher privileged level that it operates. In the past, the security researchers have done ample studies to highlight the BMC vulnerabilities. The OpenBMC project sets the stage for BMC firmware and hardware development using an open source model. Having an open source hardware interface and BMC firmware developed with open source firmware provides visibility into the utmost privileged rings of the platform security, which was always closed otherwise.

Zephyr OS: An Open Source Embedded Controller Firmware Development

This section provides a brief overview of the embedded controller (EC) that is often found in low-power embedded systems and is responsible for managing various tasks that the system firmware and an operating system can't handle. It's important to understand the EC hardware control block, its communication with the host system, etc. This knowledge is essential to establish the trust in the system boot process, as the firmware that is running as part of the EC is an independent entity in the computing system that is capable of accessing the platform components directly. The majority of EC projects are developed using proprietary code; hence, it's important to have visibility into all firmware that is part of the computing system.

Embedded Controller

The embedded controller can refer to the heart of the client and IoT computing device. The EC is the first microcontroller unit (MCU) on an embedded system that receives power when the user presses the power button or any other possible source to power on the system. The EC is responsible for orchestrating the platform power sequencing in recommended order (as per the platform design guide) so that it can release the host CPU from reset. In addition, it does lots of other things.

- *Battery charging*: Tasks includes managing the battery charger and the battery, detecting the presence of AC, and reporting its change status.

- *Thermal management*: Tasks include measuring the temperature of board components (CPU, GPU, several sensors on board) and taking action to control the fan speeds, CPU throttling, or force power off based on critical sensor data.

- *Keyboard*: The EC is also referred to as the *keyboard system controller* (KSC), which takes care of receiving and processing signals from the keyboard.

- *Hardware buttons and switches*: Tasks include receiving and processing signals from hardware buttons (typically laptop/tablet button array) and switches (laptop lid).

- *Backlight, LEDs*: The EC implements the LED's control indicators (RGB) for battery, power, AC, caps lock, num lock, scroll lock, sleep, etc. Also, it is able to control the display and keyboard backlight.

- *Peripheral control*: The EC is able to turn on and off several platform components like WiFi, Bluetooth, USB, etc.

- *Debug interface*: The EC controller provides a UART port for serial debug and a Port 80h BIOS debug port. These are primarily used for testing, debugging, and remote administration of the device.

The embedded controller is a separate chip that is soldered on the motherboard, which includes a low-power processor, memory (SRAM and ROM), several I/Os, and an interface with the host system through one of the common interfaces such as Low Pin Count (LPC), eSPI, and I2C. It's being designed as a stand-alone microcontroller that can operate in low-power mode. The EC can access any register in the EC address space or host address space. The LPC/eSPI host controller can directly access peripheral registers in the host address space. Figure 1-36 shows a generic embedded controller block diagram. The embedded controller always remains on if the system has power attached. With the release of the internal reset signal that resets the processor in the EC control block, the processor will start executing code from the ROM. The boot code part of ROM executes a secure bootloader, which downloads user code from an external SPI Flash and stores it in the SRAM. After that, the boot code jumps into the user code and starts executing.

Facts   There are two possible ways that define how the EC should access its user code from SPI Flash.

- *Master attached flash sharing (MAFS)*: In this mode, the EC won't have a dedicated SPI Flash; rather, it shares the SPI Flash with the host system PCH. EC will access SPI Flash over the eSPI flash sharing channel.

- *Slave attached flash sharing (SAFS)*: The EC will have access to dedicated SPI Flash using the SPI interface, and PCH will access SPI Flash over the eSPI flash sharing channel.

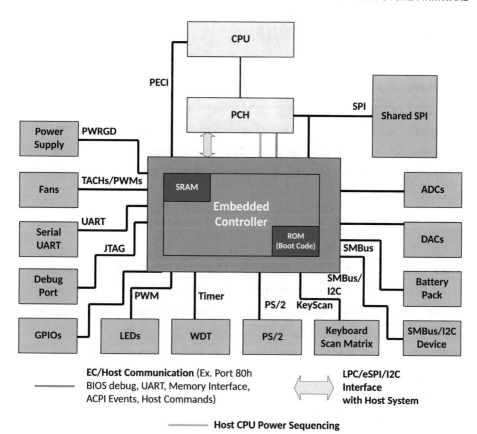

Figure 1-36. *Generic embedded controller block diagram*

After the user code starts executing, it configures the GPIOs as per the platform needs and initializes the host interface. The EC and host system can communicate with each other using EC HOST commands and trigger ACPI events for interrupting host system and memory-mapped regions shared between EC and Host CPU address space. The following is an embedded controller firmware architecture overview so you can understand the internals of EC operations that help to perform independent tasks in a timely manner.

EC Firmware Architecture

Embedded controller firmware is responsible for performing the platform power sequencing and remains active all the time even when the platform control reaches the operating system. It needs to perform several independent tasks such as thermal monitoring, battery management, keyboard control, etc. This section will provide a high-level firmware architecture overview so you can understand the innards operations being managed by the EC.

Tasks

Most of the operations being performed by the embedded controller are in the context of a task. Since embedded controllers are not multicore, the scheduling of the tasks is done using some time slicing algorithm to achieve the multitask execution. Each task has its own fixed stack size assigned. There is no heap (malloc) to use, and all variable storage is explicitly declared at build time. Each task has its given priority, and it continues to run until it exits or a higher-priority task wakes up and takes control away from a lower-priority task. At a high level, it's a loop that initiates all tasks unless there are wait eventsor a define sleep duration before resuming a task.

Callbacks

Callbacks allow you to register a function to get executed at a later point of time when a particular event occurs such as a callback to handle all button change events. Typically, these callbacks are registered by one module and invoked by different modules. If more than one callback needs to be run at the same time, then it's getting called as per the priority order.

GPIOs

The board-specific code inside the EC source is to configure the GPIOs to allow SoC power transition and system transitions. The GPIOs can be configured as inputs, outputs, and interrupts. Typically, these are getting configured as part of the board init() function or based on certain callbacks like power off() while the system is transiting its state. The interrupt handles part of each module to read the GPIO status prior to transferring the call into the handle functions.

Modules

Operations being managed by the embedded controller are grouped into modules, and each module is self-contained after the GPIOs are configured. This includes initialization sequence, state machines, and interrupt handlers. Examples of such modules are peripheral management, power sequencing, SMC host, battery management, thermal management, KBC host, etc.

Debugging

EC firmware provides a set of debug services such as serial console, exception handler, and port 80 display.

- *Serial console*: This is the traditional approach while developing or debugging EC firmware, where a serial console would be handy to indicate the problem. Also, some EC implementations use the static console buffer for ease of debugging, while the host reset doesn't clear this buffer and persists across multiple reboots. An interactive EC console would help to run various key commands and system management independent of the host system.

- *Exception handler*: If the EC firmware runs into an error, the easiest way to inform the user about the problem is by dumping the current operating stack. The exception handler contains some interesting information like the program counter (pc) and link register (lr), which indicates the code that the EC was running when the panic occurred.

- *Port 80 display*: Initialize the port 80 display and use this to indicate any error in the following format: *ECxx*, where *xx* refers to the specific error code.

Host CPU to EC Communication

The embedded controller provides a unique feature that allows you to perform complex low-level functions through a simple interface to the host CPU. The most commonly used embedded controllers include different communication channels that connect the embedded controller to the host CPU, allowing bidirectional communications. It helped to reduce the host processor latency in communicating with the embedded controller. There are different methods by which the host CPU communicates with the embedded controller.

- Host commands

- Embedded controller interface

- Shared memory map

Host Commands

The host CPU communicates with the EC by issuing host commands. These commands are identified by a command ID. When a host CPU is intended to issue a command (and data) to the EC, depending on the current operation phase (i.e., system firmware/BIOS or OS), it involves other software components. If system firmware is sending the host commands, it can directly send them to the EC, but from the OS layer, it first communicates via the EC kernel drivers, and then it receives the raw commands and sends them on the EC. The host packet is received by the EC board-specific code, which further sends the command to the common layer that runs the host command. While this is happening, the EC needs to indicate to the host that it is busy processing and not yet ready to give a response. If the host command expects a response, then the EC responds with the result and data to the host CPU. An example of a host command is to read the board ID by sending the SMCHOST_GET_FAB_ID command 0x0D to the EC.

Embedded Controller Interface

The Embedded Controller Interface connects embedded controllers to the host data bus, allowing bidirectional communications. The embedded controller is accessed at 0x62 and 0x66 in the host system I/O space. Port 0x62 is called a *data register* (EC_DATA) and allows bidirectional data transfers to and from the host and embedded controller. Port 0x66 is called the *command/status register* (EC_SC); it returns port status information upon a read and generates a command sequence to the embedded controller upon a write. Figure 1-37 shows that this interface is implemented using the ACPI specification. The figure defines more than one type of communication using the host interface.

- The embedded controller command set allows operating system–directed configuration and Power Management (OSPM) to communicate with the EC. The ACPI defines the commands between 0x80 and 0x84 to tell the EC to perform an operation. For example, the *Read Embedded Controller* (RD_EC) command 0x80 allows OSPM to read a byte in the address space of the embedded controller.

- The host waits for the Input Buffer Full (IBF) flag on the EC_SC to be 0.

- The host writes the command byte to port 0x66 and the address byte to port 0x62.

- The EC generates SCIs in response to this transaction from the SMC ACPI handler.

- The SMC command handler passes control to the actual EC SoC code. To receive data from the EC, wait for Output Buffer Full (OBF) to be set, which indicates there is incoming data.

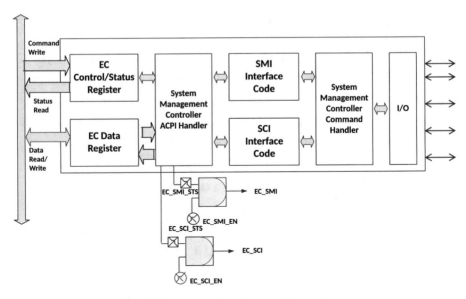

Figure 1-37. *Embedded controller shared interface*

- When the embedded control has detected a system event that must need to communicate to OSPM, it first sets the SCI_EVT flag in the EC_SC register, generates an SCI, and then waits for OSPM to send the Query

Embedded Controller (QR_EC) command 0x84. The OSPM driver detects the EC SCI when the SCI_EVT (SCI event is pending) flag in the EC_SC register is set and sends the QR_EC command. Upon receipt of the QR_EC command byte, the embedded controller places a notification byte value between 0x00 and 0xFF, indicating the cause of the notification. OSPM driver query ACPI control method with that value in the form of _Qxx where xx is the number of the query acknowledged by the embedded controller. Here's an example to explain the scenario better:

- A change in the LID switch status would trigger an GPE from the GPE bit (LAN_WAKE_N) tied to an embedded controller.

- The OSPM driver queries the EC to know the query number.

- The host system firmware has implemented a control method (_Qxx) corresponding to the OSPM query.

- The ACPI control method notifies OSPM that the LID switch status has changed to Notify (LID0, 0x80); LID0 is ACPI device entry for LID.

- The OSPM driver further calls the LID ACPI device control method to read the LID switch status (LIDS).

- LID switch status can be read using the EC ACPI command either through port 0x62/0x66 or through the LPC register.

- Upon reading from the EC, the ACPI control method passes the value to the OSPM driver, and the OS takes the necessary action.

Figure 1-38 describes this communication graphically.

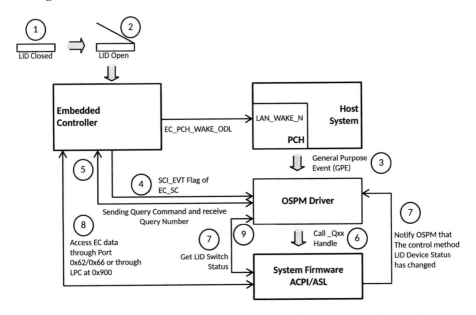

Figure 1-38. *Software implementation of the EC control interface*

Shared Memory Map

Some systems have memory regions shared between the embedded controller and the host system address space. The size of this memory region is limited and treated as read-only (RO) on the host system side. This memory is maintained by the EC to pass various interesting information such as battery status, thermal sensor data, battery information, fan speed, LID switch status, etc. A system that doesn't support this shared memory needs to send host commands to read that information.

Challenges with Closed Source EC Firmware

The firmware that is running as part of the embedded controller is working at a higher privileged level where unauthorized access won't be detected by the security controller running as part of the system firmware or an OS. Also, if proprietary EC firmware code doesn't implement Secure Boot or verified boot, then it's allowed to run even unsigned and untrusted images. There have been several vulnerabilities being reported in the past where the EC can run unsigned firmware, and having a compromised EC firmware results in a denial-of-service (DoS) attack on the system. To bring more reliability and efficiency to computing systems and allow visibility into the most privileged code that is running prior to the host CPU reset, the industry is promoting an open source and collaborative embedded controller development using the Zephyr OS.

The next section will provide details about developing EC firmware using an open source advantage, but prior that, let's understand the reference hardware design that enables independent EC development using a Modular Embedded Control Card (MECC).

Modular Embedded Controller Card

Typically, the embedded controller chip is soldered onto the motherboard, and many system firmware updates also ensure the EC firmware is upgraded. If the platform has detected a bug in the EC firmware boot code and the system firmware doesn't provide the provision to update the EC firmware, it's impossible to replace the defective EC firmware as it's integrated into the motherboard design. To mitigate this problem and have an independent, modular EC firmware development that supports various EC SoC vendors, the MECC card was developed. The host system using open source EC firmware may take advantage of the MECC specification, where different EC SoC vendors can develop and validate their solution through an add-on card rather than creating multiple hardware designs with a dedicated on-board EC. Figure 1-39 shows the MECC card design and interfacing with the host system through the MECC connector. The MECC AIC board design is an independent solution that combines the processor, memory, ROM, and different I/Os as part of the MECC board, for example, serial port for debug, SPI Flash, keyboard connector, etc., and interfacing with the host system is through the MECC (AIC) connector using the LPC/eSPI interface. Hence, it's easy to replace the AIC if broken; just upgrade the EC firmware using an external SPI programmer.

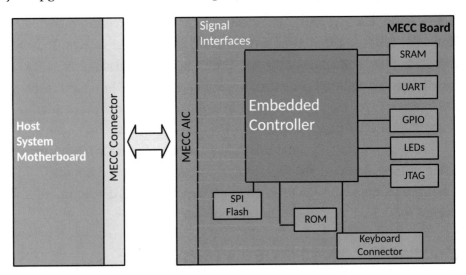

Figure 1-39. *MECC AIC interfacing with the host system*

Open source embedded controller firmware development using Zephyr-OS provides a scalable architecture that enables different MECC cards with different EC SoC vendors. The vendor added Hardware

Abstraction Layer (HAL) and EC SoC Board Support Package (BSP) support along with Zephyr RTOS.

Zephyr-Based EC Firmware

The Zephyr OS is a small-footprint kernel that is designed for use on resource-constrained and embedded systems. The kernel has support for cross-architectures and is distributed under the Apache 2.0 license. Zephyr is an open source project managed by the Linux Foundation. Zephyr provides a huge set of features.

Threads: Typically, the operations performed by the embedded controllers are task based, and hence, migrating to Zephyr for embedded controller firmware development would be effective with scheduling algorithms provided by Zephyr for creating a multithreaded environment. The creation of a thread in Zephyr uses a statically defined approach using K_THREAD_DEFINE. The thread may be scheduled for immediate execution or a delayed start. Zephyr provides a comprehensive set of thread scheduling choices that use a time slicing algorithm to achieve a multitask environment.

- *Cooperative time slicing*: Each thread should intermediately release the CPU to permit the other threads also to execute. It can be achieved using predefined sleep between tasks or explicitly releasing the CPU.

- *Preemptive time slicing*: Use the Zephyr scheduler that allows other threads to get their chance for execution without causing a starvation.

The tasks performed by the embedded controller are non-time-critical tasks; hence, cooperative time slicing is more applicable where each task would sleep for some predefined amount of the time before becoming ready to perform the task again.

Memory: Zephyr allows the static allocation of memory with a fixed-stack size. It implements memory protection and prevents the EC stack from getting overflowed, having access permission tracking for kernel objects and device drivers. Provides user-space support using MMU/MPU. A platform without MMU/MPU support combines BSP code with a custom kernel to create a monolithic image where both the BSP and the kernel code share the same address space.

Resource definition at compile time: Zephyr ensures all system resources are defined at compile time to reduce the code size and increase performance.

Security: A dedicated team is responsible for maintaining and improving the security. Also, having visibility via the open source development significantly increases the security.

Device tree: The device tree is used to describe the hardware. Information from the device tree is used to perform various device-related operations inside the BSP and/or application layer.

The embedded controller firmware development using ZephyrOS is a new and a growing area where the introduction and support of new protocols and peripherals help to go beyond the traditional I/Os from what is being available in stand-alone microcontroller units. Figure 1-40 shows the Zephyr-based EC firmware architecture diagram.

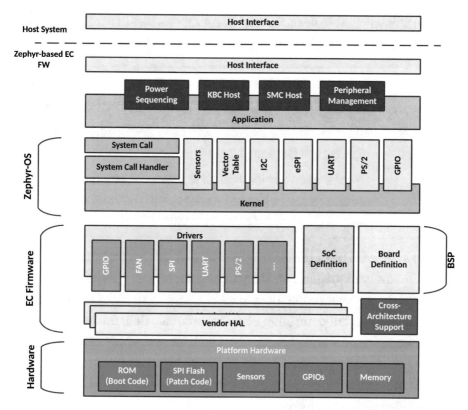

Figure 1-40. *Zephyr-based embedded firmware architecture diagram*

The modular and configurable architecture of ZephyrOS-based embedded controller firmware development is hardware and vendor agnostic. It allows switching the underlying hardware abstraction layer (HAL) and drivers based on different EC SoCs, while the middleware and logic remains intact. To use a different MECC card with different EC SoC vendors, the developer needs to add its HAL and board support package (BSP) to the Zephyr EC firmware repository.

The following table describes the components inside the EC firmware that are required while performing low-level operations:

Board	Board-specific code and configuration details. This includes GPIO map, battery parameters, routines to perform board-specific init.
SoC/vendor-specific HAL	MCU-specific code that deals with lower-level hardware like registers and hardware blocks.
Drivers	Lower-level drivers for UART, GPIO, Timer, I2C, etc. These drivers are using a device tree and vendor-specific HAL to access the underlying embedded controller hardware block.

The ZephyrOS layer provides upper-level code that manages the thread, memory management, I/Os management, etc. This includes high-level drivers that publish Zephyr APIs to allow the host interface to access the embedded controller. The host interface defines the hardware link between the embedded controller and host system (PCH and CPU) to work on a computing system. This link can be between LPC or eSPI or I2C, which is the section that covers all the basic applications of EC firmware on an eSPI-enabled platform.

Power Sequencing

This section describes the application of embedded controller firmware that handles the platform power sequencing, and at the end of this flow, the host processor is able to come out from the reset. The embedded controller firmware follows the host system platform design guideline that specifies the power sequence and its timings. Any platform state transition has to pass through this module. These events that trigger platform state transitions can be power signals that either come from a host system like ACPI system transitions or are generated by board circuitry like the power button, AC supply, etc. Refer to the following table that demonstrates system transitioning from G3 to S0:

System Transitions Between G3->S0

1. The power good (PWRGD) signal to the embedded controller hardware indicates when the main power rail voltage is on and stable. The processor part of the embedded controller will start executing code from the ROM. The boot code is used to download code (user code) from an external flash via the shared flash interface. The downloaded code must configure the device's pins according to the platform's need. Once the device is configured for operation, the user code must de-assert the system's Resume Reset signal (RSMRST#). Any GPIO may be selected for RSMRST# function. The board designer needs to attach an external pull-down on the GPIO pin being used for the RSMRST# function; this will ensure that the RSMRST# pin is asserted low by default.

2. Perform a deep sleep exit handshake, where PCH sends the SUS_WARN signal to the EC and the EC acknowledges by sending the SUS_ACK signal.

3. The EC indicates the PCH using the BATLOW signal that there is a valid power source or enough battery capacity to power up the system.

4. SLP_Sx (where x is based on the supported sleep state of the host system) signals from PCH to the EC indicate that the host system is transiting from the sleep state as per the platform guide.

5. Wait for ALL_SYS_PWRGD, the all-system power good (ALL_SYS_PWRGD) input generated from the board circuitry indicates to the EC that the SoC power rails are stable.

6. Based on this, the embedded controller will generate the PWROK signal.

7. PCH de-asserts PLTRST# after PWROK is stable. The PLTRST# is the main platform reset to other components.

8. The processor will begin fetching code from the SPI Flash via SPI interface.

Figure 1-41 shows the graphical representation of the system state transition between the embedded controller and host system.

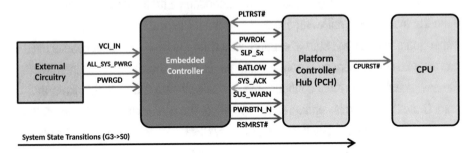

Figure 1-41. *Power sequencing with Zephyr- based EC firmware*

Peripheral Management

This section describes the embedded controller managing the human interface device, which mainly handles buttons and switches attached to the motherboard.

Button Array Devices

All sorts of buttons that are present on the motherboard and need human interaction are managed by the embedded controller. For example, the Power Button is the input to EC, which is default-driven high with a pull-up. This signal goes low upon pressing the power button and triggers an interrupt. Apart from that, *Volume up/down* buttons, Home button, etc., are also being managed by this module.

Switches

This module is also responsible for tracking the state of laptop lid switches and other modules like the screen rotation lock.

The main job of this module is to deal with the undesirable effect any mechanical button/switch has when it strikes together (either pressed and released or open and closed), causing electrical rebound before settling down after the electrical transient time. Mechanical switch debouncing is implemented using cooperative threading to track the short and long presses of all buttons registered within the system. It also sends a notification to the host. Callbacks per button/switch are registered within the GPIO driver to track state transitions for button and switches. See Figure 1-42.

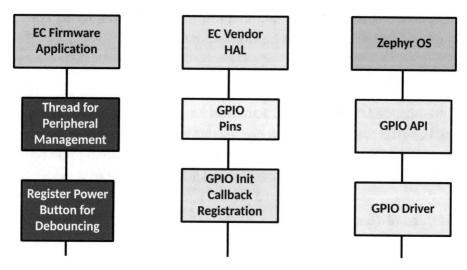

Figure 1-42. *Peripheral management with Zephyr-based EC firmware*

Facts   The embedded controller can be used to detect the docking status of the platform, whether it is in a docking station or not. Based on this status, the EC can perform additional tasks such as switching the system power source to the dock, routing signals from onboard interfaces to the dock, and reporting the docking status to the operating system.

System Management Controller

The section describes the role of the embedded controller as a system management controller, which is used to manage the following items.

Thermal Management

The EC uses the I2C/SMBUS interface to read the platform sensor data, and based on the criticality of the platform state, the EC may have PWM interfaces that can be used to control system fans.

Power Monitoring

The embedded controller ADC signal can be used to monitor the voltage, and based on the usage of the sense resistor, it can also monitor the current consumption of specific power rails. This information could be useful to monitor the battery charging and inform the user or system administrator about any potential problematic power supply condition or detection of a bad charger.

Battery Management

The EC can be used to control the charging of the battery, switch between the battery and AC adapter as the active power source, or monitor the various battery status metrics such as temperature, charging level and battery health, etc.

ACPI Host Interface

The earlier section about "Embedded Controller Interface" provided the required details to understand the host CPU and EC communication using the ACPI host interface. The EC is capable of providing an ACPI-compliant operating system with status and notifications regarding power management events. Also, it is capable of generating wake events to bring the system out from the low-power states.

The SMC host module is implemented as a cooperative thread that registers multiple callbacks within different modules to track events in the system. See Figure 1-43.

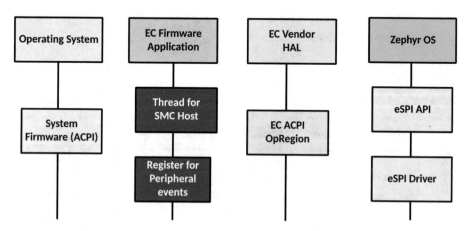

Figure 1-43. *SMC with Zephyr-based EC firmware*

Keyboard Controller

Typically, the EC is also referred to as a *keyboard system controller* (KSC), as it allows AT-compatible and PS/2-compatible support for the keyboard and mice via reads/writes to I/O ports 0x60 and 0x64. The main responsibility of this module is to inform the CPU when a key is pressed or released. It also supports auxiliary devices such as a mouse. On modern computing systems, embedded controller chips have implemented support for 8,042 commands, which means the EC can receive 8,042 commands from either the system firmware or the PS/2 operating system driver. Figure 1-44 shows the implementation aspect of an embedded controller kbchost application, where the EC firmware application can pass the received command from the operating system driver to the Zephyr PS/2 driver, which performs PS/2 communication with a mouse and/or keyboard. Alternatively, the EC firmware can also receive the command and process it prior to sending a response to the OS driver. For example, kbchost gets the command 0xD4 (Send to Mouse) at KBC Command/Status Register 0x64 that indicates the destination device; then it sends a command 0xF4 (Enable) through the KBC Input/Output Buffer Register 0x60. When the host expects to receive any response, the data arrives through port 0x60.

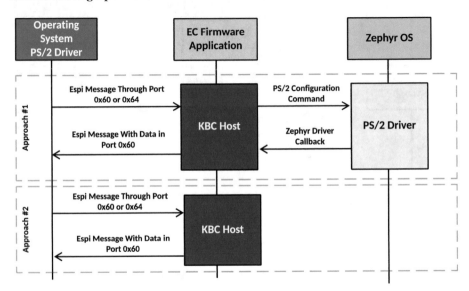

Figure 1-44. *KBC with Zephyr-based EC firmware*

Keyboard Scan Matrix

All keyboards have their keys arranged into a matrix of rows and columns; this is known as the *keyboard matrix*. Because of the number of signals required to represent those rows and columns, the external keyboard uses an on-board keyboard controller (KSC). It continuously scans the state of the whole grid; a circuit in the grid is closed when a key is pressed, and this is eventually sensed by the firmware running in the EC. Once the row and column have been determined, the EC maps the grid coordinates to a scan code, which is sent back to the EC firmware kbchost application and further sent the data to OS PS/2 driver as the eSPI message. Figure 1-45 shows the implementation of the keyboard scan matrix as part of the Zephyr-based OS.

This implementation allowed ODM/OEMs to have specific hotkeys as part of the laptop keyboard layout, which is not supported by the international keyboard standard, for example: change screen brightness, enable/disable wireless networking, control audio volume, etc.

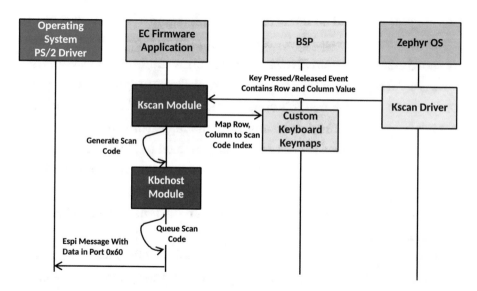

Figure 1-45. *Managing a KeyScan event with Zephyr-based EC firmware*

To summarize, the embedded controller is a special microcontroller that is part of the majority of mobile computing systems. The firmware that is running on the EC chip is operating at a much higher privilege level, which does various operations that are not possible to perform by even an operating system. This firmware started operating since platform power on and remains active even if the system is at a power-off state; hence, it's important to ensure the visibility of operations that are running part of the EC firmware. The EC firmware project is being developed with the open source Zephyr OS that has provided visibility into the EC firmware operations. The introduction of Zephyr OS makes EC development easy at the EC vendors and OEMs sides while supporting different EC SoC chips with the same host system using the MECC card.

Summary

This chapter provided an opportunity to understand the different types of firmware that exist and execute on a computing system. Typically, they are categorized as system firmware, device firmware, and manageability firmware. All these types of firmware are running at a higher privilege level compared to the kernel. In this chapter, those privileged levels are being specified as "minus" rings since any vulnerability existing in these layers is tough for any high-level security controller to detect. Hence, this chapter highlighted the need for an open source approach while developing this firmware in the future. This would finally help to restore the trust in the platform and also would provide visibility into the most privileged level firmware, which was not done before.

This chapter proposed two working principles while developing system firmware in the future for embedded systems: hybrid system firmware, where a portion of silicon vendor code is binary and communication with open source firmware is using a standard specification-defined interface, and a true open source system firmware development on an open hardware specification using a modern system programming language such as Rust. Appendix A provides the reasoning behind migrating the system firmware using Rust, an open source system programming language.

Additionally, this chapter specified the well-known mechanism for designing and developing the device firmware using closed source models like option ROM (OpROM). The legacy implementation of the OpROM might increase the platform attack surface. Hence, developing modern OpROM using the open source EDKII source code and toolchain helps to get the initial visibility into the device firmware space, but the ideal goal would be to use the open source firmware model even for developing the device-specific firmware.

The remote management for server platforms and enterprise systems demands out-of-band (OOB) access into the system using a special manageability controller to perform certain tasks when the host system is not available or demands any maintenance. The firmware that is running on these MCUs are at the highest privilege level in the ring and hence always pose the security risk if an intruder had access into the remote system. This chapter provided a brief overview of system architecture of the two widely used microcontrollers, BMC and EC, on the computing system. This will help developers perform a migration to open source firmware development for these manageability controllers in the future.

The goal of this chapter was to explain why firmware architecture is expected to evolve in the future, and it's fairly possible that the majority of firmware development will migrate to open source. Hence, it's important that developers understand the industry's need and prepare themselves for the future.

Chapter 6 represented some innovation in system firmware design and development using an open source firmware approach that addresses the ongoing concerns with extensible firmware architecture that increases the firmware boundary and inherits responsibility while booting the platform.

CHAPTER 2

Tools

"If the only tool you have is a hammer, it's hard to eat spaghetti."

—David Allen

Looking back at history, tools have been the impetus for the evolution of the human race. Starting from the Stone Age through the Iron Age and to the modern computing age, tools have eased the work that humans have to do. Having the right tools for developing a boot firmware product is absolutely necessary to ease the development effort as well, provide a flexible interface for configuration, and offer seamless upgradability. This chapter focuses on the details of the various types of tools that a system developer should be equipped with for creating their own boot firmware.

The system firmware development journey includes various tools from its creation until deployment, as shown in Figure 2-1. This book is committed to providing detailed knowledge about various tooling requirements for each phase to prepare developers to work with the prerequisite software development kits (SDKs).

Typically, to get started with firmware development, a developer has to be equipped with these tools:

- *Integrated development environment*: An integrated development environment (IDE) is software that helps

---

The original version of this chapter was revised. A correction to this chapter is available at https://doi.org/10.1007/978-1-4842-7974-8_7

© Subrata Banik and Vincent Zimmer 2022, corrected publication 2023
S. Banik and V. Zimmer, *Firmware Development*,
https://doi.org/10.1007/978-1-4842-7974-8_2

developers ease their development process. It typically is a source code editor that provides some basic functionality such as the ability to create new files, search files, replace a string in a file, and more. Based on developers' needs, there are various types of IDEs available, from basic ones such as the vim editor to advanced IDEs such as Eclipse, for firmware development.

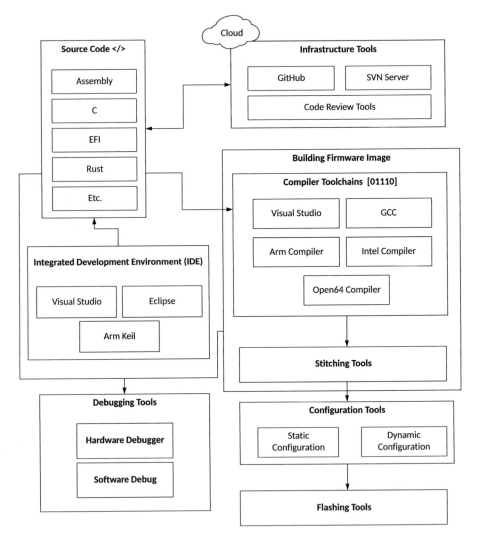

Figure 2-1. *System firmware development model*

- *Infrastructure tools*: Chapter 3 provides ample details about the usage of infrastructure tools in system firmware development. Hence, this chapter will refrain from discussing the topic.

- *Debugging tools*: Refer to Chapter 4 for a detailed overview of the debug methodology and debug tools usage on cross-architecture platforms. That chapter highlights the different types of tools used in system firmware development.

- *Build tools (compiler and stitching tools)*: Build tools are the first step toward creating a firmware image for embedded systems. This process involves taking source code as input and generating binary files as output. The next step combines all the binaries and produces the final firmware image. This process is highly dependent on the chip architecture, firmware architecture, and technology being used to create the system firmware.

- *Configuration tools*: Configurability is a fundamental right for system integrators and validation engineers working on an embedded system. Relying on the development engineers to alter the source code to allow configuration and re-generate firmware images is not a scaled solution. This approach is a bottleneck for innovation. For example, it limits the scope for performing boundary testing with a wide range of data inputs. Even not a sustained model when the goal is to enable more ODM/OEM platforms with reduced development cost. Configuration tools allow developers to generate firmware images based on SoC and board-level configuration changes without rebuilding the system firmware image.

- *Flashing tools*: The most important step to bring an embedded system to life is programming the flash parts. The purpose of flashing tools is to ensure the firmware image is correctly burned into the embedded system boot devices. The flashing process and mechanisms vary a lot, based on the underlying hardware design, target operating system, firmware architecture, technology being used, etc. A flashing tool might have a different interface and mechanism to consider based on the product lifecycle. The tooling process is different on the development side, factory side, and end-user side. Another consideration is that some firmware updates are over the air (OTA), meaning accomplished via a network.

The purpose of this chapter is to limit the discussion to the three major tooling needs (build, configuration, and flashing tools) while creating the system firmware and focus on the tools architecture across different system firmwares.

Build Tools

The most effective way to understand a system firmware architecture is by understanding its building blocks. Different firmware systems have much in common: they mostly use C, with some assembly, for example. The differentiating factors among these different system firmware are the underlying build tools.

This section provides a detailed overview of the build tools and processes of two popular system firmware products for embedded systems: EDKII and coreboot. Typically, at a high level, all system firmware packages consist of the same structures, as specified in Figure 2-2.

- Refer to the Open Source EDKII project GitHub repository:

    - `https://github.com/tianocore/edk2`

- Refer to the open source coreboot project GitHub repository:

    - `https://github.com/coreboot/coreboot`

The `BaseTools` or `Util` directory consists of build tool binaries, or source code that needs to be compiled, prior to starting to build the package. The package does *not* have a dependency on the build environment. The package might consist of two types of files.

- *Source code files*: Files get compiled to generate object files or binaries that need further processing.

- *Flash layout files*: Files are processed to combine various binaries to create the final firmware image.

The build process includes three main phases.

1. Set up the environment.

2. Build the package components.

3. Package the components to create the final firmware image.

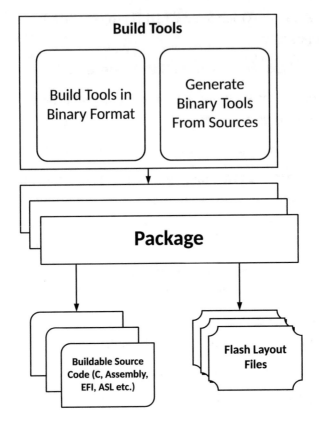

Figure 2-2. *High-level system firmware package structure*

EDKII Build Tools and Process

EDKII is an open source firmware development project utilizing the UEFI and PI specification. EDKII is intended to improve the build experience compared to its predecessor, the EDK platform. EDKII adopts modern, feature-rich tools like Python for building, providing flexibility for developers while choosing correct toolchains using intermediate text files and relying on the C source code to generate tool binaries. Figure 2-3 describes the control flow of an EDKII build.

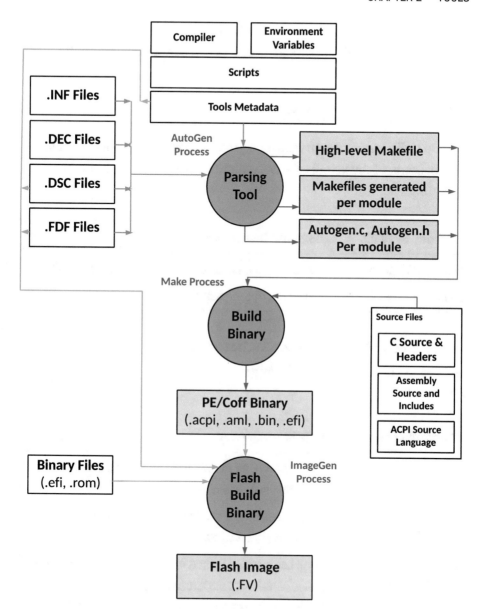

Figure 2-3. *EDKII build tools and build process at a high level*

Prior to discussing the build process and understanding how the underlying build tools are getting used, let's first understand the prerequisites to initiate the build process.

Build Environment Setup

Several build environments must be prepared prior to development for EKDII. Some of these tools are dependent on host machines and host operating systems.

Operating Systems	Compiler Tool Chains
Microsoft Windows	Visual Studio C compiler and Windows Driver Kit (WDK)
Linux	Native GCC Installation 4.4 onward

Some other build tools may also be required, depending on the source package, as part of system firmware development needs, in addition to the previous list.

Additional Compilers	Details
Nasm	Nasm is required for the EDKII build if the source package has Intel-style assembly code.
iASL	This is needed to compile ACPI Source Language (ASL) and generate .aml files.
Python	EDKII has adopted Python for several build-related tools; hence, developers are expected to install Python to run Python-based tools from source. Examples: Build, GenFds, Trim, etc.

The EDKII prebuild phase ensures that the required basic environment variables are set, by executing script files named edksetup. bat or edksetup.sh, depending on the host system. Here is a list of environmental variables that the EDKII build process depends on:

Environment Variables	Description
WORKSPACE	The first variable to be set is WORKSPACE. This variable points to the root directory of an EDKII directory tree. More than one development tree can exist, and this environment variable is used to identify the current working directory tree.
PACKAGES_PATH	This variable points out all possible required repositories for building the target project. For example, for building MinPlatformPkg, the developer needs to point to these three repositories: • Edk2 • Edk2Platforms/Platform/Intel • Edk2Platforms/Silicon/Intel
EDK_TOOLS_PATH	This points to the BaseTools directory belonging to the EDKII package. It contains binaries as mentioned in the EDK_TOOLS_BIN environment variable.
EDK_TOOLS_BIN	This is the path to point out build tool binaries. This depends on the operating system.
CONF_PATH	This is the variable to point out tool metadata files.

The CONF_PATH environment variable is used to point at the configuration files. The configuration file tools_def.txt is used to provide compiler path information, assembler information, linker information, etc., while another file, target.txt, is used to describe the build process.

ACTIVE_PLATFORM	Path to the .dsc file that represents the target embedded system
TARGET	Characteristics of system firmware like DEBUG or RELEASE
TARGET_ARCH	Underlying SoC or CPU architecture of target hardware
TOOL_CHAIN_TAG	To specify the compiler name example: GCC5 or VS2015x86
BUILD_RULE_CONF	Path to the build rule file (build_rule.txt) that specifies the build process, usage of build tools based input and output file types and specifies the type of cross-architecture platform.

At this stage, the EDKII prebuild is done with all prerequisites except the build tools, which is required to start the build process.

Build Binaries

The EDKII package consists of both the package source code and tools source code, separately. EDKII has introduced two sets of tools source code, as shown in the following tree structure:

```
|-- BaseTools
|    |-- Bin
|    |-- gcc
|    |-- Scripts
|    |-- Source
|    |    |-- C
|    |    |    |-- EfiRom
|    |    |    |-- GenFfs
|    |    |    |-- GenFv
|    |    |    |-- GenFw
|    |    |    |-- GenSec
|    |    |    |-- GenVtf
|    |    |    |-- Makefiles
```

```
|    |    |    |-- Split
|    |    |    |-- TianoCompress
|    |    |    |-- VfrCompile
|    |    |    `-- VolInfo
|    |    `-- Python
|    |         |-- AutoGen
|    |         |-- build
|    |         |-- GenFds
|    |         |-- Trim
|-- Conf
|-- CryptoPkg
|-- EdkSetupFsp.sh
|-- IntelFsp2Pkg
|-- MdeModulePkg
|-- MdePkg
|-- PcAtChipsetPkg
`-- UefiCpuPkg
```

Developers to build the BaseTools directory at least once to create build tool executables and update EDK_TOOLS_BIN before compiling the target platform package (.dsc) to generate the final Flash Descriptor (FD) file.

Depending on the host machine, perform the following command to generate executable Build Tools:

For Windows: nmake all

For Linux: make -C Edk2/BaseTools

All the required utilities will be copied into the path specified by the EDK_TOOLS_BIN environment variable. This is a manual process and expected to execute once, unless the developer cleans the entire workspace.

The build_rule.txt file is intended to provide detailed input and the expected outcome from each build tool taking part in the build process.

Let's look at a few widely used build tools in detail and their usage prior to discussing the build process.

Utilities	Description
build.py	The main interface to complete the entire build process. This tool is written in Python. The build calls the AutoGen process; then it calls make process, and finally the ImageGen process to create the final FD binary.
AutoGen.py	Another key tool in the build process; this gets called by the build command. This tool is written in Python to work as a parsing tool to parse metadata files (INF, DSC, DEC, FDF) to autogenerate C source code files, makefiles per module, and the master makefile for the project with the help of other sets of libraries such as the following:
	GenC Library: Used by AutoGen.py to create AutoGen.h and AutoGen.c after parsing the metadata files to resolve PCDs, GUIDs, etc.
	GenMake Library: Used to create a makefile for each module and the top-level makefiles that can be further processed by nmake or gmake or cmake
GenFw.exe	Part of the C source code tool. Responsible for creating UEFI Firmware Image (.efi) files based on the module types listed in the INF files as part of each module.
GenSec.exe	Used to generate a valid EFI_SECTION type based on INF files. For example, as part of the .efi binary, each module also has several sections such as name sections, GUIDed sections, version sections, etc., based on associated fields in the INF file.

(continued)

Utilities	Description
GenFfs.exe	Part of ImageGen process to create FFS files based on FDF to take part into firmware volume (FV). One can make use of the GenFds tool as well to create the FFS file.
GenFds.py	To process the files generated as part of the build binary and associated binary files that are listed in the FDF and DSC files to be part of the final Flash Device (FD) image.

In addition to the previous list, there are other useful utilities that are used for some specific purposes such as compression, generating an EFI option ROM image from the .efi file, creating a configuration file and/or patching a binary module, and creating an FD image.

Build Process

Figure 2-3 already provided the high-level build process flow for the EDKII platform, where a build command has triggered the build process. The entire build process can be divided into three major stages.

- AutoGen process

- Make process

- ImageGen process

Every build process listed here involves certain build tools (described in earlier sections), driven by a fixed set of input files, that generate output files, which are used as input to the next build process. This process continues until a final firmware file (a so-called FD file) is generated.

AutoGen Process

This process was introduced in the EDKII build infrastructure. The major drawback that EDK had was each module needed to create its own makefile (similar to the C programming logic) to link the required libraries, GUID, etc., prior to compiling a module. It is difficult for a new developer who is transitioning into an EDK-based framework for firmware development.

EDKII has introduced this concept of AutoGen to parse the metadata files as part of the target package and/or individual module to generate some C source code files, the makefiles for each module, and even the master makefile for the target project.

Parsing Tools: This process has involved more than one tool and associated libraries. All tools that are part of this build process are written in Python. Refer to the build tools discussion for more details.

- AutoGen.py: This tool is used to parse the metadata files with the help of another two libraries, GenC and GenMake, to create AutoGen.c, AutoGen.h, and other makefiles.

Input Files: At a high level, the parsing tools takes the following files as input:

File	Name	Description
.dsc	Platform Description	Each package has one DSC file to describe the build rules, libraries, and components (INF) being used.
		A platform build process starts with this file.
.dec	Package Declaration	Declares the interfaces that are being used in that package.

(continued)

File	Name	Description
.inf	Module Definition	Each module has one INF file to define the interface, source code, libraries, usage of GUID, etc.
.fdf	Flash Description File	File in each package that provides the flash layout and associated firmware volumes. Each component that is described in this file will take part in final binary creation.

Output Files: As mentioned earlier, the purpose of the parsing tool is to ease the development effort; hence, the output binaries that are part of this process are as follows:

- *Top-level makefile*: This is the makefile for the entire package that resolves all libraries, GUIDs, and any global definitions as part of the package.

- *Makefiles per module*: A C-based module can't really compile without having a dedicated makefile. The parsing tool will generate a makefile for each module based on the INF file, after resolving the required dependencies using other packages.

- *Autogenerated C source code*: The source code as mentioned in the INF files is mostly written in C, where it relies on C-based data structures. With the metadata-based implementation in EDKII, it needs a parser to create an autogenerated AutoGen.h or .AutoGen.C file based on the need to provide macro definitions and resolve external symbols for the next build process (which is the make process).

Make Process

The make process is not exceptional from any standard C-based compilation process to generate binary files that are further processed by special build tools to create EFI firmware image type files. Figure 2-4 describes the make process control flow:

> *Build binary*: This process involves standard C-compilers, assemblers, static linkers, and dynamic linkers to generate PE/PE32+/COFF images from component or module types listed in the INF files. Additionally, the GenFw tool is used to generate EFI firmware image files.

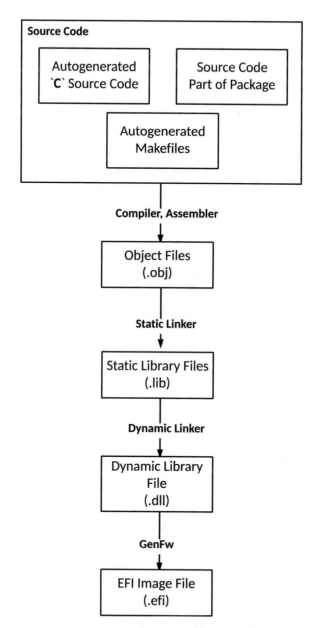

Figure 2-4. *High-level make process structure*

Input files: The make process takes two types of files as inputs. The source code belongs to the target and associated packages (C source, headers, ASM source and includes, ACPI and ASL files, etc.) and the autogenerated C source code headers and makefiles.

Output files: The purpose of the make process is to generate EFI file images that can be further used during the ImageGen process. But based on the input files, it can also generate .acpi, .aml, and .bin binaries. Figure 2-4 has provided a detailed control flow for generating EFI files based on input C source code. This process involves several intermediate steps, as shown here:

1. The standard C-based compiler has compiled the source code to generate .obj files.

2. .obj files have been given as input to the static linker to generate static library files (.lib), which further process into dynamic library files (.dll) with the help of a dynamic linker.

3. Finally, the GenFw tool as part of the $(make) phase converts the .dll into an EFI_SECTION type. The EFI file format is compatible with the PE32/PE32+/COFF format.

ImageGen Process

This phase is responsible for taking the EFI format files generated as part of the make process and parsing the package metadata files to verify whether all those EFI file types are intended to be part of the final flash image.

This process can also take binary files as input, which is not part of the target DSC file or not the outcome of the build process while creating the final firmware image. Figure 2-5 describes the ImageGen process control flow.

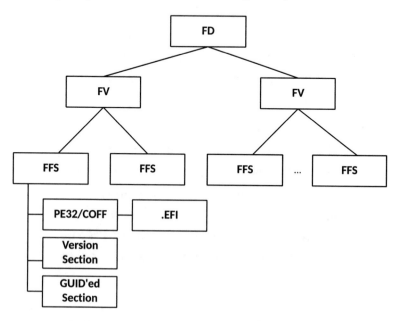

Figure 2-5. *High-level ImageGen structure*

> *Build binary:* Once the EFI section files have been created in the previous step, they need to be placed within an FFS file. GenFfs is the build tool that generates FFS files after combining those EFI_ SECTION type binaries with the FFS header. GenFds is used to construct the final firmware binary.
>
> In addition, there might be a few modules and components that are part of the DSC files that are not meant to be part of a final firmware binary like Option ROM (OpROM). The EfiRom tool builds an option ROM image from an EFI file.

Input files: At this stage, all components or modules that are part of the target platform package DSC file are now converted into build binaries. Out of those build binaries, module types with UEFI applications and OpROM are excluded from being part of the final Flash Descriptor (FD) creation process. This final build process depends on the FDF file to create the flash layout.

Output files: The FDF file section provides an overview of generating one or more firmware volumes (FVs). The FV section describes how to combine FFS files to create FV files. Multiple FV files are combined to create the final firmware image as a flash device (FD). FD tokens provide the BaseAddress, Size, ErasePolarity, BlockSize, and NumBlocks fields.

BaseAddress	$(FLASH_BASE) | gSiPkgTokenSpaceGuid. PcdBiosAreaBaseAddress
Size	$(FLASH_SIZE) | gSiPkgTokenSpaceGuid. PcdBiosSize
ErasePolarity	1
BlockSize	$(FLASH_BLOCK_SIZE)
NumBlocks	$(FLASH_NUM_BLOCKS)

At the end of this phase, the final firmware binary at a size of $(FLASH_SIZE) is ready to use the EDKII framework to flash on the target embedded system.

This section provided an overview of the build system for an EDKII-based system firmware development. The next section will focus on the build tool and its creation process using another system firmware architecture, known as *coreboot*.

coreboot Build Tools and Process

coreboot was developed based on the open source firmware development principle that relies more on C-standard build tools and build environments to generate the final firmware binary. This process doesn't require high-level build tools and is much simpler compared to the EDKII build process described in earlier sections. Figure 2-6 shows the coreboot high-level build process.

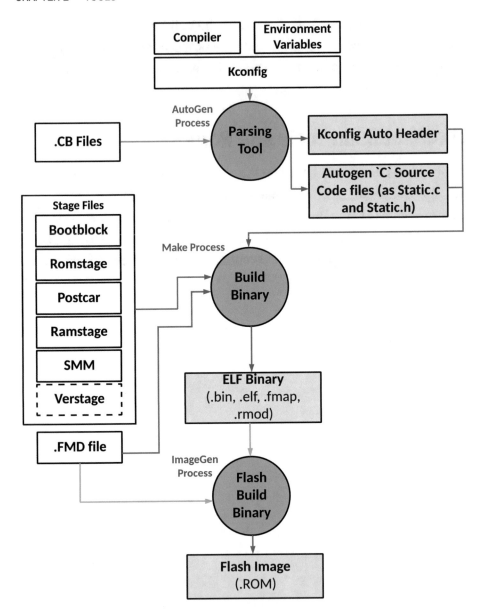

Figure 2-6. *High-level coreboot build tools and build process*

For a better understanding and to be able to compare the build process with EDKII, this section presents the coreboot build flow almost in the same manner as was presented in the previous section.

Build Environment Setup

This section provides the prerequisites to download the coreboot source code, which includes both the package source code and the source code for build tools. Additionally, it provides details about the compiler based on the host systems and environment variables that are expected to be set based on the target embedded system architecture.

The coreboot build process is based on GNU make; hence, developers need to have a Linux and UNIX-equivalent operating system on the host side with native GCC installed. GCC is the compiler for building coreboot (alternatively, one can also use LLVM/clang to build coreboot).

Some other build tools may also be required depending on the source package as part of the system firmware development needs in addition to the previous list:

Additional Compilers	Details
iASL	This compiles ACPI Source Language (ASL) and generate .aml files.
Flex	The GNU flex tool is used to parse the device tree field as it works as a lexical parser.
Bison	The GNU bison tool works as a grammar parser for device tree files.

The coreboot prebuild phase is to ensure that all associated coreboot project-related files are also getting synced from their respective repositories prior to building the target project or mainboard. These associated projects are maintained separately as part of Git submodules and checked out automatically after fresh coreboot code sync using `git submodule update --init --checkout`. The reason for maintaining these submodules separately is because they might be additional firmware projects by themselves like vboot or might be some SoC-specific closed source binary blobs like FSP, CSE, or PSP, etc., used to generate the final firmware binary.

The prebuild phase also sets up the required basic environment variables.

Here is a list of environmental variables that the coreboot build process is dependent on:

Environment Variables	Description
FIRMWARE_ARCH	This variable points to the target hardware architecture for which these files are getting compiled. Values can be used as x86, arm, etc.
KCONFIG_CONFIG	This variable points to the input config file. Typically, this is referred to as $(DOTCONFIG).
KCONFIG_STRICT	The value assigned to this variable is build/util/ kconfig/conf --oldconfig src/Kconfig. Define to enable warning as errors.
KCONFIG_AUTOHEADER	This variable points to the path and filename of the auto.conf file.

The tool chain configuration file (toolchain.inc) is meant to provide paths for compiler, assembler, and linkers based on the target hardware architecture.

At this stage, the coreboot prebuild has been done with all prerequisites except the build tools, which are required to start the build process.

Build Binaries

The coreboot package consists of both source code and tools source code separately, as shown in the following tree structure:

```
|-- 3rdparty
|-- configs
|-- Documentation
|-- payloads
|-- src
|-- util
|   |-- abuild
|   |-- acpi
|   |-- amdfwtool
|   |-- amdtools
|   |-- apcb
|   |-- cbfstool
|   |-- cbmem
|   |-- crossgcc
|   |-- futility
|   |-- ifdtool
|   |-- kconfig
|   |-- sconfig
```

To start the final firmware binary generation process based on the target hardware, coreboot needs to build the cross-compiler, such as x86, arm, risc v, etc. For coreboot, the entire build process is designed based on GNU make; hence, running a make help command would list the possible tool chain options.

To build the coreboot for all supported architectures, developers can use the following command:

make crossgcc CPUS=n [n = number of CPU cores to use.]

Additionally, developers need to build other tools as per package source support or build flow needs.

Let's understand a few widely used build tools/utilities in detail and their usage prior to discussing the build process.

Kconfig

Kconfig is a widely used tool in Linux kernel projects to allow configuration mechanisms by selecting the required modules based on developer input. Similar to a coreboot project, Kconfig is used to allow developers to select the SoC feature or platform feature to create an autogenerated file that can be given to the make process for further processing. The Kconfig utility in coreboot gets built from the source code in `util/kconfig`. The Kconfig language is designed to describe a series of menu entries, and each Kconfig line starts with keywords like `config`, `menuconfig`, `choice/endchoice`, `menu/endmenu`, `if/endif`, etc. All Kconfig symbols in the coreboot project are referred to with the `CONFIG_` prefix. Because of this advantage, the Kconfig language can be used easily to enable or disable any feature at build time. While building the coreboot project, developers are mostly familiar with the following modes to use Kconfig:

- `config`: Text mode configuration; asks developer about each configuration option

- `menuconfig`: Menu-driven configuration tool (added from Linux 2.5.45) still in Text mode

Output: After parsing all the source files, the Kconfig tool generates a `HEADER` file with a list of values inside `build/auto.conf`, which will be further used by the source code and makefiles of the project.

Sconfig

The coreboot device tree is one of the most important concepts in the coreboot project. The device tree is designed to represent the platform hardware device structure in the form of a device node that can be the bridge, the underlying bus architecture, and then finally the endpoint device. Sconfig is the tool that is used to compile the device tree files in a coreboot project to generate the static device configuration. The Sconfig utility is built from the source code inside `util/sconfig`. The Sconfig tool is internally using the Lex and Yacc tools to parse device tree files to create C source code, which can be further used by C-based compilers.

- *Lex*: The GNU flex tool is used as a lexical analysis tool that can parse the `.cb` file to identify specific text strings such as `chip`, `register`, `device`, `pci`, `on`, `off`, `domain`, `cpu_cluster`, `irq`, etc.

- *Yacc*: This is a grammar parser. The GNU bison tool is used to provide this functionality. The output of the flex tool is used as input for this tool to understand what action to take when a token is being identified. Examples: for Interrupts INT[A-D], for decimals [0-9.]+, for hexadecimal 0x[0-9 a-f A-F.]+, etc.

Output: The main goal of Sconfig is to convert the mainboard (and SoC if any) device tree files to create static C source and header files. It takes a few steps to generate desired output files.

1. `util/sconfig/lex.yy.c_shipped` is converted to `lex.yy.c` as a source file.

2. YACC takes `lex.yy.c` as input and creates the `sconfig.tab.c` and `sconfig.tab.h` files that contain the macros for the tokens.

3. The Sconfig utility is generated from the combined output from lex and YACC.

4. Finally, the Sconfig utility is used to generate `static.c`, `static.h`, and `static_fw_config.h` files.

cbfstool

cbfstool is a utility for managing the coreboot file system (CBFS) components during the final firmware image (ROM) generation process. The basic operations that cbfstool supports are add and remove modules into or from ROM images. For the platform using SPINOR as a boot device, one also needs to be aware that SPINOR memory is getting mapped into system runtime memory. Module relocation is not an option for early coreboot modules or `.elf` binaries in absence of physical memory at reset on x86 platforms. Thus, cbfstool needs to take care of two types of modules.

- *eXecute-In-Place (XIP)*: cbfs components marked as `--xip` will execute from the address where they've been mapped in SPINOR. Examples: verstage, FSP-M binary. To support XIP components with a higher SPINOR (32MB), cbfs has introduced concepts called *extended window* and *extended window size* that are mapped anywhere outside (4GB to 16MB) the system memory range.

- *Position-independent modules*: Modules can be relocated anywhere in physical memory after it's being available. The raw binaries like data or configuration files also belong to this category.

There could be more than one cbfs inside the coreboot final binary based on project design. For example, on Chrome OS projects there are three CBFSs per image: `COREBOOT`, `FW_MAIN_A`, and `FW_MAIN_B`.

cbfstool is built using the coreboot source code inside `util/cbfstool`. Inside the cbfstool directory there is source code to create other binaries as follows:

> *fmaptool*: This is the Flashmap Descriptor language and compiler. It's a tool that is able to parse the textual representation of an `.fmd` file and describe the layout of the flash chips that might contain more than one CBFS. This tool creates an intermediate file called `fmap_config.h` with the start and size of each component that would like to be part of fmap blobs. The final output of this tool is `fmap.fmap`.

> *rmodtool*: This is another tool that is part of cbfstool, which is intended to parse and convert ELF type files to *rmodules*. For `.elf` files as part of the coreboot project, those that are supposed to get executed after the physical memory is initialized and not using SPI mapped memory, they are using rmodtool to generate position-independent code and data blocks.

In addition to the generic build tools, there are few important SoC vendor-specific tools that are used to generate the final firmware binary or perform key platform initialization or reset operation as follows:

Utility	Description
ifdtool	Intel Flash Descriptor (IFD), an open source tool that is used on the Intel platform to stitch boot-critical binaries (referred to as SI_ALL in .fmd) like Intel ME, GbE, EC, and Flash Descriptor along with coreboot BIOS region, referred as SI_BIOS in the .fmd file. Developers can use this tool to override the Flash Descriptor fields as well as part of the manufacturing flow.
apcb	AMD Platform Security Processor (PSP) Control Block Tools. This tool is capable of patching an existing APCB binary into the PSP blob. A part of this tool (apcb_edit.py) is allowed to patch the AMD PSP Customization Block (APCB). A binary has been integrated into the PSP to provide the SPD information and perform the required GPIO programming to select and load the right SPD.
amdfwtool	This tool is used to inject various images needed by the PSP to complete the reset flow. This tool takes image name, size, and intended location in the firmware structure. The output of this tool is amdfw.rom, which holds headers, pointers, and added firmware images.
amdcompress	A utility to generate a compressed BIOS image for AMD Family 17h. This compressed image is added into PSP's amdfw.rom binary. The modern AMD system has the PSP, which is able to bring up DRAM prior to x86 reset; hence, the PSP decompresses (the PSP has support for zlib engine) the BIOS image into the DRAM and starts execution.

Build Process

Figure 2-6 has already provided the high-level build process flow for the coreboot platform where the GNU make command has initiated the build process. From opening up the terminal on the host system until the final firmware (.ROM) file generation process, the entire build process can be divided into three major stages.

- AutoGen process

- Make process

- ImageGen process

Every build process listed here involves picking up the correct build tools (described in earlier sections) and having a fixed set of input files, and the target is to generate the output files that can be further worked as input for the next builder script. This process continues unless a final firmware file is generated.

AutoGen Process

This process involves parsing the Kconfig source language files (.kconfig) and package device tree files (.cb) for generating two types of files.

- Autogenerated C header that holds the value of lists of Kconfig being used on the project package (CONFIG_*). The auto.conf header file is the outcome of parsing the Kconfig file by the Kconfig build tool.

- Static C source and header files are being generated as part of this process by the Sconfig tool. These files are getting used further to provide the hardware configuration snapshot to the system firmware during boot.

File	Name	Description
*.CB	Device Tree Files	Each package should have at least one `devicetree. cb` file, which allows for the board-level configuration along with providing the snapshot of the CPU and PCI bus endpoint devices. At runtime this snapshot is being used to enable/disable the hardware interface or initialize a device.

Make Process

The top-level makefile for the project and all the package makefiles are used in the *make process*. The input for the make process includes autogenerated C source and headers from the previous stage; coreboot provides assembly and C source code per stage such as bootblock, romstage, postcar, ramstage, and SMM. The coreboot build process is flexible enough to make any boot stage optional. For example, if the system firmware design doesn't need to have a dedicated ramstage as a stage for loading the payload, then coreboot can generate the final ROM image without compiling files for ramstage. These coreboot stages are independent enough in this build process to generate the ELF file after using the `FIRMWARE_ARCH`-specific compiler, assemblers, and linkers.

On the x86 platform where SPINOR is being used as a boot device and in absence of physical memory, it needs to ensure that the bootblock is able to patch at the reset-vector where coreboot is able to execute the bootblock instruction upon hitting CPU reset. In addition, there are a few stages (.ELF) that would like to load as a position-independent binary; hence, there is a need to use rmodtool to generate a special `.rmod` binary for stages that are typically getting executed after DRAM is initialized.

ACPI modules are also getting compiled using the iASL compiler and generated in this process. The fmap tool is used in this process to parse the FMD file to create a flash descriptor file with the names of possible CBFSs.

File	Name	Description
.fmd	Flashmap File	Each board package is equipped with one .fmd file to provide the description about flash layout. This .fmd file might consist of more than one region (SI_ME, SI_EC, etc.) in addition to the BIOS region, specified as SI_BIOS. Based on the project requirement, this FMD file might have more than one CBFS as well.

ImageGen Process

This phase is responsible for creating the final firmware image (ROM) after adding all those build binaries from the previous stage into the CBFS.

This process basically divided into two phases:

- *Create CBFSs*: The coreboot build process relies on the cbfstool build to add the .elf and .bin binaries into sections into cbfs as per the following example where different coreboot stages and raw binary is getting injected to create the final ROM image:

```
printf "    CBFS        fallback/romstage\n"
CBFS        fallback/romstage
build/util/cbfstool/cbfstool build/coreboot.pre.
tmp add-stage -f build/cbfs/fallback/romstage.elf -n
fallback/romstage  -c none  -r COREBOOT -a 64 -S ".car.
data" --xip
printf "    CBFS        fallback/ramstage\n"
CBFS        fallback/ramstage
```

```
build/util/cbfstool/cbfstool build/coreboot.pre.
tmp add-stage -f build/cbfs/fallback/ramstage.elf -n
fallback/ramstage  -c LZMA  -r COREBOOT
printf "   CBFS        fallback/dsdt.aml\n"
CBFS       fallback/dsdt.aml
build/util/cbfstool/cbfstool build/coreboot.pre.tmp
add -f build/dsdt.aml -n fallback/dsdt.aml -t
raw -c none  -r COREBOOT
```

- *Add SoC/CPU vendor-specific binary*: This process involves using vendor-specific binaries and tools to inject into coreboot.rom to call it the final firmware binary. For example, on the Intel platform, ifdtool is used to inject a descriptor, ME and EC, whereas on the AMD platform, an additional step has to be performed to compress the bootblock (using amdcompress) and create the build binary (amdfw.rom using amdfwtool) into PSP; it can then be added directly into the coreboot image.

At the end of this phase, the final firmware binary (ROM) at a size of CONFIG_ROM_SIZE is ready using the coreboot open source firmware model to flash on the target embedded system.

Configuration Tools

The configuration tools are intended to allow changes in the final firmware image without going through the entire build process. The scope of configuration can vary between static and dynamic based on the system where this tool is running. For example, a tool can be running as part of the host system. Taking a final firmware binary (FD or ROM) as input to modify its default configuration value is known as *static configuration*. Or, if during the runtime execution on the target hardware a native configuration interface allows modification of the configuration database, this is called a *dynamic configuration* tool.

In this section, we will discuss a few widely used tools in the scope of different system firmware architectures like coreboot, EDKII, and Slimboot that are allowed to modify the configuration database.

Human Interface Infrastructure

Legacy system firmware was lagging in terms of allowing a unified approach to configure the underlying hardware with different hardware vendors providing their own configuration tools and access mechanisms. This made it harder for system integrators to design a robust interface for end users and various other users of system firmware.

On the UEFI platform, the Human Interface Infrastructure (HII) is used to provide a flexible and standard way to configure the target hardware. HII allows the platform configuration to access the hardware interface and store the data using the form browser. The form browser is like a web page that uses display and input devices for configuration to take place. Figure 2-7 shows the high-level operational model of HII.

HII is designed to create the platform configuration in the form of a data structure that needs localized text and a GUI to interface with the user. It needs six types of components to allow platform configuration using HII.

- *HID devices*: Input devices are used for configuration in the form of localization. HII supports localization, a process that helps a product adapt to the local market. HII supports keyboard mapping to allow users to choose their own language as input.

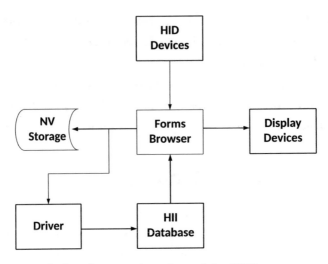

Figure 2-7. *High-level operational model of HII*

- *Display devices*: The output devices support the localization. HII supports Unicode characters, which allows it to support all possible languages to display as part of the form.

- *HII database*: The HII database is created dynamically as the system boots. The UEFI driver is required to register a list of HII packages into the HI database. The package list provides different types of binary data. The data types could be font, string, image, keyboard layout, form, etc.

- *Driver*: The UEFI driver provides the Config Routing Protocol as ExtractConfig, RouteConfig, and Callback to retrieve and save configuration information associated with HII forms.

- *NV Storage*: The NV Storage is to store any data which remains persistent even after the system is resuming from the mechanical off state. The NVRAM is getting used as the NV storage. The HII form retrieves the configuration data from NV Storage and allows modification of these parameters from the available configuration list. The EFI variable services protocol is used to access the NV Storage.

- *Forms Browser*: This is a GUI to represent the HII and allow users to configure the options. HII has its own standard architecture and language as IFR and VFR to present the browser with the help of a Unicode string.

  - *IFR* : Internal Forms Representation is the architectural binary encoding used to present the user interface pages. The Vfr compiler takes VFR files as input and generates output IFR files.

  - *VFR*: Visual Forms Representation is the source code language that is used by developers to design a form page.

The following table provides a conversion from VFR to IFR for developers' understanding:

VFR	IFR

form formid = 1,
  title = STRING_TOKEN(
      STR_FORM1_TITLE
  ),
	typedef struct _EFI_IFR_FORM {
	    EFI_IFR_OP_HEADER Header;
	    UINT16 FormId;
	    EFI_STRING_ID FormTitle;
	  } EFI_IFR_FORM;

Figure 2-8 represents a UEFI browser setup page created using HII.

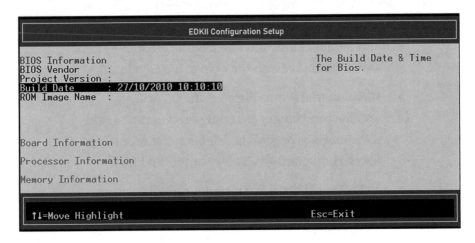

Figure 2-8. *EDKII setup browser using HII*

YAML-Based Configuration

YAML-based configuration is part of Slim Bootloader (SBL) configuration process to provide a simple and flexible method to modify the board-specific parameter to support new boards. SBL provides configuration parameters that are getting used for platform initialization and are typically categorized into memory; SoC hardware interfaces like USB, PCIE, and GPIO; and OS boot options.

SBL configuration parameters are packed in a configuration binary blob. This binary blob is stitched with BIOS regions to apply the configuration at runtime (during Stage 1B phase of SBL).

The idea of the configuration binary block is to support multiple board configurations using a single system firmware image; hence, this blob contains configuration parameters for multiple different boards. The configuration binary block starts with a configuration blob header and is followed by the configuration parameters that are organized in configuration blocks. Each configuration block contains a block header followed by the parameter structure. Each configuration block is identified by a unique tag as PLATFORM_CFG_DATA, MEMORY_CFG_DATA, etc.

In SBL firmware architecture, the platform configuration relies on YAML files. Figure 2-9 shows the high-level view of the YAML-based configuration.

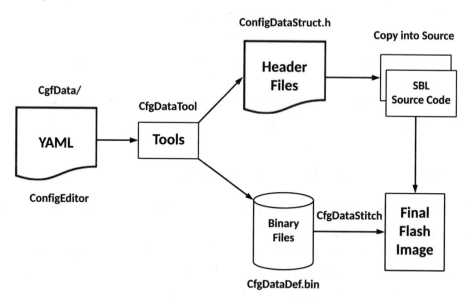

Figure 2-9. *High-level YAML-based configuration*

YAML is a data serialized language that can be used for generating the configuration blobs while working with other modern programming languages. The idea here is to create all possible configuration options in SBL source code in the form of YAML syntax inside *cfgdata*. For example, a template of Debug Consent configure is shown here:

```
- DebugInterfaceEnable :
    name        : Enable or Disable processor debug features
    type        : Combo
    option      : $EN_DIS
    help        : >
                    Enable or Disable processor debug
                    features; <b>0- Disable</b>; 1- Enable.
    length      : 0x01
    value       : 0x00
```

Users can open the CfgDataDef.yami file using the ConfigEditor GUI tool to allow the default value to be overridden.

All configuration YAML files will be processed by configuration tools like GenCfgData, CfgDataTool, and CfgDataStitch to generate configuration header files and binary blobs.

Finally, use the CfgDataStitch tool to patch the new configuration data file into the final firmware binary.

Firmware Configuration Interface

Traditionally, coreboot has limited dynamic configuration capabilities compared to other system firmware used on the embedded system. Because coreboot was designed with the principle of instant boot and a small footprint, it doesn't provide much scope for a preboot configuration environment like a UEFI browser. This eventually results in source-based modifications to enable/disable certain hardware interfaces as per system firmware users' needs.

The firmware configuration interface in coreboot is designed to overcome such limitations and allow users to configure the possible hardware interface at runtime. This interface will also help to maintain a single firmware image that can work seamlessly on different motherboards where the base schematics is the same but the I/Os might be different.

The coreboot Kconfig option CONFIG_FW_CONFIG can be used to enable this feature where the platform has decided to provide a bunch of configuration options as part of the devicetree.cb source code for runtime configuration.

The firmware configuration structure today is limited to a 64-bit value where the bitmask is used to determine the feature that needs to be configured at runtime. There are two possible implementations for enabling the firmware configuration interface in coreboot.

CBFS

A 64-bit raw value can be stored into CBFS with the name CONFIG_CBFS_PREFIX/fw_config. To enable this feature, coreboot needs to be built with the CONFIG_FW_CONFIG_CBFS option.

At runtime while the fw_config_probe() function is getting called, it will check the Kconfig option and load the CBFS filename to get this configuration value. *cbfstool* can be also used to override this binary blob at build time.

Embedded Controller

On the Chrome OS platform, the embedded controller interface will read and write the firmware configuration value using the CrOS Board Info (CBI) command. Mainboard users can select CONFIG_ FW_CONFIG_CHROME_EC_CBI options to read the fw_config value from EC CBI.

The ectool command can also be used to configure this value using the ChromeOS environment.

Firmware Configuration Table

The firmware configuration table, which is part of the mainboard devicetree.cb file, starts with a special token as fw_config and terminates with end. The SCONFIG tool is used to parse this fw_config token to generate a static_fw_config.h file after understanding the grammar, where each field is defined by providing the *field name,* the *start bit,* and the *end bit.* Inside each field block, the option is used to provide the possible option name and associated value. This example configures the EMMC boot using fw_config:

```
field BOOT_DEVICE_EMMC 22
                option BOOT_EMMC_DISABLED 0
                option BOOT_EMMC_ENABLED 1
end
```

Binary Configuration Tool (BCT)/Config Editor

The hybrid firmware development model is where the open source firmware development model gets stitched with closed binary blobs like the Firmware Support Package (FSP) to create the final firmware binary for embedded systems. Previous sections discussed in detail the possible options to configure the open source boot firmware, and this section will provide mechanisms to allow changes in the configuration settings for FSP binaries. The Binary Configuration Tool (BCT) (almost deprecated and replaced with a newer utility named Error! Hyperlink reference not valid.Config Editor) was developed by Intel to allow configuration changes in static UPD configurations. Static UPDs are a kind of configuration parameter that isn't really meant to change based on certain runtime decisions; hence, users can make use of BCT/Config Editor to open the FSP binary and modify the default UPD value as part of the SPI Flash image. This tool is not designed to manage the dynamic UPD configuration. See Figure 2-10.

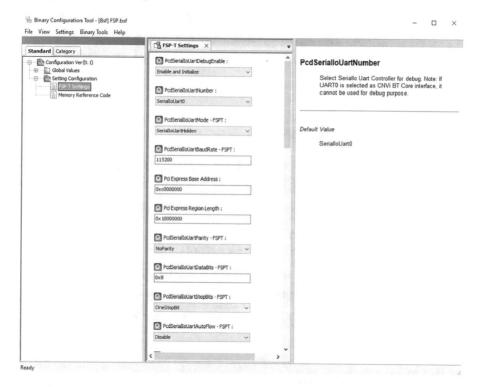

Figure 2-10. *Configuring static FSP-UPD using BCT*

Flashing Tools

In the system firmware development approach, the last but very significant tool is the flashing tool. Starting from the source code development all the way up to generating the final firmware image, the process will fulfill its purpose only if the embedded system is able to boot after flashing the final image on the targeted embedded system's boot device. The flashing tools are highly specific to the target embedded system; they need to know the hardware interface that can be used to flash into the boot device from the local or remote host. At the high level, these flashing tools can be divided into two categories: hardware-based tools and software-based tools.

In this section, we will discuss a few popular flashing tools used on the target hardware for flashing the system firmware. The assumption being made here is that all these embedded systems are using SPINOR as the boot device.

Hardware-Based Tools

Hardware-based tools are used to flash the embedded systems in some specific scenarios like a device with an empty SPINOR as the very first boot during the manufacturing process, a corrupted SPINOR, or the device being unable to boot to the OS or pre-boot console to allow flashing using a software-based mechanism. This type of tool requires the host system to be connected to the target device where the host and the target device will connect using the hardware interface like USB or serial and where the host system is running the flashing software to write into the target device SPINOR.

SPINOR Programmer

Mostly in all the latest embedded platforms, the SPINOR is the default and soldered onto the board; hence, either the board design has an SF programming header where the SPINOR programmer can be attached to flash the firmware image or you need to make use of some custom clip solution to attach directly onto the SPINOR chip itself for flashing. Dediprog SF100 and SF600 are the widely used in system programing. Programmers can flash the firmware on the target system using a USB interface.

Servo

Servo is a debug board used for Chrome OS projects for multipurpose operations. One such operations is to allow the developer to flash the CPU and EC SPINOR using the USB interface. Over the generations, the Servo hardware specification has evolved from v2 to v4. Flashrom is the utility for updating the SPI Flash using Servo while running from the Host machine as well. The utility expects to mention the external SPI programmer support using the -p option followed by the name of the FTDI FT2232 device. For example:

```
sudo flashrom -V -p ft2232_spi:type=google-servo-v2 -w $IMAGE
```

This ensures the recovery of the bricked system by flashing the EC and system firmware using Servo.

Software-Based Tools

The software-based tools don't have any prerequisites for the underlying hardware interface or any dependency over the host system. These kinds of tools run on the target device to allow read, write, or erase on the SPINOR using the pre-OS or OS environment. The following are a few popular software-based flashing utilities being used on cross-firmware projects.

Flashrom

An open source flashing utility is used across various operating systems and motherboards for detecting, reading, writing, erasing, and verifying the flash chips. The Flashrom tool can be used to flash coreboot/EFI images on the supported mainboard. Flashrom has support for various AICs like network, graphics, and storage.

It also supports a wide range of SPI programmers using USB interfaces like FTDI FT2232/FT4232H. The flashing mechanism is different from flashrom while using hardware-based tools like Servo to run as a user space application on the DUT itself.

Users can run the flashrom -p -w $IMAGE command to write the final firmware image into the SPINOR using the DUT OS command line. The flashrom source code is getting managed inside https://github.com/flashrom/flashrom, and users are expected to build the flashrom source code to generate the flashrom tool binary. While working inside the Chrome OS project repository, developers can run the following command to generate the flashrom tool:

```
cros_workon --host start flashrom; sudo emerge flashrom
```

UEFI Tools and Utility

Different vendors have created their own platform flashing tools using UEFI pre-boot services or native OS-based drivers to access the underlying SPI Flash device with the highest privilege.

AMI Firmware Update (AFU) is one popular tool (AfuEfix64.efi) used on the Aptio platform either from the pre-boot environment or from the OS layer to update the SPINOR. Many OEMs are using the uefiflash.efi binary to update the final firmware image from the EFI Shell environment as part of the shell automated script.

Summary

This chapter has provided detailed analysis of various system firmware development tools such as build tools, configuration tools, and flashing tools that a developer has to be equipped with prior to starting their own system firmware development. This chapter might also be useful for firmware developers to understand the underlying tools architecture and build process for popular boot firmware like EDKII and coreboot. This knowledge can be directly applied while creating your own system firmware using a new SoC/CPU architecture that is not yet supported by existing system firmware (EDKII or coreboot).

The book *System Firmware: An Essential Guide to Open Source and Embedded Solutions* has a case study about adding support for a new RISC-based CPU using EDKII.

We also discussed possible configuration options across different leading system firmware solutions so that developers can make the right decision when choosing the correct boot firmware for their target embedded system. Understanding flashing tools and the underlying hardware interface is useful to ensure guaranteed recovery even from the bricking state of the target device.

CHAPTER 3

Infrastructure for Building Your Own Firmware

"Talk is cheap. Show me the code."

—*Linus Torvalds*

Open source firmware development without the right infrastructure is like fighting a battle without proper weapons and trained troops. The idea behind open source development is to provide an inclusive environment across various parties, not limited to only certain companies. As source code development is an important piece while creating your own firmware for target hardware, having that code be reviewed by the open source community with the proper visibility in a timely manner is also key. This process might also involve migration, where in the future open source firmware will be used for embedded system development; hence, developers either need to open their existing infrastructures to the external world or adopt the available open source infrastructures for product development.

This chapter will provide an overview of the existing open source infrastructure offerings and help the product development team make the right decision for creating their own firmware. Additionally, this chapter will focus on reducing the onboarding gap between firmware architecture migration and open source firmware development by reviewing the code of conduct and coding standard differences between different firmware versions.

Overview of Source Control Management

Firmware development is a process that involves creating source code from scratch and modifying the source code based on the hardware behavior. In most cases, the firmware code is used to testify the hardware interface and eventually results in the platform specification.; hence, this source code development process might involve trial and error to create the final working version. Source code management (SCM) is important to ensure that the working code base never gets tampered with due to the trial-and-error part of the development process.

This process gets more complicated with more engineers working on the same project, which means there is a need to share the code in a central location rather than maintaining it on a local machine. This type of source control management is also referred to as *version control* and can work as a central database to host the source code for multiparty development. One developer might need to work on a module for developing new features, and others might need to make some bug fixes on the same module; hence, there might be a chance that while merging their individual code changes, they override each other's work by mistake. Version control helps the team to solve such problems by tracking the changes for every individual and resolves any conflicts by rebasing the changes onto the branch master.

The source control also needs to be shared for peer review. While developing the firmware with the open source community, this step is important to submit code changes for review and generate pull requests for a reviewer to review your code changes.

Based on the previous discussion, it's clear that any firmware is looking for three major features from SCM.

- A free, open-source-friendly, high-quality version control system

- A cloud-based repository hosting service that allows multiple teams to collaborate and share source code

- An application that can provide the code review functionality

Keeping these requirements in mind, let's look at the existing offerings to select the correct SCM for firmware development.

Version Control System

Using version control software (VCS) for firmware development provides flexibility for the development team to travel back and forth on a development branch without fear of losing the current project status. This process is sometimes sufficient to identify a regression by just filtering the branch based on different commit IDs and finding the culprit code change list (CL) without requiring any additional debugging.

Subversion

Subversion (SVN) is a free and open source software tool for performing source control management. SVN is considered the successor to the widely used Concurrent Version System (CVS) tool on Windows operating systems. Many open source projects such as FreeBSD and SourceForge have used SVN for code management.

SVN provides an improvement over CVS by adopting the concept of *atomic operations*, which prevents databases from being corrupted due to partial changes. Hence, most DevOps teams that relied on CVS in the past have switched to SVN for the improved features and fast response compared to CVS. Although SNV has support for almost all leading operating systems, it still provides better support with Windows OS. It provides easy plug-ins for integrating with modern IDEs, such as Visual Studio.

One of the most popular VCS tools that is used by various projects is called Git. As per the survey data conducted by Stack Overflow in 2018, Git is the dominant choice for VCS; approximately 88 percent of developers are checking in their source code using Git; the next most popular is Subversion with 16.1 percent.

Git

Git is a free and open source project originally developed by Linus Torvalds to support the development of the Linux operating system kernel. Many open source projects such as the Linux kernel and Eclipse use Git for version control.

Git is an example of a distributed VCS (DVCS) because Git supports the installation and maintenance of the source tree in the local machine without any need of a remote cloud. Unlike other popular VCSs like SVN or CVS, where the full version history resides in a single place, in the case of Git, each local repository consists of the full history of project check-ins.

Here are the underlying principles of Git:

- *Performance*: The performance of the Git while doing tasks such as committing new changes, branching, merging, and comparing different versions is much better than any other version control software.

Git was designed with the concept of a file system; hence, it makes the versioning easier compared to other SCMs. Git relies more on file content rather than on the name of the file. The filename is something that can change over the time by different developers based on project need.

- *Distributed development*: Unlike other version control management solutions, Git sets itself apart with its *branching model*. This allows for a distributed development where each developer's local repo is self-sustaining in terms of the project development history and code changes. Later these changes can be pushed into the mainline branch from the local branch. See Figure 3-1.

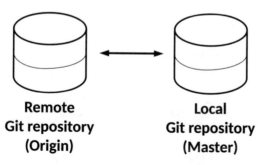

Remote
Git repository
(Origin)

Local
Git repository
(Master)

Figure 3-1. *Git distributed development model*

This distributed development model provides flexibility to developers to experiment with the source code without creating any new repository when enabling a new feature that might need to add, modify, or delete files from the working branch.

- **Security**: Git uses SHA-1 to ensure the integrity of
  the source code branch from accidental corruption.
  Starting from the content of the files, version, commits,
  tags, and other data objects for Git are secured with a
  cryptographically secure hash. The method to see the
  Git history is associated with the commit ID, which
  is also generated using a unique combination of the
  following:

  - The source code tree

  - The patent commit SHA-1

  - The author information

  - The committer information (if it's different from
    the author)

  - The commit message

Figure 3-2 shows the Git unique commit ID.

```
$ git show
commit 02bec2bd5cbef9ab5fab422b801768686e436b51
Author: Subrata Banik <subrata.banik@intel.com>
Date:   Mon Feb 15 21:42:38 2021 +0530

    lib: Add DDR5 DRAM type

    TEST=Not seeing default msg "Defaulting to using DDR4 params." with
    this CL.

    Change-Id: Ib751396ec74b1491fd08b88b07462b315c4a152d
    Signed-off-by: Subrata Banik <subrata.banik@intel.com>
    Reviewed-on: https://review.coreboot.org/c/coreboot/+/50745
    Reviewed-by: Furquan Shaikh <furquan@google.com>
    Tested-by: build bot (Jenkins) <no-reply@coreboot.org>
```

Figure 3-2. *Git commit ID with commit message*

Git Working Model

The single biggest difference on Git that separates it from other source control management software is its branching model. As shown in Figure 3-1, Git supports distributed development that allows you to create an independent local repository upon syncing the source code from the remote repository. Working on the local branch is almost similar to working on the remote repository in terms of making any code changes, adding the changes, committing the changes, and merging into the local branch. Later you can submit those changes to the remote repository.

Figure 3-3 describes the Git branching model that allows developers to share the code with each other by creating development Git branches. These Git branches are an independent line of code compared to the default branch where typically developers start their work after syncing the code from the remote repository, known as the *main* branch or *master* branch. Any changes that are part of this Git local branch don't automatically reach the master branch unless you perform a pull/push request.

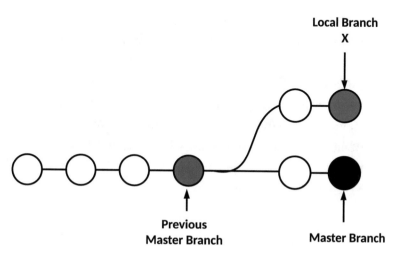

Figure 3-3. *Git branching model between remote and local branches*

At a high level, the Git working model can further divided into three major categories.

- *Remote repository*: This is typically referred to as a *unified sharable code database*, which is shareable across various developers based on either their access account or open access. The idea here is to allow seamless access of the source code beyond the local repository; hence, anyone in this world can contribute to the source code or even browse the code. This remote repository can hold one or more than one project repository. Typically it is the job of the DevOps team to create a remote repository for project development so that development resources can be shared, but this eventually reduces the development time.

- *Local repository*: After the DevOps team has provided you with the remote repository where you can check in the project files and folders, you still need to have a way to browse or modify the source files or directory structure in your local system. To support this, Git provides *cloning*, a mechanism by which developers can sync the source code from remote repositories (referred to as the *origin*) to their local machine. By default the source code resides in the branch known as the *master* branch. Figure 3-4 shows this cloning model to create the local repository.

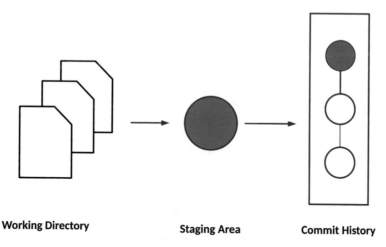

Working Directory   **Staging Area**   **Commit History**

Figure 3-4. *Git workflow between working directory and staging area*

- *Working directory*: After syncing the source code from the origin to the master branch, the developer creates the local branch to ensure an unpolluted master branch. Developers are now free to modify the changes as per the project requirements. These changes reside in files and/or directories that are still not merged into the local branch.

  a. *Staging area*: The staging area is for the intermediate process by which the developer can prepare the snapshot of the local changes into the working directory prior to committing them into the local branch to keep track of those changes as part of the project change history.

Figure 3-5 provides a few examples of widely used Git commands and working relationships between these work streams (remote repository, local repository, and working directory) while using Git for source code management across teams.

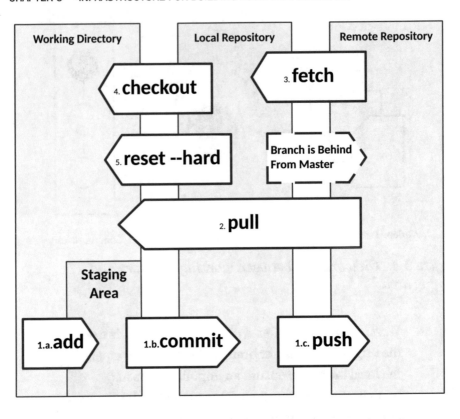

Example #1: git add   Example #3: git fetch   Example #5: git reset --hard
Example #2: git pull   Example #3: git checkout

Figure 3-5. *Git workflow between working directory and*
staging area

Data Structure

The internals of Git were designed with keeping the file system concept in mind, which later extended to support a full set of features expected from a traditional SCM. Here, a detailed understanding of the information is stored by each commit uniquely in the form of a file system. Git has two data structures: a *stage or cache index,* to provide information about the working directory and the revision supposed to be committed next on the working directory; and an *object database*. Each Git object consists of three pieces of information: type, size, and content. The size is the size of the contents of the file. Git uses three types of objects: commit, tree, and blobs.

Commit object: A commit object contains the metadata such as the tree, parent, author, committer, and commit information. The following diagram shows the commit object description (from the open source coreboot project):

commit	0603902..
tree	733f5fd..
parent	492a79..
author	Subrata
committer	Subrata

Developers can use the git show command with the --pretty=raw option to get more details about the commit object.

```
$ git show -s --pretty=raw 0603902
commit 06039025250e0908c8da63f879eafd2b3581db19
tree 733f5fd080bb87a9880441f9041ac17e4def6e64
parent 492a792d3872ee2683db169fb011daf87b71bff9
author Subrata Banik <subrata.banik@intel.com> 161528439 +0530
committer Subrata Banik <subrata.banik@intel.com>
1615439203 +0000

    soc/intel/common/block/cpu: Use tab instead of space

    Convert the lines starting with whitespace with tab as
    applicable.
```

```
TEST=Built google/bryaO and ADLRVP with BUILD_TIMELESS=1:
no changes.
```

```
Signed-off-by: Subrata Banik <subrata.banik@intel.com>
```

Here is a description of the fields that are part of the commit object from the previous example:

- `tree`: The SHA-1 name points to the tree object. Each commit object is linked to a dedicated tree object to represent the contents of the directory at the time this commit is being made.

- `parent`: The SHA-1 name refers to the previous commit rather than the current one. If the current commit doesn't have any previous comment, then the parent commit is "nil," and the current commit is considered to be a "root" commit.

- `author`: The name string is the name of the author who wrote this code change.

- `committer`: The name string refers to the name of the person who committed the code change. In some cases, the author name and committer name could be different, such as if the author has sent the code changes to the committer to check into the database.

- `comment`: This describes the purpose for this code change.

Tree object: Each commit object points to a tree object, and each tree object further holds multiple points to blobs and other tree objects. Typically, a tree represents the directory structure in the project database and contains a list of filenames. Each filename points to a blob. The following diagram shows the tree object description (from the open source coreboot project):

tree	733f5fd..	
blob	ec0f95b..	Makefile
tree	db803ce..	src
blob	14879c1..	README.md
tree	3f4fd34..	util

Developers can use the git ls-tree option to get more details about the tree object based on a SHA-1 name for a tree.

```
$ git ls-tree 733f5fd080bb87a9880441f9041ac17e4def6e64

100644     blob     11a617328327dba48d5a68fcfec9335b527fcaa2    .gitignore
100644     blob     4350a2c9b520e0823da8f8a67484d5a889cf56e3    .gitmodules
040000     tree     9f0a9bb5b6f925d2b88f80d9d6fbbfa4fac61736    3rdparty
100644     blob     8b1cb226085cf0aae8a9d2ee57a6bf0d43510009    AUTHORS
040000     tree     1437f7116a9948d875a76c12a497c66d15ee5153    Documentation
040000     tree     a4f77350eb9cd4e68e0fddae80446ab159ba32ef    LICENSES
100644     blob     0e283ca1a347aaba1639b3b4372b796bb6792396    MAINTAINERS
100644     blob     ec0f95b59556d5dcbfd95bd02a7fa2642d068d9c    Makefile
100644     blob     f46de4615fd73d8ebe63032ba51df500d12e5e83    Makefile.inc
100644     blob     14879c14842f2ab7e83bd724b5daaff1520f4ddc    README.md
040000     tree     571aac417263272b8f41589579bbffc7d36b191b    configs
040000     tree     f61b04b99db2adef68871e3171c8fb41b589f47c    payloads
040000     tree     db803cee61fbb5aa6f05f1b8ba8e02dfc161fb90    src
040000     tree     3f4fd34dfd29bb9b58eea83518977406efe3a091    util
```

Blob object: Each file listed in the tree points to a binary data object called a *blob*. The blob contains the compress contents of the file at the time of the commit. The blob file doesn't have any name, timestamp, or metadata; hence, just renaming the filename doesn't change the blob object that file is associated with. The following shows the blob object description (from the open source coreboot project):

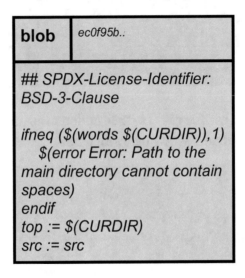

Developers can use the `git show` option to get more details about the blob object based on a SHA-1 name for a file.

Let's look at a small example to understand the working relationship of these data objects across various Git commits.

Here is a sample project directory and file structure that are managed under Git SCM:

Project HEAD	With Latest Commit on HEAD
| ```
$ tree
.
|-- io.h
`-- x86emu
  |-- fpu_regs.h
  `-- x86emu.h
1 directory, 3 files
``` | ```
$ tree
.
|-- io.h
`-- x86emu
  |-- fpu_regs.h
  |-- regs.h
  |-- types.h
  `-- x86emu.h
1 directory, 5 files
``` |

Figure 3-6 is the example of git commit and associated data objects to show how it's being managed to track changes in the Git commit history. The last commit (*399689b..*) has added two new files (regs.h and types.h) into the project directory, so two new blobs are shown in Figure 3-6 under the blob data object column.

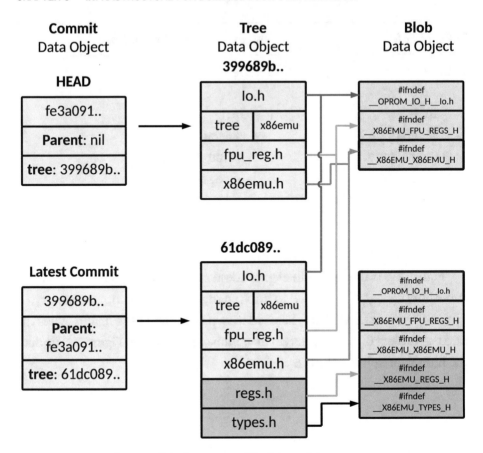

Figure 3-6. *Relationship between Git data objects*

The rest of the blob doesn't change with the latest commit; hence, the tree links to the blobs from the previous commit. This method of reusing the blobs between commits helps to make the internal Git operations faster with optimized space.

Setting Up Git

Using Git as a version control management software for firmware development has many benefits that we have already discussed such as a distributed development mechanism, flexibility, and wide community support for code maintenance without extra cost. Git is a universal tool that is available on almost all possible operating systems and is easy to install and use.

Installing Git on Windows

Windows users can download the stand-alone installer for Git from `https://gitforwindows.org`.

After successfully downloading the installer package, developers can start the installation, and the Git Setup installation wizard will prompt for the default installation path and the default settings to complete the installation, as shown in Figure 3-7.

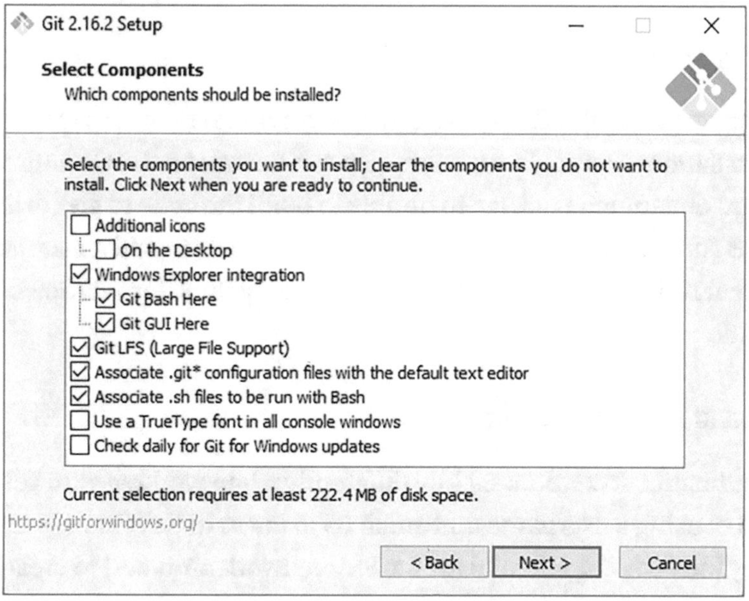

Figure 3-7. *Git Setup installation wizard with default settings*

At this stage, Windows users can open Git Bash to start syncing the source code from the remote repository or pushing the code into the remote branch. Prior to that, the user needs to configure the username and email to allow Git to use this information to add during `Signed-off-by` when running git `commit -s`.

```
$ git config --global user.name 'Subrata Banik'
$ git config --global user.email hello@git.com
```

Installing Git on Linux

With the Linux distribution package, the user can choose to make use of either apt or yum to install the Git package.

From the Linux terminal, install Git using apt-get on Debian/Ubuntu.

```
$ sudo apt-get update
$ sudo apt-get install git
```

Or make use of dnf/yum to install Git on Fedora.

```
$ sudo yum install git
```

After installing the Git package, users can run git `--version` to verify the installation version. Linux users also can download the Git source code and dependent package to be able to build the code to create the Git installer. After successful installation, the user needs to add a username and email ID in a similar manner to what's being done for Windows Git installation.

Create and Register Git SSH

User authentication works slightly differently when working with Git. Instead of using a username and email ID to log in to Git, Git uses an SSH key (an access credential for the SSH network protocol) to create a public/private key pair to initiate a trusted communication with the remote branch. SSH keys are generated using a key cryptographic algorithm (typically, RSA) for which the SSH command line has included the key generation tool. The public key is registered with the Git remote repository, while the private key is stored on the development machine. The combination of public/private key pairs will help users to pull/push the source code changes from/to remote repositories.

The process for creating the SSH key is the same across different operating systems (note: on Windows OS, users need to use the Git Bash shell to run these commands). Typically, these operations are taking place inside the .ssh directory (create it if it is not available by default).

Step 1: Use the SSH keygen tool and run the following command:

```
$ ssh-keygen -t rsa
```

This command will create a new SSH key pair and prompt you to enter a file in which to save the key. Users can either specify the new file location or press Enter to accept the default path as /Users/<user_name>/.ssh/id_rsa.

Step 2: Additionally, it will ask to enter the passphrase, which may work as an additional layer of security in case someone has access to your development machine and might access the remote repository. Adding a passphrase will reduce the risk even with a physical attack.

```
$ ssh-keygen -t rsa
Enter a file in which to save the key (/Users/Subrata/.ssh/
id_rsa): [Press enter]
Enter passphrase (empty for no passphrase): [Type a passphrase]
Enter same passphrase again: [Type passphrase again]
Your identification has been saved in /Users/Subrata/.
ssh/id_rsa.
Your public key has been saved in /Users/Subrata/.ssh/id_
rsa.pub.
```

The new SSH key is now registered, and users can make use of the Git repository.

Git Cheat Sheet

This section provides lists of basic, useful, and advanced Git commands that might be helpful for new users who have migrated from other SCM versions to Git and started managing the project database. From my experience, while migrating the project from internal or closed source SCM to open source Git, the initial few weeks are tough because of the number of Git commands used for pulling/pushing the repository, rebasing, resetting the HEAD, etc. Ideally this effort will be useful for developers and eventually save development time as well.

Basic Commands

`git init <directory name>`	This is the first step to bring a directory under Git control. Run this command with a directory name specified to create an empty Git repository. Not specifying the directory name will result in initializing Git into the current directory.
`git clone <repo>`	Run this command to clone the remote repository specified with the repo into the local machine to create the local repo. The remote repository can be located in a remote machine and accessed via HTTP or SSH.
`git diff`	This command shows the unstaged changes in the working directory.
`git log`	List the entire commit history from the local repo using the default format. Appending `--oneline` will show each commit to a single line, and `-p` will display the full diff of each commit changes.

(continued)

Basic Commands

`git status`	Show the current changes in the working directory. This command lists the files in three categories as staged, unstaged, and untracked.
`git add <file(s)/ directory name>`	Run this command to stage all the changes from the working directory to the local repository.
`git rm <file(s)/ directory name>`	Run this command to remove a file(s) or directory from the working directory to the local repository.
`git commit -s`	Commit the staged snapshot and add a description about the changes. Use `--amend` instead of `-s` to modify the existing commit.
`git format-patch -<commit count>`	Run this command to create patch files from the current branch HEAD based on the commit count. It's a useful command to share working patch files between teams without review.
`git am <patch-file>`	Apply `patch-file` generated from the `format-patch` command on the local repo. All changes as part of this command will be part of the staged changes and in a committed state.
`git apply <diff file>`	Apply changes from the diff file to the working directory. All changes will be listed under unstaged files.
`git rebase -i <base SHA-ID>`	Interactively rebase the current branch onto the base SHA ID. Users can specify the mode of changes for each commit using rebase.

(continued)

Basic Commands

`git rebase` `--continue`	Run this command to migrate to the current branch's latest commit after finishing the rebasing process.

Undo Commands

`git revert` `<commit id>`	Create a new commit by reverting any previous commit specified by the commit ID.
`git reset` `<file>`	Remove the file from the staging area to the unstage area without overriding the changes being made to the file.
`git reset`	Use this command to undo the changes from the staging area to match the recent commit.
`git reset` `--hard`	Use this command to undo the changes from the staging area to match the recent commit and overwrite all changes in the working directory.

`git reset`
`--hard`
`<commit id>`
	Move the current branch HEAD backward to a commit specified by a commit ID. This process will eventually delete all uncommitted changes.

`git undo`	A good thing about Git is that there's a "undo" command that is capable of recovering from an undue state, such as correcting the last commit to include that small change. Revert a whole commit because that feature isn't necessary anymore.

Managing Branches

`git branch`	List all the branches in the local repo. Specify a branch name to create a new branch.

(continued)

Basic Commands

`git checkout -b <branch>`	Create and check out to a new branch specified with the branch name. Don't use the `-b` flag if an existing branch is available with the same branch name.
`git merge <branch>`	Merge a branch into the current branch.
`git reflog`	Reference the log (reflog) to record the changes made on the tips of branches and other references in the local repo. This is a useful command to travel between various changes in the local branch without impacting the remote repo.

Accessing Remote Repository

`git remote add <remote name> <remote url>`	Create a new connection to a remote repo.
`git fetch <remote name> <branch>`	Fetch a specific branch from the remote repo.
`git pull <remote name>`	Fetch the code from a specific remote repository into the current local branch.
`git push <remote_name> <branch>`	This command pushes the branch specified with the branch name to remote. If the branch name is not specified, then it will push changes ahead of HEAD in a local branch to the remote repository.

Version Control Repository Hosting Service

Earlier we provided details about version control and using Git because it's the most efficient way to handle version control management. Unless you have a hosting service to manage your version control outside your local machine, it's not possible to allow a wider audience to contribute to your project development and review the activity. This section discusses a version control repository hosting service to manage more than one Git version control efficiently.

A most common way to explain the version control hosting service is that it's like LinkedIn, a web-based hosting service for your professional work where you can add your work details, experiences, achievements, etc., for others to see and comment on. Similarly, GitHub is a web-based version control repository hosting service for Git. Git allows you to manage the version control over a local host or server, whereas GitHub provides a cloud-based hosting service that lets you manage your multiple Git repositories after creating a free account on GitHub.

GitHub

GitHub is a web-based Git repository hosting service that allows all of the distributed development features, version revision control, and source code management functionality of Git as well as its own features. GitHub provides a graphical user interface so that an individual Git repository can be remotely accessed by an authorized person from any computer without cloning the code into a local machine. From the user standpoint, it looks as if a hub that allows docking of several different Git repositories that users can browse. Figure 3-8 shows the high-level GitHub work model with hosting various Git repositories.

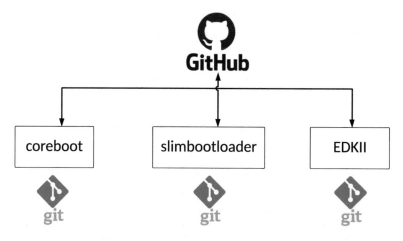

Figure 3-8. *GitHub work model*

GitHub provides a no-cost user profile for accessing the basic open source repositories (it also has an access control method to restrict unauthorized user access). Typically, GitHub accounts come with an abundant storage space that allows users to host their working project and allows the open source community to review, modify, and share feedback by creating separate Git branches. This also helps to build the professional profile to know the developer's proficiency.

Unlike Git, GitHub recommends its users work on a specific branch while developing any new feature. This makes it possible for entire teams to work together in a single project even without being bottlenecked on each other while implementing the code changes. With each new code change, a new branch is created; these branches are like copies and won't get merged into the master branch unless the user chooses to raise a pull request for review. As mentioned earlier, GitHub not only inherits features from Git but also has few unique features over Git to make it more powerful.

- *Fork*: This is a copy of a repo in your own user account where you can make the changes without affecting the original project. Suppose your account doesn't have access to write into a repository; then this feature allows you to copy one user's repository into your own account and modify it. Later you can raise a pull request to the project owner to allow merging into the original project.

- *Pull request*: Unlike Git, this *pull request* is different from what `pull` does in Git. This allows a GitHub user to share the code changes with the project owner once the change is ready after copying the original project repo. Using pull requests, you can notify others about changes you've pushed to a branch in a repository on GitHub. Once a pull request is opened, you can discuss and review the potential changes with project owners and add follow-up commits before your changes are merged into the master branch. This is equivalent to reviewing record creation in Gerrit.

  - *Pull*: Just for reference, `git pull` is a convenient operation that a user does while working at the Git command line for getting the latest changes from the remote repository.

- *Merge*: After the user has raised the pull request and the project owner has approved the changes, the project owner can merge these changes found in your repo into the original repository just by clicking the "Merge pull request" button.

Users often get confused between the original purpose of Git and GitHub as they're tightly coupled, but here are the differences between Git and GitHub:

Git	GitHub
Git is a command-line software/tool.	GitHub is a GUI enabled, web-based repository hosting service.
The purpose of Git is to track the changes being done in the different local repositories to provide the VCS and SCM.	GitHub provides an abundant storage space to upload several Git repositories. GitHub not only inherits features from Git like VCS or SCM but also has its own few key features like forks, pull requests, and merges.

Code Review Application

In earlier sections, you learned how to use the version control system on local machines and make it available in the cloud for much wider access. The power of Git and GitHub also provides a responsibility to its users (developers and maintainers) to make sure each code change goes through a proper review process and there is a way to track the review comments. Assume a developer came back a year after the code submissions and asked a very basic question about the integrity of the code. Without a backup system that points back to the code review database, it would be difficult to answer such questions. Hence, there is a need to have a code review model as well as part of the firmware development infrastructure.

In general, one could argue that GitHub by default provides options to review the code changes as soon as someone adds changes and raises a pull request. But there are some serious concerns while reviewing the code in that format where one might lose track of the comments in the code, and viewing the exact code changed since the last commit is really difficult. There are some offline tools that will allow you to manually diff the code changes, but doing this for every pull request makes the reviewer lose interest in reviewing the code.

Gerrit

Gerrit is a free web-based open source software application that provides the code review functionality. The purpose of Gerrit is to make the code review easier and more efficient. Gerrit application serves as an intermediate between developers and the Git repositories. It also can be viewed as a web-based Git repository hosting service for code review purposes.

Unlike GitHub, Gerrit doesn't support multiple commits under a single pull request. The fundamental idea for Gerrit is that one code change is like one node in the overall commit. For example, once you are done with your code changes and generate a commit using the `git commit -s` command, you will add the unique change ID to track the changes and submit the code for review using `git push <remote-name> HEAD:refs/for/master`. Gerrit will generate a unique commit ID for each code change being submitted, and any incremental changes on top of that commit ID using the same change ID would create a new patchset. Because each patchset is treated separately in Gerrit, any review comments given for a particular patchsets would be part of the tracking process unless the developer has addressed the comments and marked them resolved.

At a high level, this process is much simpler compared to the GitHub review process where a developer first needs to fork the remote repo into the user's own account and then clone that code into a local machine, create a branch, make the changes, push the changes, and then finally create the pull request for review. With Gerrit, developers just need to clone the remote repo, do the changes, and push it directly into the master branch for review. Here are the primary functions of Gerrit that make it a powerful review medium:

> **Asking for code review**: Gerrit provides a simple and open code review process. Submitters can add the reviewer name (or email ID), and Gerrit will

notify the reviewer once they have been added. Also, this is a very open cultured environment where anyone can add to a Gerrit review. See Figure 3-9.

Figure 3-9. *Gerrit My Review view from Gerrit dashboard*

- *Reviewing the code changes*: A Gerrit code review provides a nice side-by-side representation to compare the original and modified code. Each code change ranges from -2 to +2 (by default the code review starts with the Code-Review as 0), and a code review requires a minimum Code-Review +2 (looks good to me, approved) vote to get merged into the mainline. We will discuss code review etiquettes in the "Code of Conduct" section. If the reviewer has some concerns, then the reviewer could initiate a discussion by adding a review comment for each new line of code added. See Figure 3-10.

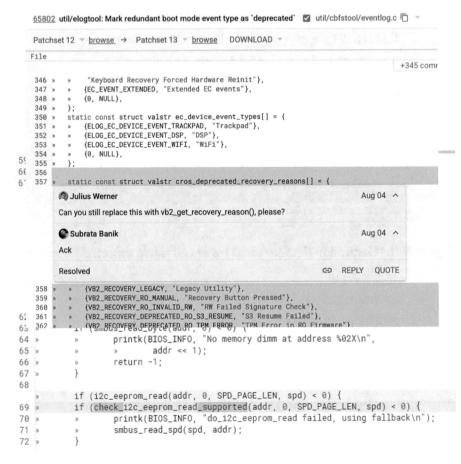

Figure 3-10. *Gerrit adding review comments*

- *New patchset*: If the reviewer is not satisfied with the code review and added the code review comments with a suggestion to improve the code qualification, then the submitter would need to push a new patchset to address those review comments. This process continues until the submitter resolves all review comments and the reviewer has casted the vote to let go of this code change.

In Gerrit, each patchset refers to a separate code review.
Each time the submitter addresses the review comments
and updates the commit using `git commit`
`--amend`, it regenerates the new commit hash. The
difference between the old commit hash and new
commit hash will allow Gerrit to show the delta code
between two patchsets. This process is very efficient
while reviewing significant big code changes that involve
multiple files; hence, reviewers don't need to review
all the code changes every time. Rather, the difference
between the current (n patchset) and previous patchsets
(n-1) would help to list the modified files between
those two patchsets. If there are no changes in those
two patchsets (may be a rebase), then a Gerrit GUI will
explicitly mention "nothing new to see." See Figure 3-11.

Figure 3-11. *Multiple patchsets to address review comments*

- *Submitting code changes*: After the code review is done and the patchset has required the correct number of votes for Code-Review, All-Comments-Resolved, and Verified (and others some third-party plug-ins if applicable like IP scan, etc.), a project maintainer can allow the code changes into the mainline of the repository by clicking the Submit button. This process of allowing code changes into the master branch of the project repository might need special access permission.

If the purpose is just a code review in a much simpler and efficient way and ensures that the code review process is being maintained separately from managing the Git repositories, then Gerrit is the best option for you while developing your own firmware for embedded systems.

Best Known Mechanism of Source Code Management

SCM not only provides the version controlling mechanism but also provides a flexible, collaborative code development environment that is a must-have for the firmware development approach using the open source firmware development model. SCM is a huge boost for the engineering team to be able to manage the code development and project history without any additional resource code. Here are some best known mechanisms to handle the SCM efficiently:

> *Commit frequently*: Commits don't cost anything to anyone, and they're easy to create. Don't try to combine unnecessary code changes into one commit just to avoid meaningful multiple commits if possible. Ideally developers should make the commit as an incremental approach toward the

firmware development process. Frequent and small commits also help while debugging the issue by using git bisect.

Latest to upstream master: Working in a distributed development environment, it's important to always be in sync with the latest upstream code. It's been seen that many developers don't bother updating their local copy with the latest upstream master code. This eventually creates a problem while trying to commit a change sitting in a local copy that is far behind the latest upstream master. Hence, it's recommended to update the local copy on a regular basis to avoid merge conflicts.

Provide details in commit: Commit is the face of the underlying code change, and everyone might not have the time and interest to go through the entire code while using git bisect. Having a meaningful commit message with ample details allows developers to understand why the code changes are being made and what is in the code at a high level without deep dive into each commit.

Make use of branches: Git provides a powerful branching model where developers can create their own branch derived from the master to continue their development. This process ensures the master always remains untouched or unpolluted. Once development is done on a specific branch, then it can be merged into the master.

Prompt addressing review comments: Avoid outstanding review comments for more than 24 hours. It's the patch owner's responsibility to ensure all of the review comments are addressed. Don't leave your patch at the half-done stage. If you think your patch is not progressing in the review, seek help and ask for review. Also, avoid rebasing the entire patch tree repeatedly. It's painful for reviewers as it will spam their inboxes.

Code of Conduct

Working on a firmware project using an open source firmware development model means collaborating with a wider technical community. This community involves a mixture of professionals with different domain expertise, volunteers, and students from all over the world. They all are working together for their mutual interest in making the virtual workplace inclusive to connect with people, learn from each other, and provide mentorship as and when required.

Such a diverse environment might also lead to a communication gap and unpleasant situations if not managed with some standard protocols, which are also referred to as a *code of conduct* (CoC). The CoC provides some basic ground rules that the community should follow to make the workplace free from bad experiences. The point of defining the CoC is to bring equality to folks with vast technical knowledge and experience, even to the youngest contributor who has just started their professional journey in firmware. Here is some common community etiquette that every individual can follow:

- *Be friendly and supportive* in all possible forms of communication including the Gerrit code review, mailing lists, IRC chat rooms, reporting bugs, and virtual or physical meetings in events or conferences.

- *Be open* while giving comments and receiving comments as well. In the majority of cases, unpleasant situations happen during the code review.

  For each code change, the Gerrit code review provides a range between -2 to +2. The way it works is if the reviewer gives -2 to a code change, it means there is something very wrong fundamentally, and the reviewer doesn't accept the code change and also forbids the code changes from being merged into the mainline. Typically, reviewers should provide ample details to justify the -2 vote and provide a path forward to overcome this vote in the coming patchset. A -1 vote shows the same preference as -2 but on a slightly lighter note where reviewers don't want to merge this code change as is. A good reviewer not only casts their vote but also provides equally good review comments for the submitter so that the submitter can move ahead with the code changes and fix the problem. Note: in general, each code change has its own purpose, so it's better not to create a roadblock for others.

- *Be sensitive* about the fact that due to the distributive development approach of open source firmware, many active project contributors are not native English speakers; hence, they might have misunderstood the review comments or provided some comments that might appear rude.

- *Be careful* with any words that might spread hatred, commenting on someone's sexual orientation, gender, race, religion, educational qualification, color, or disability. Also, avoid inappropriate physical contact and unwelcome sexual attention during face-to-face meetings.

If you come across any of these situations, then please reach out to the concerned team via email. Typically, all open source communities have strict CoC policies to ensure that the community doesn't encourage unacceptable behavior. The best practice to avoid such unpleasant situations is to stop such issues at their core, and once an issue is raised, people are expected to comply immediately. Making the same mistake in a repetitive manner might result in a temporary ban or permanent block from the community.

Although this is not the exhaustive list of *dos* and *don'ts* in the open source firmware development community, while you are focusing on creating your own firmware, these are basic guidelines to make developers and reviewers understand their roles and responsibility while they are taking part in such technical communities.

Coding Standard

The purpose of this book is to provide all the required details to prepare developers for architecture migration from closed source firmware development to open source firmware development. In this migration process, one important thing that remains unnoticed is the coding standard.

Developing firmware is more than just writing the code that will work on embedded systems. Rather, the firmware engineer also needs to ensure there is a long-term maintenance plan for the written code. This process involves the following:

- Define a coding style that can be easily adopted by all developers, even the most recent ones, with a minimum learning curve.

- Write code in such a way that provides ample information about the change requirements.

- Code maintenance should be independent of the original author; that means the written code can be maintained by others without having detailed knowledge about the intricacies of the code.

- Provide documentation wherever possible to explain the accurate code changes to minimize the learning curve for new engineers.

The most popular firmware uses the C programming language because of its simplicity, flexibility, and wide adoption in embedded systems. But the problem that the C programming language faces is the inconsistent ways it's used among various developer groups. This lack of uniformity in developing firmware using C makes it harder to use unless a unified coding standard is enforced.

Although each firmware has its own coding standard and guidelines for developing the source code, this section will discuss the open source firmware development approach using coreboot. The topics covered in this coding standard include the following:

- C language rules and guidelines

- Naming conventions

- Commenting rules

- Standard way to create commit message

Ideally these guidelines will be helpful for engineers migrating their architecture from closed source firmware development to open source.

The major benefit that coreboot provides to its developers is the similarity with the Linux kernel coding style. Hence, it's easy to adopt among developers.

Indentation

The idea behind indentation is to make it easy for the developer to look at the code. It helps to define where a block of control starts and ends. Tabs are eight characters, and hence indentations are also eight characters. Refer to the following example:

```
int azalia_enter_reset(u8 *base)
{
>>        /* Set bit 0 to 0 to enter reset state (BAR +
          0x8)[0] */
>>        return azalia_set_bits(base + GCTL_REG, GCTL_CRST, 0);
}
```

Using eight characters for multiple indentation levels in a switch statement would be difficult; therefore, you can align the switch and its subordinate case labels in the same column. Refer to the following example:

```
>>        switch (src) {
>>        case EC_SMI_BATTERY_LOW:
>>            >>        printk(BIOS_DEBUG, "Battery low. Shutting
                        down\n");
>>            >>        outl(ACPI_PM1_CNT_SLEEP(S5), ACPI_PM1_CNT_BLK);
>>            >>        break;
>>        default:
>>            >>        printk(BIOS_DEBUG, "EC_SMI event 0x%x\n", src);
>>        }
```

The intention here is to provide better code readability for the developer; hence, it's recommended not to make a cluttered single line, which is tough to read and understand. The following example shows the difference between bad and good programming practices, although the compiler grammar would be able to understand both:

Bad Programming Practice	Good Programming Practice

int a = 1, b = 2, c, d;
c = a + b; d = b - a;
if (expression is true) return true;
      return false;
	int a = 1;
	int b = 2;
	int c = a + b;
	int d = b - a;
	if (expression is true)
	      return true;
	return false;

vim is a widely used source code editor for the Linux OS. In addition, there are many advanced feature integrated development environments (IDEs) available like Eclipse that make life easy for developers and don't leave space at the end of lines; also, avoid having unnecessary blank lines between two source code lines.

coreboot supports a special file for configuration called *Kconfig*. This file consists of several configuration tokens called *config*. config supports mixed indentation where all definitions are indented with one tab but help text is indented with an additional two whitespaces. Here's an example:

```
config CONFIGURABLE_CBFS_PREFIX
>>      bool
>>      help
>>      ..Select this to prompt to use to configure the prefix
        for cbfs files.
```

Maximum Columns per Line

Coding standards are also necessary to make it easy for reviewers to understand the code with a single glance. Having a longer code line with too many characters in it makes it harder to follow the purpose of that line and reduces the code readability.

Typically, many firmware coding standards recommend limiting the single line by 80 columns. In the latest version of coreboot, this limit is

96 columns per line. If you need to write a longer line than 96 characters, then make use of the newline character to break the line onto the next line. There are some exceptions such as printk functions, where breaking such functions onto multiple lines is not recommended as it will break the ability to grep a user-visible line while debugging.

Using Braces

For conditional statements there is a need to combine all the required actions under the statement to make it more readable. In the C programming language, braces are used for this purpose. Here's an example:

```
if (!rom) {
        printk(BIOS_ERR, "%s failed\n", __func__);
        return current;
}
```

This applies to all conditional statements such as if, switch, do, while, for, etc., where the opening brace is the last character on the line, and the closing brace is first on the next line.

You don't need to use unnecessary braces for a single statement, as follows:

```
if (!rom)
        rom = pci_rom_probe(device);
```

The previous recommendation doesn't apply if a conditional statement doesn't have a single statement in both cases. The following example uses braces even if one conditional statement still has a single statement:

```
if (dock_present()) {
        printk(BIOS_DEBUG, "dock is connected\n");
```

```
        dock_connect();
} else {
        printk(BIOS_DEBUG, "dock is not connected\n");
}
```

The starting of the brace rule certainly doesn't apply for functions where the opening brace starts at the beginning of the next line, as shown here:

```
void __noreturn pcidev_die(void)
{
        die("PCI: dev is NULL!\n");
}
```

Need for Spaces

This is why you need to use spaces:

- *Recommendation for keywords and functions*: Typically, you will use spaces after most of the keywords such as if, else, switch, do, while, and for, but there are exceptions like sizeof, typeof, etc., which look similar to a function call. Refer to the previous examples where whitespace is used between if and expression. Also, note that there is no whitespace between the function name and passing argument. Do not add spaces around (inside) parenthesized expressions.

Bad Programming Practice	Good Programming Practice

if(!rom)
  rom = *pci_rom_**probe** (device)*;
  addr -= **sizeof** *(*struct cpu_info);
	if (!rom)
	  rom = pci_rom_probe(device);
	  addr -= sizeof(struct cpu_info);

- *Recommendation for operators*: Use one space around the most binary and ternary operators, but there are exceptions like no space after the unary operators, no space before the postfix increment and decrement unary operators, and no space after the prefix increment and decrement unary operators. Also, there is no space around the period (.) and arrow operators (->).

Bad Programming Practice	Good Programming Practice

unsigned int *a=1;*
unsigned int b = 2;
unsigned int *c= ! (++ a + b --)*
	unsigned int a = 1;
	unsigned int b = 2;
	unsigned int c = !(++a + b--)

Naming Conventions

Each firmware programming standard has its own naming conventions for defining variables (local and global) and function names.

- *Recommendation for variable name*: Avoid using CamelCase while defining a new variable, for example: VariableNameIsTmp. Use variable names that are short and meaningful.

It's recommended to make limited usage of global variables and to have a descriptive global variable name to use across different functions. In the case of UEFI, a global variable should start with m followed by a variable name.

The scope of local variables is limited; hence, variable names also need to be short.

- *Recommendation for function name*: The function name should represent an action, so the name should be something that makes it clear what it does, for example, do_something() instead of tmp_function(). Here is the rule of thumb: variable names are often nouns, and making function names verbs in the code can be more readable.

```
void cpu_set_max_ratio(void)
{
    /* Check for configurable TDP option */
    if (get_turbo_state() == TURBO_ENABLED)
        cpu_set_p_state_to_turbo_ratio();
}
```

Typedefs

Using typedef is controversial among different firmware.

As per the coreboot coding standard, it's recommended not to use typedefs for structures and enums, whereas in UEFI, it's mandatory to use typedefs and not use structs in source files.

coreboot Coding Style	UEFI Coding Style
| ```
struct reset_mapping {
    uint32_t logical;
    uint32_t chipset;
};
struct reset_mapping map;
``` | ```
typedef struct {
    uint32_t logical;
    uint32_t chipset;
} reset_mapping;
reset_mapping map;
``` |

The only exceptions to this recommendation are u8/u16/u32/u64 types in coreboot, these are *typedef* of the standard datatypes like unsigned int/long, etc.

Commenting

Comments are good, but over-commenting defeats their purpose. The only purpose that commenting serves is to let the code live on for many years; in other words, comments are helpful to understand the code at a high level without going deep into it. The recommendation is to provide what your code does in comment sections rather than being explicit about how it's doing it. Also, avoid commenting on each line, which makes code look ugly. The coreboot style for commenting is the C89 /* ..*/. The following is an example of the preferred approach for commenting:

Short Comments	Long Comments
| ```
/* This structure will be used
to
  describe a community or each
  group within a community. */
``` | ```
/*
 * This structure will be used
to
 * describe a community or each
 * group within a community.
 */
``` |

Write a Good Commit Message

Earlier sections provided required information on how to improve the project code quality by adopting a coding standard as per the target firmware architecture (we discussed coreboot in detail). A good firmware engineer not only bothers to write quality source code but also gives equal importance to commit messages as commit messages are significantly helpful while debugging a problem.

From my experience, folks spend a good amount of time writing the code and reviewing the code, but when it comes to writing a commit message, people lose their interest. Here's a funny example of how back-to-back commit messages lost their purpose and were meaningless:

ID	Commit	Date
123..	*Create infrastructure to get System Time*	*10 Hours Ago*
456..	*Add API to implement time routines*	*8 Hours Ago*
789..	*Calling API*	*6 Hours Ago*
ABC..	*Add some new APIs*	*4 Hours Ago*
DEF..	*Missed to add few APIs hence adding those here*	*3 Hours Ago*
A1B..	*Don't know why I'm adding this code but it's needed*	*3 Hours Ago*
2C3	*Everything is working now with this CL*	*2 Hours Ago*

Here are the seven golden rules when creating a great commit message:

- Maintain a separate submit from the body with a blank line.

- Try to limit the subject line to 50 characters.

- Capitalize the subject line.

- Don't end the subject line with a period.

- Write the subject line in imperative tense.

- Don't exceed the body beyond 72 columns per line.

- Use the body to explain what's new and why it's changing and how.

Figure 3-12 shows a sample commit message that adheres to these recommendations.

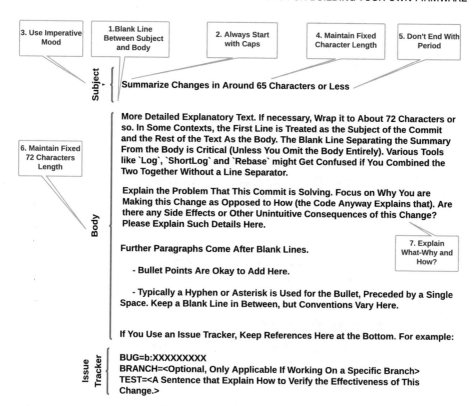

Figure 3-12. *Sample commit message following the golden rule*

Figure 3-13 shows the actual commit that was submitted for a Gerrit review after following the golden rule, as described in Figure 3-13. A quality commit message always increases your chances to get a quick review and required vote to merge compared to a partial or an incomplete commit message.

```
vc/google/elog: Record vboot FW boot information into elog

This patch calls into vboot API (vb2api_get_fw_boot_info) to retrieve
FW slot boot information like (tries count, current boot slot, previous
boot slot, previous boot status and boot mode).

Upon retrieval of the vboot information, elog callback from ramstage
records the info into the eventlog.

Additionally, this patch refactors the existing event logging mechanism
to add newer APIs to record vboot firmware boot related information.

BUG=b:215615970
TEST=Build and boot google/kano to ChromeOS and run below command to
check the cbmem log:
Scenario 1:
localhost ~ # cbmem -c | grep VB2
[INFO ]  VB2:vb2_check_recovery() Recovery reason from previous boot:
         0x0 / 0x0
[INFO ]  VB2:vb2api_fill_boot_config() boot_mode=`Developer boot`
         VB2:vb2api_get_fw_boot_info() fw_tried=`A` fw_try_count=0
             fw_prev_tried=`A` fw_prev_result=`Success`.
....

Scenario 2:
localhost ~ # crossystem recovery_request=1
localhost ~ # cbmem -c | grep VB2
[INFO ]  VB2:vb2api_fill_boot_config() boot_mode=`Manual recovery boot`
         VB2:vb2api_fill_boot_config() recovery_reason=0x13 / 0x00
         VB2:vb2api_get_fw_boot_info() fw_tried=`A` fw_try_count=0
             fw_prev_tried=`A` fw_prev_result=`Unknown`.
```

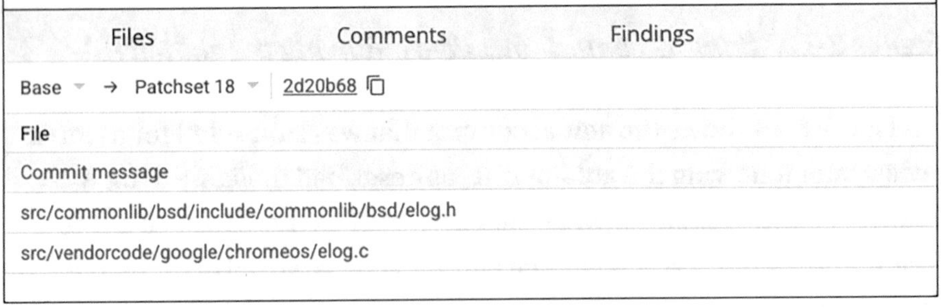

Files	Comments	Findings
Base ▾ → Patchset 18 ▾ 2d20b68 ⧉		
File		
Commit message		
src/commonlib/bsd/include/commonlib/bsd/elog.h		
src/vendorcode/google/chromeos/elog.c		

Figure 3-13.   Actual Gerrit commit based on the golden rule

In conclusion, this section provided the basic principle behind creating a qualified source code by adhering to a specification. It's recommended that all users should follow this specification without failure. By default many development environments/studios have integrated the checkpatch-like script that does the coding style check and expects to run this script while creating the code changes prior to submitting the code for review.

Summary

This chapter helped you understand the value of infrastructure tools while doing the firmware development. Typically, software/firmware engineers place a high precedence on creating source code and fixing bugs on embedded systems. Maintaining the source code and sharing across multiple teams are also equally important in the firmware journey. Source control management is an invaluable tool for firmware development. This chapter provided a detailed analysis of the best possible SCM available for open source development and its feature sets. Many engineers use Git, GitHub, and Gerrit in their day-to-day activity but are unable to understand the working relationship between these infra tools and choose the best one for their needs. Finally, this chapter highlighted the basic developers rights while working in a distributed development environment, including the best practices to create the code changes by adhering to the coding standard and submitting the code changes that help your chances of getting code merged into the remote repository after a quick review.

CHAPTER 4

System Firmware Debugging

"Programming allows you to think about thinking, and while debugging you learn learning."

—Nicholas Negroponte

If system firmware development is an art, then debugging that firmware is a fine art. The debugging process primarily depends on a thorough understanding of the platform capabilities (for both the SoC and board design), system architecture, and system boot state. Additionally, requires an appropriate debug methodology to deliver a solution. Embedded systems are highly customized to address the market needs. As the smartphone, tablet, personal computer, and household robot markets expand, silicon and platform designers have a challenge to provide ample hardware capabilities to debug the platform at the many different stages of the product life cycle. In addition, most embedded systems have a limited dedicated debug capability due to their small form factor (SFF) and fewer hardware revisions possible between prototype and mass production (MP).

System failures are expected at any phase of the product development cycle and even after the product launch while the device is in use. Firmware, being the closest possible entity to the underlying SoC and

© Subrata Banik and Vincent Zimmer 2022
S. Banik and V. Zimmer, *Firmware Development*,
https://doi.org/10.1007/978-1-4842-7974-8_4

hardware, is responsible for diagnosing a defect and providing a solution if possible. System firmware running into those embedded platforms has its own debug architecture and methodology that needs an adaptations based on the target hardware. For example, the system firmware debug methodology will undergo changes from the early stages of product development (proto, engineering validation test [EVT]) in an open case or bench environment to the advanced/final stage (design validation test [DVT] to platform MP) in a closed case.

The system firmware needs to inherit a variety of debugging methodologies to overcome such dynamics to the platform hardware design and provide SoC architecture-agnostic solutions. This functionality may need to be implemented at the firmware architecture level to ensure easier migration of system firmware without any visible impact on platform debug capabilities.

At a high level, these debug capabilities can be divided into two categories.

Hardware-assisted debugging: The key reason to use hardware-assisted debugging methods is the nature of the defects, such as if the detects are seen early in the boot phase, where software-based debugging is not feasible, or there is a need to access a CPU register in a multithreaded environment where attempting to enable software-based debugging might result in unpredictable system behavior.

This hardware-assisted debugging can be further divided into the following subcategories:

- *Generic debugging*: The kind of hardware debugger is attached neither with any SoC or CPU architecture nor with any OxM-specific hardware. These debug aids are very generic and can be applicable based on the hardware interface.

- *SoC/CPU-based debugging*: The hardware debugger used in this process is very specific to the target CPU or

SoC architecture. No matter which target SoC or CPU
you want to debug and which debugger you choose to
use, there will always be some common features that
every debugger will offer. For instance, every debugger
will provide ways to do the following:

- Connect to the target hardware

- Download the software programming on the
  host system

- Allow start, stop, and step through program
  execution

- Dump memory and register contents

- *ODM/OEM hardware-based debugging*: This approach
  is independent of the target CPU or SoC architecture.
  This method will rely more on utilizing the common
  hardware capabilities that OxM hardware is proving to
  access the underlying hardware resource. For example,
  Closed Case Debug (CCD) is a widely used method on
  all Chrome platforms irrespective of the underlying
  SoC architecture like ARM, AMD, or Intel. Typically,
  hardware vendors use the common practice methods
  across CPU designs while creating such common
  hardware debuggers.

Software-based debugging: The idea is to be able to debug firmware
without any additional cost or hardware-based tools. The most widely
used debug method in the system firmware development model is to
utilize the software-based methods or firmware's own capabilities to
debug the defects. Firmware development, debugging, and providing
resolution toward the coding issues has always been one of the most
time-consuming aspects while working in a product development

cycle. Debugging is sometimes a complex affair due to multilayered communication between various boot firmware, the host CPU, and the underlying IP firmware communication in a multithreaded environment. The most common method that developers or debug engineers are using to monitor the execution flow is printf. This approach may be useful in most cases where the developer is highly aware of all layers of the system firmware stack or when the problem is known to a single code block or module in question. Keep track of all the different types of problems or unexpected dependencies with other components in the firmware stack; the system firmware should be equipped with different debug methods. This software-based firmware debugging can be further divided into subcategories as follows:

- Traditional breakpoints

- I/O-based checkpoints

- Serial messages or serial buffers

- Preboot environments

- Runtime debugging

    - ACPI debug message or ACPI buffer

    - Windows Debugger (WinDbg)

    - GNU Debugger (GDB)

This chapter will present an in-depth overview of system firmware debug techniques on embedded systems for the x86 and ARM architectures. The topics discussed in this chapter will identify the debug methodology used for different microcontrollers as part of the hardware block. Additionally, it will present the different ways to debug coding issues and show debugging techniques for complex issues such as cache eviction, finding the local variable value in a multithreaded environment, and techniques to help bring different components of the embedded system stack to maturity.

Figure 4-1 illustrates a typical ARM-based platform block diagram with possible hardware components associated with it. The idea here is to show the different debug capabilities that each hardware block is permitting. For example, the system firmware running on the ARM CPU can use a serial UART to debug the CPU, and the embedded controller (EC) ROM can be used to debug the EC interfaces such as the battery information, sensor values, key sequence, etc. The physical security chip, TPM, can also have its own serial console to debug those private registers and have special access to the CPU and EC SPINOR as well. A hardware-based debugger can be used over Serial Wire Debug Port (SW-DP) to allow accessing CPU registers and memory blocks; similarly, a native USB debug interface can be used to route CPU, EC, and TPM debug interfaces to avoid dedicated debug interface needs on hardware. Other devices such as storage, panel, and audio codec firmware need special driver-based access methods that can be done using higher-level debuggers like the Windows Debugger (WinDbg) or special debug kernel drivers for Linux-like OSs.

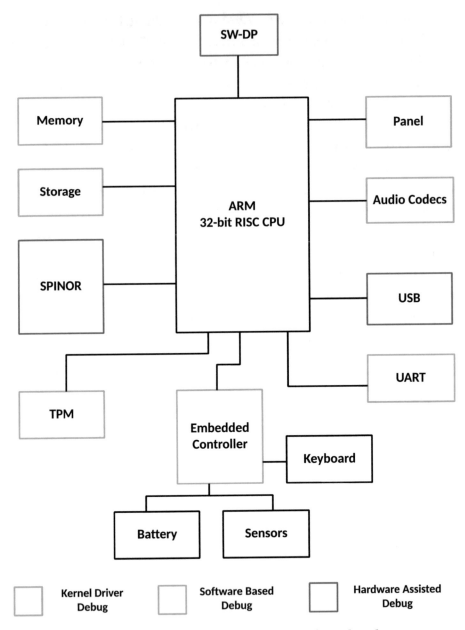

Figure 4-1. *Debug view of an ARM-based platform hardware*

Let's start with a detailed analysis of each debugging method and its debug aid in this section.

Hardware-Assisted Debugging

As mentioned, the most advanced form of system firmware debugging is utilizing the hardware capability. Typically, this form of debugging is a combination of the hardware interface exposed as part of the CPU architecture and a connector on board, enabling the SoC or CPU capability using the native firmware and high-level software. In many cases, this debugging method requires a debugger and a cross-development environment. Based on the complexity of the problem, which requires a debug aid, a debug engineer might decide to use this approach over traditional ones. Every SoC vendor has their own hardware debugger and associated software that can be used while debugging the target hardware. The major consideration point in this approach is the cost: the cost involved to purchase the hardware debugger, the amount of debug signals needed to get routed on the board layout to allow hardware debugging, and the purchasing cost of a software license to allow cross-development.

In this section, we will discuss the widely used hardware-based debug aids in the system firmware development and debugging process. As explained, all the hardware-assisted debug tools can be divided into three categories.

- Generic debugging

- SoC/CPU architecture-specific debugging

- OxM hardware-specific debugging

Generic Debugging

This method involves investing a higher cost into purchasing oscilloscopes like hardware equipment along with other tools. The only consideration point is that the cost involved here is a generic investment, so the same hardware can be used across different embedded systems.

Oscilloscope

A traditional misconception around debugging the embedded system is that it *always* relies on the hardware rework to bring out various probe points and attach them with an oscilloscope. Debugging with an oscilloscope is not a scalable solutions due to various reasons.

- It requires dedicated rework to attach the probe points to monitor the signal. The test points might be present at different sides of the board, which makes it difficult to handle a reworked board efficiently.

- Debugging with oscilloscope has a limited scope; hence, oscilloscope users are also equipped with other hardware instruments like the following:

  - Digital voltmeter

  - Logic analyzer

  - Protocol analyzer

- The main purpose of the oscilloscope in early embedded system development is to discover signal anomalies. Typically, the correct expectation from hardware validation is to probe around the design and to get a sense of whether any anomalies exist.

Figure 4-2 provides a debugging scenario where oscilloscope-based debugging is useful for embedded system development cycles. Prior to communicating with onboard third-party components like TPM, a touchpad, etc., using a standard firmware routine, if hardware compliance ensures the device is meeting its power/initialization sequence guideline, would help to avoid any anomalies throughout the embedded system lifespan.

Benefits: Figure 4-2 is from a real-life problem that occurs early during the boot phase where an oscilloscope is used to verify if the endpoint hardware attached to the SoC is able to send the acknowledgment upon receiving the CS signal.

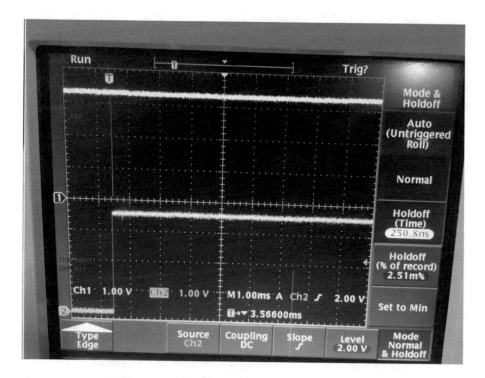

Figure 4-2. *Verifying signal integrity between Chip-Select (CS) and Interrupt while communicating with an I/O Device.*

Protocol Analyzers

It's the fact that Modern embedded system designs are getting complicated. Devices belonging to the advanced technology families like PCIe, USB, NVMe, SATA, I2C, and SPI are getting attached to the motherboard design (as shown in Figure 4-1). The protocol analyzers are the answer to performing the test solution for these computer buses and network communication standards. The protocol analyzer is an indispensable tool for embedded engineers.

A protocol analyzer works by capturing the data across the communication bus in the embedded system and then displaying it using GUI tools. With the help of a protocol analyzer, hardware engineers can design an embedded system, while firmware engineers can develop any new firmware module for these hardware interfaces listed earlier, and validation engineers can test the hardware product.

A protocol analyzer is a combination of dedicated hardware and software tools. The hardware captures the data, and the software displays the captured data. The hardware block typically needs three-way communication such as the following:

- *Connecting to DUT*: An interface that is attached to the device under test to capture the data.

- *Connecting to HOST*: To show the captured data in real time, it needs another interface to the HOST CPU. Engineers are using the HOST machine to detect the anomalies if any are in the bus communication.

- *Input interface*: This is an optional interface to attach the external devices like USB or Ethernet, which emulate attaching the device directly to the DUT.

Let's take a look at some popular protocol analyzers used during the system firmware development and debug phase:

- **USB protocol analyzer**: The most commonly used communication protocol in the computer machines is the USB protocol. The USB protocol analyzer is also referred to as a USB sniffer; it is a connection between the host computer and the DUT to capture and decode raw bus data and event information in a human-readable format. This information is useful to identify the bus errors.

- **I2C protocol analyzer**: In embedded system design, there are more devices that are getting attached with the I2C protocol due to its low power and simple bus communication. The I2C protocol analyzer can be used to debug any communication issue where the slave device address is not known or sees a timeout-related error.

- **SPI protocol analyzer**: This is another commonly used hardware interface in embedded systems where the SPI protocol analyzer can be used to connect multiple slave devices.

- **PCIe protocol Analyzer**: A PCIe bus is the default *de facto* industry standard for any high-speed communication between the CPU and motherboard component. Each PCIe specification has its own criteria in terms of speed, operating voltage, etc., to meet the PCIe compliance test for certification. This tool is used to monitor and interpret data transferred over a PCIe bus and generate error reports.

Benefits: The protocol analyzer provides output in the form of a report that covers the error type, recommendations, and directly captured data format. Traditional test tools relied on oscilloscopes for doing such compliance tests, which need manual effort and are eventually time-consuming. To reduce the product development cost and to meet a faster time to market (TTM), a protocol analyzer is the only logical solution. See Figure 4-3.

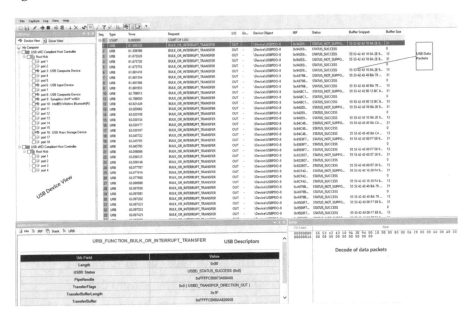

Figure 4-3. *USB protocol analyzer to trace USB bulk transfer*

SoC-Specific Debugging

For embedded system developers and security researchers, a SoC/CPU-based debugger is the *minimal requirement* while debugging. This method is capable of providing access to microprocessor registers and system memory while the system is operational. There are different SoC debug interfaces being explored to allow debugging on different hardware phases efficiently. For example, during the early development cycle, because the hardware is bare metal, the platform remains open chassis, which makes debugging comparatively easier. A more sophisticated form factor design at the later phase of the product cycle makes the debugging harder. Hence, SoC vendors are trying to improve the debuggability and validate and test the platform's scope even for the product at the final MP stage efficiently.

This section will provide an idea about all the possible hardware debuggers and their control methods across popular CPU architectures.

This debugging process on embedded systems is referred to as *cross-debugging*. Cross-debugging in an embedded system is a development model that involves two different computing machines working together. The target hardware, which is intended to get debugged, is not supposed to have any debug tools installed on it. For this reason, in the cross-debugging model, the development host system is where all the required debug tools are installed. The software running on a host development system that provides access to the target hardware using the standard user interface might belong to a different architecture. In a nutshell, the debugger is a combination of hardware and software tools that work together to provide a user interface. It lets developers harness the benefits of the underlying CPU, GPU, and/or APU with a single program.

Hardware Interface

In a cross-debugging model, a debug communication channel between the host and target needs to be established on the target hardware device. Figure 4-4 shows a typical debug setup between the host and target hardware.

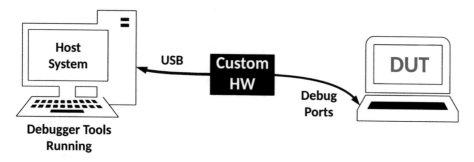

Figure 4-4. *Typical hardware-based debug setup*

The debug port is the interface between the host and the DUT debug access port. For embedded systems, the *de facto* standard for hardware-based debugging and accessing the hardware registers is the Joint Test Action Group (JTAG). The IEEE 549.1 standard defines a "Standard Test Access Port and Boundary-Scan Architecture" for Test Access Port (TAP) used for testing printed circuit boards (PCBs). This standard is commonly referred to as the JTAG debug interface. Since its origin, the JTAG debug interface has become a widely used interface for debugging the system firmware. Figure 4-5 shows a JTAG debug probe connected to a CPU. The JTAG interface allows access to the various systems on chip (SoC) test access ports (TAPs) like CPU and PCH. The JTAG protocol provides a serial interface to add to a chip device. The host system running the debug tools can use the serial link to reach those TAPs to access memory and registers that are running on the target hardware chip logic.

Today most of the embedded devices are equipped with a JTAG port to support early hardware debugging and firmware development. The JTAG-based debug port doesn't require any special firmware programming to access the TAPs; hence, this mechanism can be used while debugging early CPU reset issues and early platform boot stages like SEC and PEI for UEFI and bootblock and romstage in coreboot.

Figure 4-5. *Debugger attached to the JTAG debug port*

Depending on the specification of JTAG, typically this interface
supports four PINs as follows:

- **TMS**: Test Mode Select

- **TCK**: Test Clock

- **TDI**: Test Data In

- **TDO**: Test Data Out

In modern embedded systems, every device is equipped with
multicore CPU architecture. Hardware-based debugging is absolutely
necessary to debug CPU features such as SGX, VMX, etc. In such a
multicore boot environment, hardware debuggers should be capable of
halting all possible cores using a single JTAG scan chain. Figure 4-6 shows
a daisy-chained technique that CPU designers can use where the output of
the one core is acting as the input to the next core.

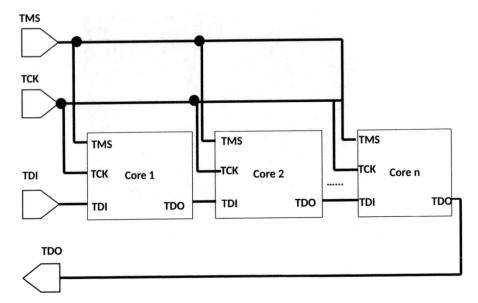

Figure 4-6. *Daisy-chained JTAG interface for multicore CPU architecture*

Different SoC vendors are utilizing this JTAG interface to create their own hardware debug tool.

- The Intel architecture has with different hardware debuggers for open-case and closed-case debugging using the JTAG interface.

- ARM architecture processors come with JTAG support as well. Sometimes it supports another debug interface with a lower PIN count such as *serial wire debug* (SWD).

eXtended Debug Port

The traditional way to do hardware-assisted debugging on Intel platforms is to use a proprietary 60-pin connector known as eXtended Debug Port (XDP), an extension of the JTAG specification. XDP communications are based on the physical connectivity assumption that the host machine running the debugging tools is a closed case but the target hardware under test is an open case. The XDP pod sits between those two layers, as shown in Figure 4-7. The host machine running the debug tools is connected via a USB interface. The debugging tool workflow passes through the proprietary USB protocol to the XDP pod, where the XDP pod is designed to translate the host tool workflow into JTAG probe mode. The DUT side of the pod is directly connected to a specific debug port on the motherboard. The debug port has access to all TAPs that are available in the SoC, CPU, and PCH. This method of hardware debugging is expected to expose more debug signals on the motherboard or silicon products; hence, these XDP transports are primarily used in open cases or during early product development.

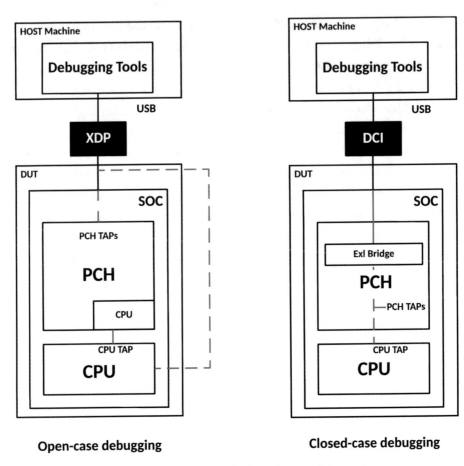

Figure 4-7. *JTAG-based open and closed case debugging*

Direct Connect Interface

Over time, more sophisticated devices and smaller form factors have
challenged the SoC side to have a simpler debug hardware interface with
the same capabilities. Also, open-case debugging may not always be the
scalable solution for the product development life cycle. Direct Connect
Interface (DCI) is the solution for such problems where the assumption
is that both sides of the debugger are now enclosed systems. On the

host side, it still uses the same connection as XDP, but on the DUT side, it connects to the JTAG interface using a new transport layer named Embedded DFx Interface (ExI). ExI works as a bridge behind the USB controller, which is responsible for passing the debugging tool workflow to the target via the proprietary USB protocol. In this mode of debugging, the control and data pass through the ExI bridge to gain access to JTAG and probe mode.

The primary goal here is to allow debugging closed-case OxM platforms like sealed tablets, smartphones, laptops, etc., where debuggers don't need to access to the XDP header on the motherboard. Figure 4-7 provides the high-level architectural difference in closed-case compared to open-case debugging.

Serial Wire Debug

On embedded systems the JTAG interface is the default standard for attaching debuggers. The major drawback in this protocol is the higher number of signals, which may not be possible for smaller and compact form-factor hardware. To solve this problem on microcontrollers with low pin counts, an alternative debug interface was created known as *Serial Wire Debug* (SWD). SWD uses only two wires, a clock wire and a data wire. The connector pins are as follows:

- *SWDCLK*: Serial Wire Debug Clock signal sent by the host.

- *SWDIO*: Serial Wire Debug Input Output is a bidirectional signal used to carry data between the host and debug port. The data sent by the host is getting sampled at the rising edge and sampled by the debug port (DP) during the falling edge of the SWDCLK signal.

Figure 4-8 provides an architecture overview of the SWD interface and access mechanism.

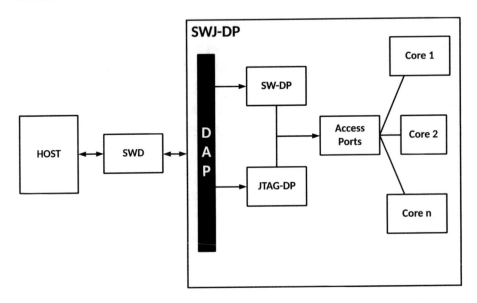

Figure 4-8. SWD architectural overview in multicore CPU environment

Unlike the JTAG interface, which uses a daisy-chain topology to connect multiple debug components, the SWD interface uses a bus called Debug Access Port (DAP). The external debug interface connects to the DAP through a DP. There are three different debug ports available to access the DAP.

- *JTAG Debug Port (JTAG-DP)*: This is similar to the JTAG interface and protocol to access the access ports (APs).

- *Serial Wire Debug Port (SW-DP)*: This uses the SWD protocol to access the AP.

- *Serial Wire/JTAG Debug Port (SWJ-DP)*: This allows external debuggers to attach to SoC using either JTAG or SWD DP. It provides a mechanism to select between the JTAG and SWD interfaces. It allows an easy migration between the JTAG and SWD interfaces where

SWDIO and SWCLK can be overlaid on the JTAG TMS and TCK pins.

Multiple access ports can be attached to the DAP. This APs can further access different debug components, for an example:

- *JTAG access port (JTAG-AP)*: This allows access to JTAG equipped cores.

- *Memory access port (MEM-AP)*: This provides access to system memory, bus-based debugging, and device registers such as AMBA Advanced High-performance Bus Access Port (AHB-AP) or AMBA AXI Access Port (AXI-AP) or AMBA Advanced Peripheral Bus Access Port (APB-AP)

Software Interface

After understanding the different hardware interfaces to connect hardware debuggers between the host system and target device for debugging, it's time to take a look at different debugging tools provided by various CPU vendors while accessing the debug ports to get into system memory or registers.

The first step in this cross-debugging setup is to have the required debugging tools installed on the host machine. Typically, every SoC vendor provides the flexibility of installing the debugging tools on all leading operating systems. Debugging the system firmware requires access to various different debug components like CPU registers, device registers, system memory and local variables, etc. A cross-debugging session with an integrated development environment (IDE) would make it very simple.

On AMD platforms the debugging is done through CodeXL, whereas on the Intel architecture, it's the Intel System Debugger, and on the ARM-based platform, the ARM debugger as part of ARM Development Studio is used for debugging the embedded systems.

CodeXL

CodeXL is the comprehensive tool suite used on AMD-based platforms
to access the CPU, GPU, and APUs with a single program. It includes
powerful GPU/CPU/APU debugging and CPU and GPU profiling as well. It
works as a stand-alone application on both Windows and Linux OS.

After downloading the installer package on the host system and
installing the package, developers can start using CodeX. The CodeXL GUI
window should appear as Figure 4-9 with debug explorer view notes.

Figure 4-9. *CodeXL debug mode: no project loaded*

The CodeXL debugger will allow developers to access the runtime
behavior of the target hardware based on the control programming
buttons while debugging.

These controls are as follows (left to right): Debug Mode, Switch to Profile Mode for GPU, Analyze Mode, Start, Pause and Stop Debugging, Step In, Step Over, and Step Out.

In order to perform source code based debugging, you need to connect the target device and load the debug symbols to map the program running in the target device memory to its original source file. Figure 4-10 shows the source code view after starting the debugger program as described earlier and then hit the Break button to interrupt it program execution to inspect the current execution state (i.e., memory view, register view etc.).

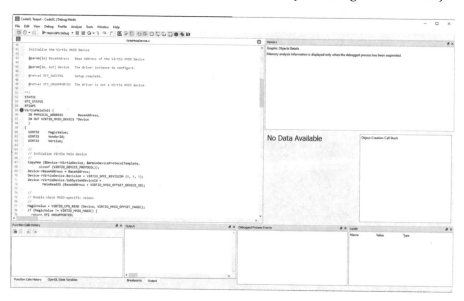

Figure 4-10. *CodeXL source code view*

Intel System Debugger

The Intel System Debugger is the GUI-based system software debugger to allow access to the system state, processor registers, platform device registers, and system memory via a JTAG-based hardware interface. The debugger GUI provides complete control over the debugging process by allowing the basic functions such as stepping in, stepping through, and displaying memory by clicking the menu toolbar button. The GUI also supports source code debugging after loading the symbols files of the same program running into the target hardware memory.

Figure 4-11 shows the options to connect the target hardware debugger after loading the Intel System Debugger. After successfully connecting with the target hardware, the debugger command will modify from xdb_D> to xdb_R> unless the developer uses the following control programmer buttons to pause the execution on the target system:

These controls are as follows (left to right): Connect, Disconnect, Load/Unload the debug symbols, Reset the target system, Start, Pause and Stop debugging, Step In, Step Over, and Step Out.

***Figure 4-11.** Intel System Debugger: connecting the debugger*

The Intel System Debugger also allows source code–level debugging for any bootloader, even coreboot, which is an open source firmware project. To start debugging coreboot with the Intel System Debugger, developers need to load the symbol files manually. Figure 4-12 shows the default loading process by selecting File ➤ Load/Unload Symbol File after halting the target.

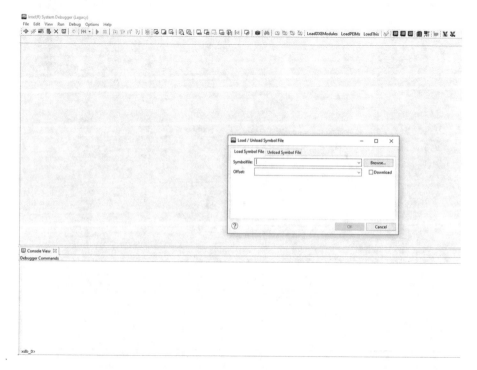

Figure 4-12. *Intel System Debugger: loading the symbol files*

After loading the necessary .debug files, you can start debugging coreboot. Figure 4-13 shows how to debug coreboot using the Intel System Debugger where developers can make use of the source code viewer to view the assembly code, CPU registers, local variables, memory dump, and access to the global descriptor table (GDT). Developers can make use of the debug console or directly override the registers or memory values.

Figure 4-13. Intel System Debugger: source code debugging

Arm Debugger

Arm Debugger is capable of providing a GUI-based environment that
allows users to debug the complex SoC bringing-up scenarios and debug
multicore environments like symmetric (SMP) and asymmetric (AMP) and

also heterogeneous systems. Figure 4-14 provides a high-level overview of ARM DS-5, a powerful development toolkit with an IDE for ARM-based processors, an ARM compiler, support for a simulation model for software development without the target hardware, streamlined tools for analyzing software performance, JTAG debug, and trace support.

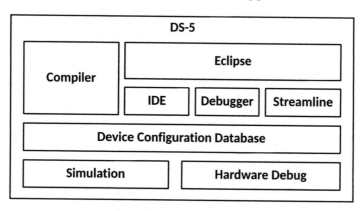

Figure 4-14. *ARM-DS5: development studio*

All these debugging tools are the same in terms of the underlying capabilities such as the register access, memory access, etc. Here is a list of common semantics used by different debuggers irrespective of CPU architecture:

Debugger Features	Description
Connection type	All debuggers will give you the option to connect to the target using different methods, for example single-core and multicore access using the JTAG daisy-chain method and SWD star topology. The idea is to halt all available cores using a single command.

(continued)

Debugger Features	Description
Loading program	Most debugging sessions are focused on debugging some type of program. This process might involve loading a program into the target device, or the target is already loaded with a program while debugging connects or loads the same program on the host side to allow source code debugging. In most system firmware debugging processes, the SPINOR already has the program preloaded, and in the debugging process either the SPINOR is mapped into system memory or the system firmware is responsible for copying them into memory.
Reset target	Being able to reset the target hardware is the minimum expectation from a hardware debugger. Allowing the target to reset will help to restore the target to a known working state. The CPU architecture-specific part is the reset mechanism, which is different across different SoCs.
Run control	Most debuggers provide run control options such as start, pause or stop, step in, step through, and step out. These options will impact the state of system registers, memory, local variables, etc.
Breakpoints	Almost all debuggers are capable of setting breakpoints. There are two types of breakpoints that developers can use while debugging. • *Hardware breakpoints:* Special hardware registers are used to create logic that halt the CPU execution. • *Software breakpoints:* It's much easier to create software breakpoint by adding an assembly instruction. Implementing breakpoints on embedded systems is CPU architecture specific.

(continued)

Debugger Features	Description
Watcher	Also referred to as watchpoints, this is a feature that many debuggers provide to set a watchpoint on a particular memory value or I/O port value. Execution on the target system will autobreak upon hitting the watchpoint either on memory or on I/O watched addresses.
Semihosting	Some custom debuggers provide this option where the target hardware can make use of I/O facilities on the host machine. For example, a program running on the target machine will use the host system console out to redirect the console message. This feature is useful while doing remote debugging where all required outputs are coming into single units applicable on the host system.
Registers, memory (system memory), special bus like PCI, AMBA, etc.	These allow access toward all possible CPUs, PCH registers, system memory, and special bus architecture. Depending on access points, the debugger will allow you to view and modify the system memory and registers.
Low-power mode debugging	Debuggers are equipped with a special mode when the OS has put the system into lower power mode and all cores are in power-down mode. The other low-power, always-on microcontroller APs can be used to monitor limited device registers without impacting the device's operational state.

OxM-Secific Debugging

The major drawbacks in SoC-specific debugging are the cost of hardware
debuggers, usage of proprietary software tools (in many cases, available
only under nondisclosure agreements), and lack of applicability of these
in cross-architecture debugging. To solve this problem, many ODM/
OEMs have come up with more generic approaches that can be used for
hardware-based debugging even on cross-architecture platforms. This
section provides an overview of a few low-cost, handheld debug tools.

AMIDebug Rx

System firmware developers have been relying on *checkpoint cards* to
debug early boot stages where the serial console is not available. This
debug method is tightly coupled with open-case debugging where a PCI-
based card is attached to the motherboard. AMIDebug Rx is designed as a
replacement for the PCI port 80 POST checkout card and makes port 80–
based debugging a scalable solution on closed-case devices as well.

AMIDebug Rx is built around the debug port feature on USB 2.0 EHCI
controllers. To enable this mode of debugging, system firmware is needed
to program USB 2.0 controller PCI configuration space and implement
base address register (BAR) address space for communication. Typically,
system firmware has a native USB 2.0 debug driver that uses the "USB
debug port" to transmit the checkpoint data on the device.

XHCI Debug Capability

The XHCI debug capability (Dbc) is an open specification part of the
XHCI host controller that allows low-level system firmware debugging
over USB without any additional cost. Figure 4-15 shows the Dbc interface
connecting two systems; one system is the debug host and another is the
DUT as the debug target. After the Dbc is initialized, it will present the

device target as a debug device through a debug USB port. This method can be useful to replace the proprietary UART implementation on different motherboard designs.

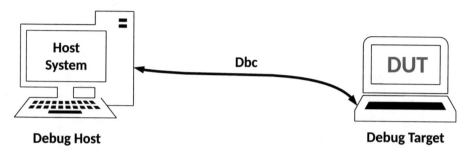

Figure 4-15. *Dbc connection between debug host and target*

Figure 4-16 shows an example of the Dbc software architecture, which is completely independent of the XHCI interface that is typically developed by system software for other USB device-class communication.

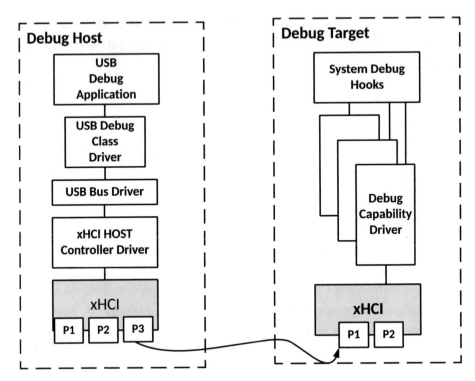

Figure 4-16. *Dbc debug software stack*

The USB debug application is running as part of the debug host. The debug host provides a USB debug capability class driver that will communicate with the device target after the debug device is enumerated. At a high level, the debug device can expose all its debugging capabilities as part of the debug driver. The debug capability driver is expected to be loaded immediately after power-on to let the system firmware debug process use this method.

Closed Case Debug

Legacy Chrome OS devices were using a custom debug header known as *Servo* to access the CPU and EC serial console, SPINOR, etc., in a generic way across cross-architecture platforms. Newer Chrome OS devices have introduced a multipurpose secure microcontroller, referred to as H1 and running an embedded OS called Cr50. The debugging method using Cr50 is called *closed-case debug*, which replaces the need to have a dedicated servo header to allow access to the CPU, EC UART, and SPI interface on the device under test.

The Chrome OS devices and H1 microcontroller are communicating using a custom USB Type-C cable called SuzyQ. The debug architecture has been built around the USB Type-C specification. Figure 4-17 shows the debugger architecture and communication flow.

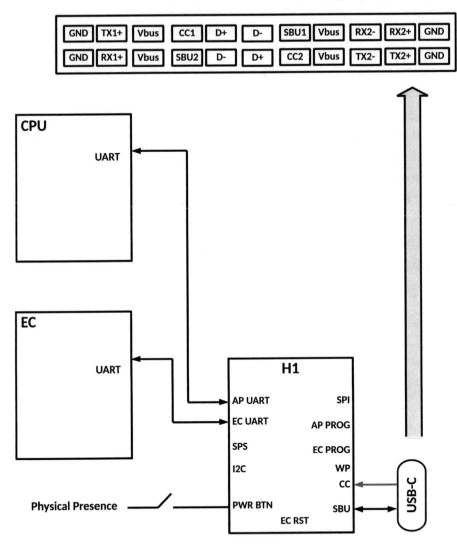

Figure 4-17. *CCD accessing the CPU and EC UART*

To put the Cr50 into the debug mode, the SuzyQ cable needs to connect to Chrome OS devices, and users need to specify the *physical presence*. The H1 includes two pins that can detect the debug accessory signature on the CC1 and CC2 pins. After detection, Cr50 enables a USB full-speed USB 2.0 slave interface that connects to the SBU pins on the USB-C connector. Cr50 makes several USB endpoints available to the host to communicate with the consoles. For example, Figure 4-17 shows the access of the CPU and EC UART. In addition, Cr50 also allows access to the H1 console.

Software-Assisted Debugging

The most cost-effective debug method in the system firmware development model is utilizing the software and firmware's own capabilities without being dependent on hardware debuggers. Adapting hardware debuggers has its own difficulties during later stages of SoC and/or product development where many CPU interfaces are required to be disabled by default; hence, it needs a special firmware image to enable all the required debug interfaces. In many cases, the timing-related issues are not possible to replicate with a hardware debugger attached due to an induced delay in the debug workflow between the host to the target access points. For such reasons, firmware developers need to rely on their traditional debugging techniques and skill sets to identify a defect and provide a solution.

This section will highlight a few known good debugging methods that developers are using on embedded systems and that are even applicable across architectures.

Traditional Breakpoint

Traditional breakpoints are the most common debugging technique being used developers to track the code flow. While debugging the unknown defects, every developer is trying to get ahold of the code flow without adding any new piece of code. There are different ways to introduce breakpoints.

Usage	Method to Apply a Breakpoint
In assembly files	The most difficult code block in system firmware to debug is the assembly instructions. The most common usage of the breakpoint in assembly code is `jmp`.
	The syntax for JMP is `JMP <label>`. The level specifies an address to which the code will jump upon execution. In this case, `.` specifies the current address; hence, this special symbol works as an *infinite loop* unless the developer overrides the program counter (PC) or instruction pointer (IP).
In C Files	It's much easier to apply the breakpoint in a C-based programming file. Developers can either choose to generate a break on the CPU or execute an infinite loop.

```
void CpuBreakpoint (void)
{
    __asm__ __volatile__ ("int $3");
}
void CpuDeadLoop (void)
{
    volatile uint32_t  Index;
    for (Index = 0; Index == 0;);
}
```

A debugger may be used to skip past the loop and continue the code execution if needed.

I/O-Based Checkpoint

Another traditional and popular debug technique for system firmware debugging without impacting much of the program execution flow is POST codes, also known as progress codes. The I/O ports on the X86 platform,

0x80 and 0x81, are used for such debugging while checkpoint cards can be either a PCI add-in card or an onboard LED display or rely on EC to sample the POST codes at regular intervals. Every BIOS vendor has their own predefined error codes or POST code implementation to identify the underlying system firmware block if executed.

Usage	Method to Apply an I/O Checkpoint
In Assembly, C files	Implementing the I/O checkpoints depends on the underlying assembly instructions due to an out operation to write into the legacy port. Put any byte value intended to write into CONFIG_POST_IO_PORT(Port 0x80) into AL.

```
movb    $value, %al;
outb    %al, $CONFIG_POST_IO_PORT
```

In ASL files	This method helps debug runtime communication issues between the OS and firmware layer. For example: performing sleep state transitions (S3 to S0 and vice-versa). While debugging, ACPI source code (ASL) writes into the debug port (address 80h) using ACPI operating region. Here is the code snippet to illustrate this operation.

```
OperationRegion(PRT0,SystemIO,0x80,1)
Field(PRT0,WordAcc,Lock,Preserve)
{
  P80B, 8
}
Method(D80H,1,Serialized)
{
  If(LEqual(Arg0,0))
  {
    Store(Arg0, P80T)    // Write into the Port 80h
  }
}
```

For hybrid system firmware development models with integration of closed-source binary blobs (FSP), it's important to clearly understand the postcode debugging model for FSP.

FSP outputs 16-bit postcode to indicate which API and inside that which module is getting executed. The postcode is in the following format:

Bit Range	Description
Bit 15 : Bit 12 (X)	Indicate the phase/API under which the code is executing
Bit 5 : Bit 18 (Y)	Indicate the module
Bit 7 (ZZ bit 7)	Reserved for error
Bit 6 : Bit 0 (ZZ)	Individual codes

Figure 4-18 represents the 16-bit postcode usage model in FSP.

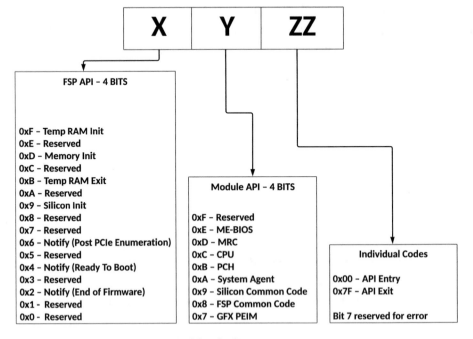

Figure 4-18. *FSP Postcode block diagram*

Serial Message or Serial Buffer

The most trusted debugging method on embedded systems is using printf and redirecting the output over the serial UART of the processor. Based on the motherboard designer, there could be different hardware interfaces that the system firmware needs to provide while making use of serial UART. Here are some examples:

- *Legacy CPU UART ports*: On an X86 platform, this makes use of 0x3F8 or 0x2F8 legacy ports to get serial consoles. System firmware (in this case coreboot) uses CONFIG_DRIVERS_UART_8250IO and 8-bit I/O-based serial drivers to set up the console and read and write operations.

- *PCH UART ports*: Another alternative for serial console debugging is using MMIO-based UART controllers on modern chipsets. System firmware (in this case coreboot) uses CONFIG_DRIVERS_UART_8250MEM_32, which is 32-bit MMIO access for setting up the console for debugging.

- *UART over SuperI/O*: Many motherboards designed with SuperI/O controllers also provide access to serial ports for debugging. The developer needs to select the applicable driver for the SuperI/O controller. For example, the *delta lake* OCP platform is using Aspeed SuperI/O and hence enabling the corresponding driver by selecting CONFIG_SUPERIO_ASPEED_AST2400 Kconfig (for coreboot as the underlying boot firmware).

While developers are comfortable using the serial console for debugging and redirecting various messages to the serial console using printf, they don't even realize the problem that this debugging technique often causes. Many times developers complain that the issue is seen with only the release build but not with the debug binary. They are ignorant about an unseen delay due to redirecting those debug message characters into a serial port using native serial UART driver implementation. In a single-threaded environment, calling a serial write method would eventually pause the execution until every intended debug character is successfully transmitted to the serial console. As all microcontrollers inside the SoC are running their own firmware, such a delay might be useful for restoring their state into a good working condition compared to a release binary, without any delay in execution.

The best method to overcome this problem is to rely on a serial buffer rather than a serial message. System firmware would create a reserved memory during POST, and a native serial write implementation would write into that memory rather than writing to the serial port. One would argue that it is a waste of system resources if the system hangs prior to fetching this serial buffer. The counter argument is that using some basic hardware debugger functionality to retrieve this memory is the best solution to reduce the gap between the debug and release system firmware binaries while debugging a defect.

Preboot Environment

All modern system firmware is equipped with a basic preboot environment to provide minimum access to CPU registers, system memory, and chipset registers prior to booting to the OS such as EFI Shell, Embedded Boot Loader (EBL), u-root console, depthcharge console, etc. The preboot environment serves as an important debug vehicle to narrow down an issue between the system firmware and OS. It provides open access to all chipset registers without connecting any hardware debugger prior to boot to OS; hence, developers can dump the required registers in the firmware space to ensure the recommended hardware registers have been programmed correctly by system firmware drivers.

ACPI Debug

The majority of modern operating systems are adhering to the Advanced Configuration and Power Interface (ACPI) specification. This forces the adaptation responsibility on the underlying system firmware as well. The ACPI specification has introduced a whole new language called the ACPI Source Language (ASL) to implement the required communication in the firmware layer. Debugging this layer is more challenging because of its usage model. For example, the ASL implementation doesn't conform with native C-based serial libraries that typically get used across firmware debugging. The communication is at runtime level and hence can't make use of boot services data or protocols. Developers need various different techniques to debug ACPI source code.

Method	Details
Serial console	The system firmware needs to implement a whole new serial I/O function in ASL so that the runtime firmware drivers can make use of it while debugging. coreboot has a unique implementation called APRT and ADBG in UEFI to redirect any debug string to serial.
Serial buffer	This method overcomes the limitation of the serial console implementation due to its serialized implementation and might cause anomalies while loading the kernel driver. The system firmware reserves runtime memory so that both system firmware and OS ACPI driver can access it.

(continued)

Method	Details
Debug using the kernel	The ACPI Component Architecture (CA), Linux ACPI core, and ACPI drivers can combine to generate the debug output. Kernel developers can enable the `CONFIG_ACPI_DEBUG` Kconfig to start getting more advanced options for `acpi debug`.

For example, use the following command-line argument to enable all `acpi` debug output:

acpi.debug_layer=0xffffffff acpi.debug_level=0x2

Windows Debugger

Windows Debugger (WinDbg) is a free, powerful debugger available as part of Windows OS to allow debugging the kernel, user mode drivers, and applications. It also provides the provision to load and analyze the crash dump. WinDbg is a host-based software debugger and is capable of working in different modes based on developers' needs. In stand-alone mode, WinDbg can be used to debug an application or kernel driver after loading either the executable or the driver source files.

Figure 4-19 shows an example of how to use WinDbg to debug an application after importing the debug symbols (PDB) from the Microsoft debug server. WinDbg is also a useful tool to debug the DUT using USB, a network, or a serial interface. This method is used frequently to debug early kernel hang or blue screen of death (BSOD), a normal phenomenon on Windows devices. Figure 4-20 shows the required configuration changes both at the DUT and host sides to enable kernel debugging over USB.

```
Microsoft (R) Windows Debugger Version 10.0.10586.567 X86
Copyright (c) Microsoft Corporation. All rights reserved.

CommandLine: "C:\Users\sbanik\OneDrive - Intel Corporation\Documents\VisualeBios\VisualeBios\VisualeBios\VisualeBios.exe"
Symbol search path is: srv*
Executable search path is:
ModLoad: 00400000 0040d000   image00400000
ModLoad: 77980000 77b1a000   ntdll.dll
ModLoad: 757d0000 758b0000   C:\windows\SysWOW64\KERNEL32.DLL
ModLoad: 763c0000 765bf000   C:\windows\SysWOW64\KERNELBASE.dll
ModLoad: 776c0000 77858000   C:\windows\SysWOW64\USER32.dll
ModLoad: 76d90000 76da7000   C:\windows\SysWOW64\win32u.dll
ModLoad: 77690000 776b1000   C:\windows\SysWOW64\GDI32.dll
ModLoad: 758b0000 75a0d000   C:\windows\SysWOW64\gdi32full.dll
ModLoad: 75f80000 75ffc000   C:\windows\SysWOW64\asvcp_win.dll
ModLoad: 75cb0000 75dd0000   C:\windows\SysWOW64\ucrtbase.dll
ModLoad: 778b0000 77961000   C:\windows\SysWOW64\MSVCRT.dll
ModLoad: 5e9a0000 5ea2d000   C:\windows\WinSxS\x86_microsoft.windows.common-controls_6595b64144ccf1df_5.82.18362.1440_none_bb640f8dec8ee1cc\COMCTL32.dll
ModLoad: 75a10000 75a89000   C:\windows\SysWOW64\ADVAPI32.dll
ModLoad: 75af0000 75b66000   C:\windows\SysWOW64\sechost.dll
ModLoad: 75d00000 7668b000   C:\windows\SysWOW64\RPCRT4.dll
ModLoad: 75140000 75165000   C:\windows\SysWOW64\SspiCli.dll
ModLoad: 75130000 7513a000   C:\windows\SysWOW64\CRYPTBASE.dll
ModLoad: 75190000 751f0000   C:\windows\SysWOW64\bcryptPrimitives.dll
(f128.f280): Break instruction exception - code 80000003 (first chance)
eax=00000000 ebx=00264000 ecx=ef060000 edx=00000000 esi=005828c0 edi=7798687c
eip=77a2ecd2 esp=0019fa20 ebp=0019fa4c iopl=0         nv up ei pl zr na pe nc
cs=0023 ss=002b ds=002b es=002b fs=0053 gs=002b        efl=00000246
ntdll!LdrpDoDebuggerBreak+0x2b:
77a2ecd2 cc              int     3
0:000> la
start    end         module name
00400000 0040d000   image00400000   (deferred)
5e9a0000 5ea2d000   COMCTL32        (deferred)
75130000 7513a000   CRYPTBASE       (deferred)
75140000 75165000   SspiCli         (deferred)
75190000 751f0000   bcryptPrimitives  (deferred)
757d0000 758b0000   KERNEL32        (deferred)
758b0000 75a0d000   gdi32full       (deferred)
75a10000 75a89000   ADVAPI32        (deferred)
75af0000 75b66000   sechost         (deferred)
75cb0000 75dd0000   ucrtbase        (deferred)
75f80000 75ffc000   msvcp_win       (deferred)
763c0000 765bf000   KERNELBASE      (deferred)
765d0000 7668b000   RPCRT4          (deferred)
76d90000 76da7000   win32u          (deferred)
77690000 776b1000   GDI32           (deferred)
776c0000 77858000   USER32          (deferred)
778b0000 77961000   MSVCRT          (deferred)
77980000 77b1a000   ntdll           (pdb symbols)        C:\ProgramData\dbg\sym\wntdll.pdb\2F569EE7D177CA609E61E00686922CFD1\wntdll.pdb
0:000>
```

Figure 4-19. *Debugging Windows applications using WinDbg*

Follow these steps on the DUT side to configure for debugging:

1. Press Windows Key+R to open the Run box.

2. Type **msconfig** to enable the debug configuration.

3. Select the Boot tab and then select "Advanced options."

4. Select the Debug check box.

5. Select the Debug Port options, either COM and USB. In the case of a USB interface, specify the USB target name. See Figure 4-20.

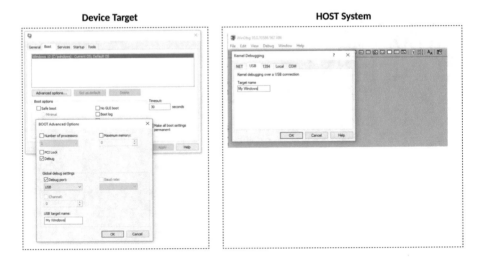

Figure 4-20. *Kernel debug mode using WinDbg*

Follow these steps on the Host side to configure for debugging:

1. Open WinDgb.exe.

2. Go to the File menu and select Kernel Debugging.

3. Specify the same hardware interface and name if the target debug port is USB.

Now reboot the DUT to start kernel debugging; developers will be able to see the kernel modules are getting loaded using the host system debug console.

GNU Debugger

The GNU Project Debugger (GDB) is a command-line debug tool that runs on Linux and other Unix-like embedded operating systems. Figure 4-21 shows a GDB session.

```
(gdb) help
List of classes of commands:

aliases -- Aliases of other commands
breakpoints -- Making program stop at certain points
data -- Examining data
files -- Specifying and examining files
internals -- Maintenance commands
obscure -- Obscure features
running -- Running the program
stack -- Examining the stack
status -- Status inquiries
support -- Support facilities
tracepoints -- Tracing of program execution without stopping the program
user-defined -- User-defined commands

Type "help" followed by a class name for a list of commands in that class.
Type "help all" for the list of all commands.
Type "help" followed by command name for full documentation.
Type "apropos word" to search for commands related to "word".
Command name abbreviations are allowed if unambiguous.
(gdb) █
```

Figure 4-21. *GDB: command-line interface*

GDB offers an extensive set of features including debugging other software or executable files, accessing the register contents to help optimize the program, inspecting the usage of variables and altering those values at runtime, stopping the program execution and performing step operations, adding breakpoints, analyzing the crash, and allowing remote debugging between DUT and host systems using either a network or a serial interface. Independent system firmware modules are being developed using Assembly, C, Go, and Rust-based languages and can make most use of GDB during the early development stages to optimize the development cost and increase the product quality.

Summary

This chapter provided detailed information about the popular hardware and software debuggers and their usage on cross-architecture platforms while debugging a defect. It also provided some guidelines and tips on how to identify a problem and choose the right debugging method between hardware-assist and software-assist after considering the cost factor, the stage of product, and the criticality of the defect. Based on my experience, during critical debugging, debug engineers spend the most time trying to figure out the best method to attack the problem.

This chapter was a good starting point for developers and embedded system engineers to understand the underlying architecture of various hardware debuggers like JTAG and SWD and their interfaces across different CPU architectures. This information might be useful while migrating the system firmware development across various SoC architectures.

CHAPTER 5

Security at Its Core

"It takes 20 years to build a reputation and few minutes of a cyber-incident to ruin it."

—Stephane Nappo

Today most computing devices (laptop, smart phone, smart appliances, etc.) are connected to the Internet, which poses challenges for the device manufacturers because they have to think about platform security. For any device, platform security is a combination of hardware, software, and associated configurations. Users are always equipped with these devices, and they are used to perform financial and/or personal data transfers. Hence, the security specification demands continuous evolution. Firmware, being closest to the hardware, assumes the primary role of enforcing the security configuration because it is within the Trusted Compute Boundary (TCB). Firmware is also responsible for abstracting the operating system from the underlying hardware, which provides more reason to ensure that the communication channel is secure.

This chapter focuses on designing the boot firmware, keeping security in mind. As the industry is moving toward more cloud-driven services, we need to ensure that the firmware communication is secure within the firmware space and even from the OS to the firmware using trusted APIs.

© Subrata Banik and Vincent Zimmer 2022
S. Banik and V. Zimmer, *Firmware Development*,
https://doi.org/10.1007/978-1-4842-7974-8_5

A typical computing system handles a variety of assets owned by users, software vendors, OS vendors, OEM vendors, and silicon vendors. It is essential that the components in the computing system are trusted to handle these assets, lest these assets are compromised.

The building blocks of the computing system can be categorized into the following groups:

- *Silicon or hardware (hardware)*: This includes the system on-chip or micro-controllers or application-specific integrated circuits (ASICs).

- *Firmware (firmware)*: This is the first piece of code executing on the hardware and is essential for configuring and operating the hardware. Typically, without the firmware, the hardware device will not operate.

- *Software (software)*: This is the component on the computing system through which users typically interact with the hardware. The firmware is a subset of the software; the firmware has very limited or no interactions with the user.

Attackers are constantly looking for vulnerabilities in all areas of a computing system for information theft, espionage, ransom, sabotage of nation-state security, etc. Thus, it is paramount that security objectives are built into every facet of a computing system to ensure that complex systems can be built from the ground up with the appropriate security requirements. While developing a product, the security cannot be an afterthought. Security is fundamental to any computing system and needs to be designed into the entire stack of a computing system (hardware, firmware, and software).

As noted, as hardware and software stacks become more robust, attackers are increasingly researching vulnerabilities in firmware stacks. It is more effective to hide exploitation tools such as rootkits in the firmware because the firmware on a computing system is typically not updated frequently and antivirus tools are unable to scan the firmware components in a system. A rootkit in the firmware can be used to compromise information such as memory contents, system storage contents, etc., and can effectively alter the operation of the system by compromising the hardware configuration and controlling the software that executes on the computing system. There are several published reports, papers, and articles on firmware attacks.

A secure computing system implies that the hardware, firmware, and software can all be trusted to handle various assets as per the defined security objectives. Starting from the foundation of the computing system, the hardware is considered to be immutable. Attacks on the hardware requires physical access to the computing system. Software (e.g., an operating system, word processor, etc.) is loaded after the hardware comes up and the firmware is executed. Continuing to build on this foundation, assuming the hardware is immutable, it is important that the firmware be secure to ensure that the rest of the stack loaded by the firmware is also secure.

Facts   Hardware can be attacked using physical attacks such as fault injection through voltage/thermal differentials, etc. You can learn more about physical attacks from the bibliography.

Attacks on software by exploiting bugs, etc., is beyond the scope of this book. You can learn more about software vulnerabilities and security from the bibliography.

This chapter focuses on aspects of the firmware security relevant for a secure computing environment.

Revisiting the Definition of Firmware with a Security Mindset

Typically, a platform (as shown in Figure 5-1) consists of several hardware components that may or may not be equipped with underlying firmware. As discussed earlier, the components without firmware are just hardware blocks and considered to be immutable. For the components with firmware in them, the firmware can be obtained from various nonvolatile storage attached to the computing platform such as system storage, platform boot flash, component-specific flash on the board, components in-package, or components on-die flash. During the boot or runtime of the computing system, the hardware component powers on and retrieves the underlying firmware from the nonvolatile storage and executes this firmware. Once the firmware executes, any additional high-level software like an operating system is loaded by the firmware and jumps into it. The software stack is used by the user to interact with the hardware and access resources on the computing device.

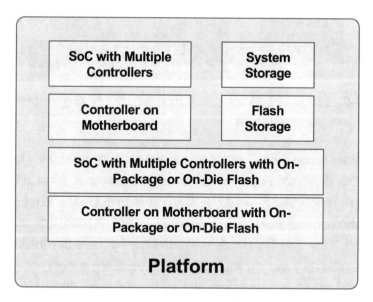

Figure 5-1. *Block diagram of a typical platform with controllers and firmware storage components*

Why Is Firmware Security Required?

As described earlier, there are various assets on the computing system that are required to be protected from unauthorized access. The software stack is used to access these assets. Hence, there is a requirement to ensure that only a "trusted and known" software stack always executes on the computing system. The software stack to execute on the computing system is controlled by the firmware stack, as explained in the book *System Firmware: An Essential Guide to Open Source and Embedded Solutions*. Figure 5-2 illustrates a simple flow diagram showing the dependency. As shown in the figure, the ROM is responsible for bringing up the firmware, and the firmware in turn is responsible for bringing up the software.

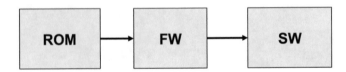

Figure 5-2. *Simple block diagram showing the flow of booting up in a typical computing system*

The ROM is considered hardware; attackers may potentially be able to attack the ROM to control the hardware. But they may do so at the cost of having the computing system "fail" because to get to the ROM and tamper with it, the attacker has to conduct a deep physical attack. On the other hand, if the attacker is able to control the software by attacking the firmware, then they can get control of the computing system.

In addition to the assets accessible by the software, the computing system also includes vendors' (OEM, silicon/hardware) assets and configurations like boot configuration, system debug configuration, security configurations, etc., that need to be protected from adversaries. These assets are typically controlled by the firmware executing in the system.

Furthermore, as the software stack (e.g., like operating systems) becomes more robust, attackers are continuously exploring other areas in the computing system to exploit vulnerabilities. The firmware stack is the next logical target for adversaries to hide malicious code and also get more control of the entire system, as described in *System Firmware: An Essential Guide to Open Source and Embedded Solutions.*

Thus, the security of the firmware components in a computing system is a fundamental requirement. Without the right implementation of proper security protections for firmware components, it is not possible to ensure assets can be protected from adversaries, and more importantly, potentially attackers can take over the entire system easily.

Threats and Issues

The lack of firmware security can potentially expose the computing system to various vulnerabilities. The risks similar to the vulnerable software stack apply. For example, adversaries can do the following:

- Spy on activities in the computing system

- Siphon data from the computing system

- Access and control computing system remotely

- Potentially cause bodily or monetary harm (e.g., attacks on utility grid, ransomware, etc.)

- Make the computing system inoperable

There are many examples of attackers taking advantage of firmware vulnerabilities to attack a computing system and the environment it is located in. A few examples are described in the "Reference" section of the book. The general perception is that firmware is easier to attack because firmware vendors do not develop firmware with a security mindset from the bottom up. Furthermore, monitoring and controlling firmware security is a difficult problem. Hence, it is important to ensure that every firmware component in a computing system is kept up-to-date based on the firmware vendor's recommendations.

Security Primer

In this section, we provide a short overview of the security concepts used to describe the security design principles for firmware security.

Terminology

For the examples in this section, we will use two users, Alice and Bob. These two parties want to exchange information securely. The attacker, Eve, wants to access the information, modify the information, replay the information, pose as an imposter, and so on, to affect the secure channel of communication between Alce and Bob.

Integrity

Figure 5-3 shows a scenario where Alice wants to send data (D) to Bob but wants to ensure that when Bob receives D, Bob can verify that D has not been tampered with. This security property is called *integrity*, and it can typically be achieved using techniques such as message authentication codes (MACs). The MAC of data D is computed and transmitted along with the data by Alice. Bob then computes the MAC of the data upon receipt of the message and compares that with the transmitted MAC by Alice to ensure that the integrity of data is maintained during the transmission.

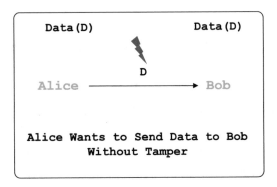

Figure 5-3. *Integrity property for data transfer from Alice to Bob*

Confidentiality

In Figure 5-4, Alice wants to send data D to Bob and wants to ensure that only Bob can read the clear-text data D. This security property is called *confidentiality* and is typically achieved using symmetric (or asymmetric) encryption techniques such as NIST's Advanced Encryption Standard (AES) algorithms. In symmetric encryption, both Alice and Bob have a key known only to both of them. Alice encrypts D using the key to create the encrypted message cipher_D, which is transmitted over the channel. Bob uses the same key to decrypt the cipher_D text to get access to the clear-text data D.

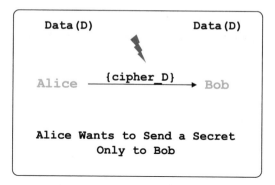

Figure 5-4. *Confidentiality property for data transfer from Alice to Bob*

Authenticity

As per Figure 5-5, Bob wants to ensure that the data received is actually from Alice and no one else. This is called the *authenticity* security property and is typically achieved by using an RSA signature on the data to be sent by Alice. Bob can verify the signature to ensure that the content is indeed sent by Alice.

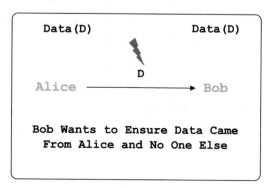

Figure 5-5. *Authenticity property for data transfer from Alice to Bob*

Anti-replay

In Figure 5-6, Bob wants to ensure that the data received from Alice is fresh and is not a playback of older data from Alice. This is called the *anti-replay* security property, and it is typically achieved by sending a monotonically increasing value along with the data sent by Alice. Bob can check if the monotonic value property is valid for every piece of data obtained from Alice and determine whether malicious data was injected into the channel between Alice and Bob.

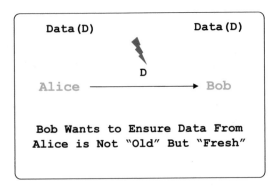

Figure 5-6. *Antireplay property for data transfer from Alice to Bob*

Availability

With the *availability* security property, Alice wants to ensure that data can be made available to Bob whenever Bob makes a request to Alice. This property can be designed by ensuring Alice is always available to process requests from Bob. Aspects such as loss of connection, loss of power, etc., at Bob's end that are not under control of Alice are out of scope for this security property for Alice. See Figure 5-7.

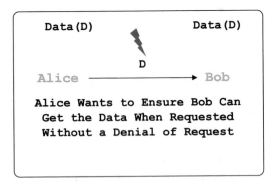

Figure 5-7. *Availability property for data available to Bob from Alice*

Anti-rollback

An important security property for computing platforms with firmware is the ability to control what version of the firmware is executing on the platform. This is important to establish the overall security posture of the platform. In this context, it is important to ensure that the firmware always executes the latest version as released by the firmware owner, and the system is designed such that a rollback to an older version of the firmware is not possible. This security property is called *anti-rollback*.

Root of Trust

The root of trust is terminology used in this section repeatedly. The root of trust can be hardware, firmware, or a software component that is inherently trusted and is secure by design. The root of trust provides the foundation on which security and trust is built for a system.

Threat Modeling

There are different ways to find security issues in firmware, like static code analysis, fuzzing or dynamic testing, penetration or red team testing, or just waiting for reports to be filed to conduct further analysis. A more formal method for identifying potential security issues is to conduct *threat modeling*. The process of threat modeling allows the designer to identify security objectives and assets with security properties and create requirements with security as one of the foundations. Threat modeling helps the designer understand better the questions of "What is the design?" and "What can go wrong?" and "How to mitigate?" and continue an iterative process on these questions until certain objectives are met to satisfaction.

The key question in threat modeling is "What can go wrong?" This question is quite open ended and difficult to address for a typical designer/engineer. To address this, many formal methods/processes to identify what can go wrong have been created. One such example is the STRIDE method, which stands for Spoofing, Tampering, Repudiation, Information disclosure, Denial of service, and Elevation of privilege. More details on the STRIDE process for threat modeling are available in the "Reference" section of the book.

Adversary Modeling

An adversary is defined as any entity not authorized to access or modify an asset or who works to defeat any protections on the asset. It is important to understand the capabilities of the adversary to understand what can go wrong during threat modeling. A rather simple adversary (e.g., an unprivileged software adversary) with the following capabilities (the adversary model prescribed by Intel) may not have the ability to compromise firmware assets as this adversary is unaware of the presence of firmware in the computing platform:

- Can read memory mapped into the address space by the system software

- Can write memory mapped into the address space with the write privilege granted by the system software

- Can execute Ring 3 instructions from memory mapped into the address space with the execute privilege granted by the system software

Therefore, it is important to understand the right capabilities of the adversary and use them for the right threat modeling. Once the adversary model is clear, the threat modeling then becomes a question of "What can go wrong if the adversary has this capability?" This leads to more clarity into threat modeling and aids in defining the right security design to mitigate against attacks by the adversary on the assets.

A taxonomy of adversaries based on capabilities is the foundation for any security analysis and the appropriate security design.

Security Assumptions

Assumptions are one of the key parameters of the design of security solutions. Security design is based on mitigating attacks on assets; it is practically impossible to list all the attacks possible on an asset to begin with; hence, a design for security always starts with the key assumptions on which the design is created. The assumptions can be aspects like "physical attack on the hardware needs sophisticated and expensive equipment that this becomes a barrier to attack," "reverse engineering the key for encryption will take enough time that the value of knowing the clear text key is lost," etc.

Approach to Security Design for Firmware

Designing the security solution for a system requires the designer to understand various aspects of the system to provide a comprehensive solution to address the security issues. This is the same with security for firmware on a computing system. The following is a typical approach to take to develop the security design:

1. Understand the system architecture.

2. Create the list of assumptions on which the security design will be based.

3. Create the list of assets in the system and their appropriate security properties.

4. Create the threat models for the assets.

5. Create security design to address the threat models.

Obviously, in the context of security, a designer can never provide a perfect solution. The security design is not constant and has to continuously improve by iterating over steps 2–4. As the designer learns more about new attack vectors that modify the assumptions and the threat

models, new solutions/technologies have to be created or devised to
address the new findings.

This section creates an understanding of the security for firmware
based on the previous approaches.

- Understanding the components in a system that
  contain firmware

- Understanding the threats in scope

- Understanding the assets

- Describing security design concepts that address the
  threat models and continuously assess the design

Platform Configuration for Firmware

This section will review the basic framework of a computing platform that
includes firmware for various components in the platform.

A typical computing platform consists of a motherboard with the
following components on it:

- One or more system-on-chip (SoC) components

- One or more microcontrollers

- Multiple sensors

- Flash storage and memory devices

- Cooling units, power supply

- Input/output devices, etc.

The microcontroller and SoCs themselves may have SRAM in them for
firmware or software to use for execution. In addition, the microcontroller
or SoCs may also have flash memory in them either as on-die flash
memory or on-package flash memory. As described in previous chapters,

the firmware for the computing platform is resident either in the flash storage on the board or in on-die/on-package flash. Depending on where the firmware is at rest, where the firmware executes at runtime, etc., the security properties for the firmware is determined.

For example, let's assume that a certain piece of firmware has confidentiality properties, implying that the firmware should be protected from being visible in the clear to anyone except the components that are allowed to execute the firmware. In this example, consider if the firmware is resident in the flash on the motherboard; then this firmware has to be encrypted because an adversary with physical access to the system will be able to "dump" the content of the flash on the motherboard using simple tools such as a "dediprog." On the other hand, if the firmware was resident in the on-die flash, it may not be necessary to encrypt the firmware because it is deemed to be more difficult to do a physical attack on the die.

Firmware with Security Mindset in a Computing System

Before we get into the details of what security constructs are required for firmware security, let's first understand what attacks are in scope for the discussion and how to address them. Figure 5-8 shows attack vectors for various firmware components in the platform. Let's look at each of them.

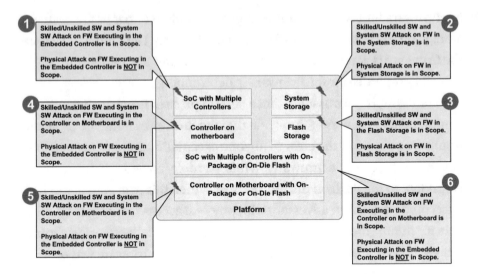

Figure 5-8. *Block diagram showing attack vectors in scope for discussion*

In Figure 5-8, for the callouts marked as 1 and 4, the firmware is assumed to be loaded into a controller and executed locally in the controller. For the callouts marked 2 and 3, the firmware is stored at rest in either system storage or flash storage.

Attack vectors in scope for firmware at rest do the following:

1. The firmware at rest needs protection from getting tampered with by any skilled or unskilled software, system software, or firmware. It ensures that any attacks like illegal or unwanted firmware updates are prohibited from tampering with the firmware to brick the system.

2. The firmware at rest must be able to detect physical attack on the firmware in the storage. An attacker with physical access to the system may be able to modify the firmware directly in the storage; while

preventing this attack can be expensive for typical computing systems, being able to detect the attack is sufficient to ensure that illegal or unwanted firmware cannot be loaded into the system.

Attack vectors in scope for firmware at runtime do the following:

1. The firmware in runtime must be protected from skilled or unskilled software/system software or firmware tampering the firmware at runtime. This ensures that the firmware executes as expected and does not cause the system's security to be compromised.

2. The firmware in runtime must be protected from physical attacks; this ensures that attackers cannot use physical side channel attacks, probe attacks, etc., to modify the runtime firmware and cause the system security to be compromised.

To address these attack vectors, the following security properties are typically attached to each firmware:

- *Authenticity*: This security property ensures that firmware that executes on a computing system is always coming from the right authority.

- *Integrity*: This security property ensures that firmware that executes has not been tampered with by an attacker.

- *Confidentiality*: This security property ensures that firmware cannot be obtained in clear text while at rest or during execution. Typically, this security property is required for firmware executing in computing systems such as set-top boxes, etc., as the cost of compromise of the firmware can lead to media content being compromised.

- *Availability*: This security property ensures that firmware is always available, so the system can function even if the firmware complies with the previous security properties but may have bugs causing the system to malfunction or stop functioning.

- *Access control*: This security property ensures that only the authorized firmware can access certain resources, and other components in the computing system cannot access these resources. For example, the fingerprint sensor data can be designed to be made available only to the security engine firmware and no other component in the system.

Typical technologies used to accomplish the previous security properties are secure boot, trusted execution environment, firmware resiliency, security assurance, etc. The rest of this section highlights the design constructs that are typically used and how to achieve security for firmware components in a computing system.

Before we delve into the security design constructs, let's look at a few resources required in the hardware to achieve the security properties highlighted earlier. Figure 5-9 shows the hardware resources available to an embedded engine in a computing system. Note: similar resources may be available to the firmware for the application processor as well.

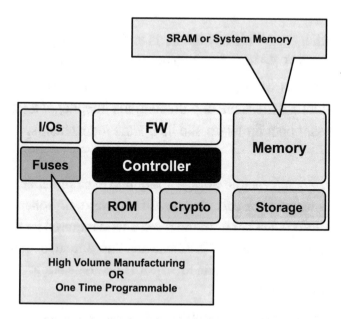

Figure 5-9. *Typical resources available to an embedded engine in a computing system*

Let's understand these components in detail.

- *Read-on memory (ROM)*: This is typically known as Boot ROM as well. It is a nonvolatile memory that contains the boot code, fetched and executed by the controller immediately after coming out from reset. Ideally, the boot ROM contains a minimal code block that requires the controller to come to life. A simplest embedded system might only have ROM that is sufficient for the platform to complete all the required hardware initialization prior to loading the high-level software without the overhead of a post-production or in-field firmware update.

291

Facts   National Institute of Standards and Technology (NIST) publications NIST SP 800-147, "BIOS Protection Guidelines for Clients," and NIST SP 800-147B, "BIOS Protection Guidelines for Servers," address the issue of protecting the integrity of a platform's host processor boot firmware and its update mechanisms.

- *Memory*: A volatile storage is required to complement the memory-restricted nature of hardware controllers while coming out from the reset. This is required for the runtime execution of the firmware. There are two main types of memory: static RAM (SRAM) and dynamic RAM (DRAM).

- *SRAM*: This type of random access memory uses flip-flop circuitry to keep the data. Unlike DRAM, this memory type doesn't require periodic refreshing. It is typically used for the cache and internal registers in powerful microprocessors and on several other microcontrollers.

- *DRAM*: This is most widely used as main memory in the computer system. This type of random access memory uses memory cells (made of a tiny capacitor and transistor) for storing the data. DRAM has to be refreshed periodically to avoid data leaking due to slow discharge of the capacitors. DRAM memory is much cheaper compared to the SRAM and hence more often used on computer systems.

Facts   By the nature of its operational model, DRAM is a soft target for security attack. Rowhammer is one such security exploit that took advantage of memory cells to possibly change its contents by repetitive neighboring cell access that caused leakage in their charge.

Figure 5-10 shows the different types of DRAM memory types being used on the embedded system.

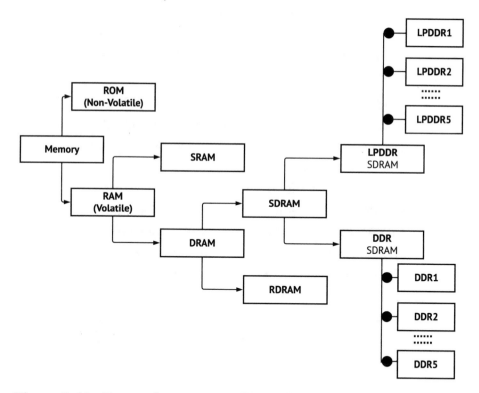

Figure 5-10. *Types of memory used in embedded systems*

- *Storage*: In computer systems, storage devices are referred to as *secondary memory*. The information stored persists across multiple power-cycle, power-off, etc., scenarios. It's also important to highlight here that, based on the boot criticality of the firmware components, there are many firmware versions that reside even in the storage devices like eMMC, NVMe, etc. The nonboot critical firmware needs to get loaded into the hardware controller using OS software driver models rather than pre-boot communication methods. For example, the AsoC Linux kernel driver is capable of registering the digital signal processing (DSP) and firmware.

- *Crypto*: Hardware-based cryptographic primitives are required to accelerate or isolate assets from the other resources. The objective of crypto in firmware space is to increase the security while ensuring seamless firmware updates for the in-field devices. The firmware update process involves downloading a binary image, which may include code, data, configuration and/or calibration value, authentication information, and other product details, etc. Now a security threat always exists on the asset since the update operation has initiated; hence, the cryptographic algorithms provide the means to protect the privacy of the content and also verify the integrity and authenticity.

- *I/Os*: Logically, at a high level, an embedded system can be considered to be separated into two blocks, the lower layer and higher layer. Figure 5-11 illustrates the high-level system view to understand the I/Os.

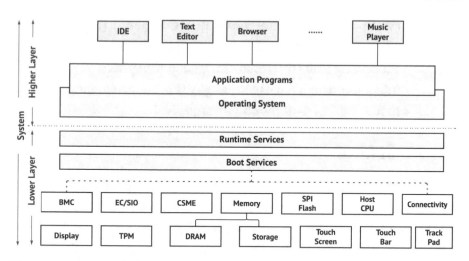

Figure 5-11. *High-level system view*

In the *lower-layer* section, the I/Os are typically the external components in the motherboard that are initialized/configured by the firmware for making it accessible by the *higher-level* software/applications.

- **Fuses**: These are the control knobs tuned by the hardware vendors (including SoC manufacturers) to configure the engine at manufacturing. Depending on the design and system requirements, hardware vendors allow fuses to be programmed and configured by the underlying firmware. These fuses are for debugging, manufacturing, managing feature enabling/disabling requests, etc. Efficient use of these fuses while debugging to trace any underlying hardware communication. Additionally, these fuses help adhere to the security recommendation during manufacturing. The fuses allow configuring a particular feature without revamping the hardware controller in the factory. There are tools to configure the fuse to satisfy the end-user requirement. For example, the airport kiosk system utilizes the Intel Next Unit of Computing (NUC) without any specific use case for keeping the Image Processing Unit (IPU) enabled. Hence, the system integrator would have to leverage the advanced tooling to turn off IPU features on the target device.

Access Control

The concept of access control was defined earlier. The goal of access control is to ensure that assets are protected from other components in the system. For example, in a bank, the safe/locker is not allowed to be accessed by any one other than a group of employees. Similarly, in a computing system, access control is used to block access to unauthorized users.

In the context of firmware security, access control in a system is used to determine which entity can access the storage area (i.e., the firmware at rest area), access the memory in the controller, access assets of the controller, and so on. This access control design ensures that only authorized components that are identified by construction are trusted by the controller, and the firmware executing on the controller will allow access to resources within the firmware. This concept is used as a security design concept to protect the resources of the firmware on a controller or system.

Secure Boot or Firmware Authentication

As discussed earlier, the typical boot of a system starts with the ROM, followed by mutable code loaded from the storage such as firmware, firmware applications, and/or software depending on the controller or computing system. The concept of Secure Boot ensures that every piece of mutable code loaded from the storage is securely verified before it is executed. Secure verification includes verifying the authenticity of the firmware, integrity of the firmware, security version number of the firmware, and any confidentiality properties of the firmware. To prevent attackers from tampering with the firmware, it is required that Secure Boot be rooted in the hardware. Secure Boot ensures that attacks on the firmware at reset are now addressed.

Consider the high-level Secure Boot flow shown in Figure 5-12. The ROM is considered as a root of trust for the Secure Boot flow. As the ROM is considered equivalent to hardware, by design it is difficult to attack the ROM and requires the attacker to have physical access and use special equipment to conduct an attack on the ROM. All modern and future systems are adding capabilities to thwart physical attacks. You can learn more about these new techniques in the "Reference" section of this book. The ROM as the root of trust is responsible for starting the Secure Boot trust chain by securely verifying the first piece of mutable code read by the ROM from the storage for execution.

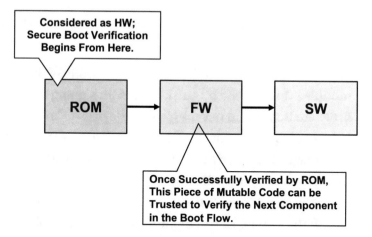

Figure 5-12. *High-level Secure Boot flow*

The system diagram for a typical implementation of secure boot is shown in Figure 5-13.

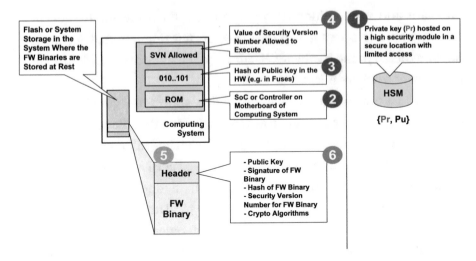

Figure 5-13. *System diagram for a typical Secure Boot implementation*

The following are the different components that are part of the Secure Boot system architecture:

- *High security module (HSM)*: The responsibility of this module is to store the private key used for signing the firmware binary and never exposing the private key to any user. Typically, this module is kept in a restricted area, and only authorized users are allowed to use this system to sign the firmware binary. This is one of the key assumptions for the security of a Secure Boot flow. If the signing key is compromised, then the only option is to use a different private key, and this requires potentially providing new computing systems into the field.

- *ROM*: As described earlier, the read-only memory is considered as the root of trust.

- *Fuses or one-time programmable region*: This component is required to hold the hash of the public key part of the key pair generated by the HSM. Storing the hash of the public key in the hardware gives the binding between the secret private key used to sign the firmware binary and the system on which the verification is conducted.

- *Storage for replay protection*: The security version number is different from a typical version number. The security version number is updated only when a security issue is fixed, whereas the firmware version number can be updated if a new feature is added or a functional bug is fixed. This storage in the hardware is used to provide the minimum security version number that can execute on the system. This number is updated by the firmware during the firmware update process.

- *Firmware in storage*: To ensure that the firmware is verified correctly, a header or verification record or manifest is attached with the actual firmware binary. This header typically contains the security information used to verify the binary.

- *Header*: The header contains information such as the actual public key used to verify the signature; the result of signing the firmware binary (called the *signature*) using the private key at the HSM location; hash of the firmware binary to ensure that firmware is not tampered; the security version number of this firmware in the storage; and so on. All the information in the header is used by the verifier to ensure that the firmware binary is exactly what the manufacturer intended from a security perspective.

As discussed in Figure 5-12 with the high-level Secure Boot flow, the ROM starts the Secure Boot chain by verifying the first piece of firmware read from the storage. The ROM reads the firmware binary and the header and then uses the contents of the header to verify the security properties of the firmware binary. Let's go through a simple process:

1. The hash of the public key in the header is compared with the hash in the hardware storage. This ensures the binding between the HSM and the hardware. Only if this step is successful, go to the next step.

2. The signature in the header is verified using the public key in the header. Only if this step is successful, go to the next step.

3. The hash of the firmware binary is compared with the hash in the header; if successful, go to the next step.

4. The security version number in the header must be equal or greater than the security version number in the hardware; if successful, go to the next step.

5. All the security properties are properly verified, so continue with the next stage of boot.

In the previous flow, if any of the steps fail, then depending on the design of the system, the boot of the system can fail, and the system can be designed to go into recovery.

As discussed earlier, the goal of secure boot is to ensure that any firmware binary executing on the controller/system is verified before it can be loaded for execution. The mechanics of the Secure Boot process can be applied to any controller with its own ROM or a root of trust in the system that controls the security for the controller.

Security Assurance

As we discussed earlier, the security of firmware is a task that is not something that is ever complete; it is an evolving problem as more features are added to the firmware and also as the following occur:

- Sophisticated attack vectors become more accessible to everyone.

- New techniques are created to attack firmware. Given this, it is important for any firmware vendor to have a solid security development life cycle (SDL) plan. This plan must include the following:

- *Architectural analysis*: Security starts with understanding the architecture and what problem is actually being solved. Hence, it is important to constantly reevaluate the architecture when significant functional changes are added to the firmware. This will help you understand if existing security assumptions continue to hold or new assumptions need to be created.

- *Code reviews*: The security architecture and design are only as good as the code that is developed to implement the architecture. Hence, an open source firmware development approach will help address this along with detailed code reviews to be conducted with the design and development teams to ensure that all security assumptions and dependencies are properly documented and implemented.

- *Code scan using tools*: While code reviews are great, some fundamental problems in the security of the design or implementation can be caught using tools such as BlackDuck, etc. The goal of these tools is to analyze the code and binaries to determine common security vulnerabilities and provide alternatives.

- *Security validation*: This is an important step in the SDL process. Functional validation ensures that the firmware functions as expected and it is easy to create test cases to cover all the functional aspects of the design. The test cases help unearth bugs that can be fixed. But these functional tests do not test for the "security" of the firmware. The goal of security validation is to create tests to break the security architecture aspects of the design, break the security assumptions, try to expose assets, and so on.

For example, let's assume a design in which a user is required to provide a login and password to access the firmware options. Functional testing would ensure that an user can provide the login and password correctly and ensure that a wrong login/password combination does not allow access. However, typical functional validation does not capture aspects such as the following: What happens if the user provides a login that is longer than allowed? What if the user provides special characters as a login or password? And so on. Some of these conditions can potentially cause misbehaviors in the system and expose security vulnerabilities.

Security assurance is an important aspect of the life cycle of firmware required to ensure that vendors are constantly monitoring and improving the security of the firmware.

Firmware Update and Resiliency

Another important construct required to ensure the security of the firmware is the ability to keep the firmware updated to the latest version that has all the known security issues addressed. One of the key issues firmware vendors face is how to deploy the updates; a full-fledged system is required with a server to push the update, and the firmware on the targeted device must accept the update and verify the update before writing the update into the storage where the firmware is at rest. However, these issues are being addressed comprehensively lately because of the concerns of attacks one can launch with compromised firmware.

Security for the firmware update process is required to ensure that unauthorized firmware is not written into the storage and potentially cause the system to brick. Verifying the update pushed by the server is similar to the process described earlier. Similar steps are used to ensure that the firmware modules received from the update server are valid and can safely be written into the storage area.

While the security for the update process ensures that firmware pushed by the update server is valid, there can still be nonsecurity issues with the pushed update. For example, functional bugs that have escaped validation can cause the system to brick or stop functioning. Hence, it is imperative for the security of the system that the firmware design considers resiliency. NIST 800-193 spells out the requirements for a design that considers firmware update and resiliency. Modern computing systems are designed to meet the NIST 800-193 requirements.

Summary

The firmware on a system is critical for the operation of a system. Attackers are constantly looking for not only new methods but also new entry points into the system, and the firmware (being a critical foundation of a system) is one entry that must be protected with strong defenses. Yes, attackers will constantly be looking to identify vulnerabilities and exploit them, but the right foundation for security is that firmware vendors have to be nimble to address the exploits and ensure the systems are not compromised and also resilient.

This chapter highlighted different security constructs such as assurance, secure boot, update, and resiliency that are used to create the foundation for firmware security. Ideally you will find a suitable space in your product development journey to be able to apply this knowledge when implementing your own system firmware to ensure the firmware is secured. You can learn more about the technical details of security advisories in the book's "Reference" section.

CHAPTER 6

Looking at the Future of System Firmware

> *"If everything you try works, you aren't trying hard enough."*
>
> **—Gordon Moore**

The evolution of system firmware over the last three decades has involved inheriting lots of complexity to support the underlying hardware and complement the limitations in legacy operating systems in a more flexible way for device manufacturers. This has resulted in unnecessary complexity in the entire system firmware boot process, requiring significant development cost and time to restructure the firmware design. This trend of designing complex system firmware has continued, without realizing the current end-user demands, offerings from modern hardware, and more competent operating systems that have overcome such legacy limitations. Boot firmware does not necessarily need to do a lot work, as it used to do in the past. Rather, future system firmware should have boundaries with end users and industry needs.

System firmware goals will evolve in the future, and if we could foresee those goals and align the designs of all available boot firmware (BIOS), then this would improve the ecosystem of future firmware. There are

© Subrata Banik and Vincent Zimmer 2022
S. Banik and V. Zimmer, *Firmware Development*,
https://doi.org/10.1007/978-1-4842-7974-8_6

several key areas inside the system firmware premises where the industry is looking to improve firmware design. The fundamental principles that future system firmware will focus on are as follows:

- *Performance*: In the modern computing era, billions of devices are connected to the Internet and doing trillions of data transfers per second. Turning a device off to perform a system update is too much to ask for. For example, if a Facebook or Google server has a scheduled reboot and the system restoration time is way higher then expected, it would significantly impact users and business. Hence, the minimum ask from future firmware would be an instant boot.

- *Simplicity*: For any solution to get accepted by the wider community, it has to be simple enough that it doesn't expect too much from its users. Since the origin of the boot firmware, it has been maintained by a closed set of communities. Hence, it's easy to implement system firmware with a high-level programming language and build a specification around it. But this results in resistance in the open community to accept such complex solutions and adapt to them. Also, the community wants to explore the best methodology to get rid of such complex solutions; hence, the idea is to use a basic programming language and software engineering methods, rather than being attached to something that needs specific skill sets.

- *Security*: Over the years system firmware has been the method to provide access from the operating system (OS) to the hardware layer due to its operational privilege level. ODM/OEMs are using legacy techniques like System Management Mode (SMM) and Option ROM (OpRom) to perform platform device initialization, which remains unnoticed by the high-level monitoring layer like OS-driven security policies. This might expose security risks. The expectation from future hardware and SoC would be to define security into its core so that firmware can avoid having such legacy implementations, which not only increases the firmware footprint but also might increase the security risk.

- *Open source*: Any future firmware development and maintenance is expected to be in an open and inclusive environment, rather than limited to a few companies to make the decision on behalf of everyone. Having visibility into open source is kind of a blessing in many ways. It helps to resolve the trust issue that is normally there with any proprietary system firmware. Open source generally helps users adapt to a specification and provides a continuous feedback path for improvements. Reducing development cost is also another key benefit of open source for device manufacturers.

- *Exploring hardware*: In the past, firmware has been designed to ease the communication with the underlying hardware. Hence, when it comes to designing an efficient platform with reduced firmware space and an instant boot experience, device manufacturers usually pick the easiest solution by introducing a pre-initialized hardware controller. This results in a higher bill of material (BoM) cost and puts an extra burden on end users. But the real exploration would be on utilizing the existing CPU capabilities and offerings in hardware or refactoring the hardware capabilities to design a better platform with combined hardware-firmware innovations, without increasing the platform BoM cost.

This chapter focuses on such key forward-looking firmware initiatives that have been built around the principles discussed earlier.

- *Designing LITE firmware*: The real need of firmware is to perform essential hardware initialization to boot the platform to the operating system. But the firmware boundary has grown so much in the last decade that sometimes it's referred to as "beyond BIOS." This chapter will cover how to design a LITE boot firmware to shrink the firmware boundary.

- *Designing a feature kernel*: The book *System Firmware: An Essential Guide to Open Source and Embedded Solutions* provides details about the payload and its usage model. The only purpose that a typical payload serves is to pick the correct boot services like console input, console output, and block device or network device to boot to the OS (and additionally perform some crypto-related operations to verify the kernel partitions prior to loading). In addition, there could be some ODM/OEM-specific customization to allow users to configure the BIOS. The feature kernel concept is to utilize the kernel as part of the payload to reduce the firmware boundary and use early OS-like environments to further boot to the OS.

- *Design multithread boot firmware*: In the past, boot firmware has been designed to work over a single-threaded environment. Modern and future processor designs are more capable of supporting more logical processors. But because of the legacy design of system firmware, it never works in a multithreaded environment to provide better opportunities for future boot firmware and reduce platform boot time.

- *Innovative hardware design*: Today system firmware looks more complicated because of the underlying SoC and/or hardware design. Ideally, the system firmware should just be responsible for performing basic CPU and chipset initialization, and the rest hands over the control to the operating system. But because of several factors such as not having enough memory to access hardware resources early in the boot process and the need to set up temporary memory to continue the hardware access, such cyclic dependencies in hardware design limits the innovation in firmware and tries to make system firmware act as legacy firmware. This chapter will discuss the possible innovation in hardware or SoC architecture to make the future firmware get rid of this legacy.

Designing LITE Firmware

Basic Input/Output System (BIOS) was originally meant to perform basic hardware (CPU and chipset) initialization during the boot process and when booting to the operating system. Over time, to support complex SoC and platform designs, the BIOS has also become reasonably complex and mammoth in nature. Today, the de facto successor to BIOS is Unified Extensible Firmware Interface (UEFI), which is also known as "beyond BIOS." Having said that, there are some ecosystem concerns due to its closed source nature.

Because of the increasing concerns of security, complexity, and closed firmware, the industry is heading toward platform development under the open source umbrella, by an initiative driven by the Open Compute Project (OCP, https://www.opencompute.org/). This effort has led market leaders to also adopt open source firmware development approaches.

This provides an opportunity for the OEM/ODM to pick a suitable BIOS for their platform from a wide range. As discussed earlier in this book, there are currently three main successors to the BIOS: coreboot, Slimboot, and UEFI.

Typically closed source BIOSs for client and server platforms have the following shortcomings:

- The firmware has become an operating system.

- The system firmware is archaic, complex, and often quite buggy.

- Closed source firmware is hard to maintain and can't forward/backport features and fixes.

- Vendor-specific tools are used in the case of closed source firmware.

- Closed source firmware has a large number of features and complexity required to support shrinkwrap operating systems and the vagaries of 'compatibility' therein.

- Closed source firmware has more challenges in robustness, ability to debug, and flexibility in both build and deployment.

OEM/ODMs are looking forward to overcoming these barriers by adopting open source firmware approaches. Open source firmware provides the opportunity to achieve feature parity, support for many generations of equipment, and curating both unified and adaptable toolkits.

coreboot is the most popular and is an extended firmware platform, built on the principles of open source software; it provides key advantages from having various CPU architecture support available by default to all OxMs.

As a firmware developer, what matters most is how to initialize various hardware intellectual property (IP) blocks in order to boot a SoC and hand it over to the operating system (OS). This process involves writing various components/IP initialization code for different SoC. But today any system firmware, be it open source or closed source, has unnecessary or redundant and complex blocks to perform hardware initialization. The majority of those complex and redundant hardware initialization blocks were introduced when operating systems were not as advanced as today and there was not much hardware knowledge to perform platform initialization. Here are some examples:

- *PCI enumeration and resource allocation*: All boot firmware does PCI enumeration and resource allocation before booting to the operating system. In reality, PCI enumeration was required in the BIOS space only when the operating system was not capable of doing it. It was late 1999 when Linux had limitations to performing PCI device initialization, and the BIOS was responsible for the PCI configuration.

- *Multiprocessor initialization*: Boot firmware does CPU core initialization, brings APs out of reset, and runs some basic tasks such as range register programming with DRAM-based resources. But because of the BIOS topology of running in a single-threaded environment, it never uses those APs to run tasks in parallel. In the past, operating systems were unable to perform SMP initialization. Hence, it was kind of a requirement to perform those initializations in the boot firmware space. But today Linux-like kernels are capable of doing SMP setup at an early stage of OS booting.

311

- *Provide runtime services*: System firmware has provided runtime hooks to operating systems using SMI handlers. Recently, many security researchers have strongly discarded this practice of using runtime services via SMI.

- *Storage block initialization*: At the end of boot firmware initialization, it's expected that firmware should initialize the block devices like UFS/emmc, NVMe/SATA or USB to boot to the kernel. This means that system firmware should have the required storage drivers in it to perform those initializations. Having those advanced drivers inside the firmware space makes it more complex and increases the maintenance costs as well. For example, to boot from NVMe, one has to add NVMe driver support in the firmware space. But in general that support has already been added into Linux-like kernels by default.

With the previous examples, it's clear that there are many redundant blocks that exist inside system firmware today. Different individuals writing the same initialization code for different firmware blocks will increase the enabling time, as well as the validation time and the review time. All SoC vendors have to support all possible BIOS solutions; hence, we're not gaining anything by doing repeated work in system firmware. Rather, it is increasing the liability of validating it across platforms.

Design Principle

Let's focus on implementing solutions with respect to the open source firmware space, i.e., coreboot. (Similar designs can be made for UEFI and Slimboot as well in the future.) coreboot is an extended firmware platform that delivers a lightning-fast and secure boot experience on modern computers and embedded systems. Figure 6-1 provides a simplistic view of the coreboot flow and other population boot firmware so you can understand the size impact of each BIOS phase and where this philosophy of LITE firmware can fit in.

Figure 6-1 and 6-2 provide the typical boot flow of the boot firmware for any SoC platform and the estimated size for each stage. Without having a detailed understanding of its boot flow and where the majority of boot time and boot firmware footprint lies, it would be difficult to design the LITE firmware solutions.

Note   The boot flow between coreboot and the Slim bootloader are similar, where the bootblock can be referred as Stage 1A, romstage as Stage 1B, and ramstage as Stage 2; hence, the estimated size for those stages are almost identical.

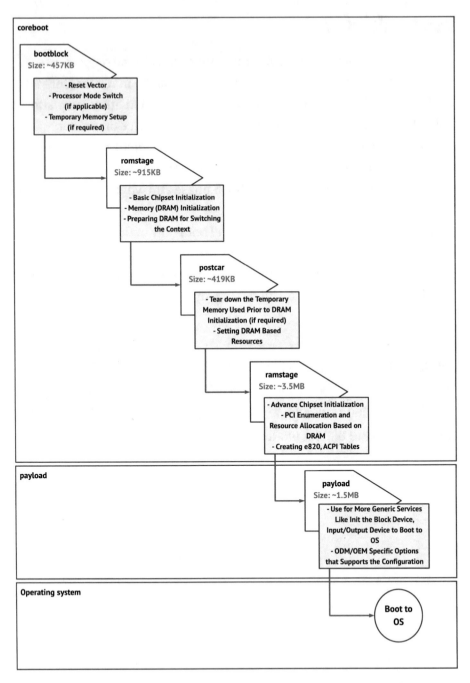

Figure 6-1. *Typical coreboot flow with size of each boot stage*

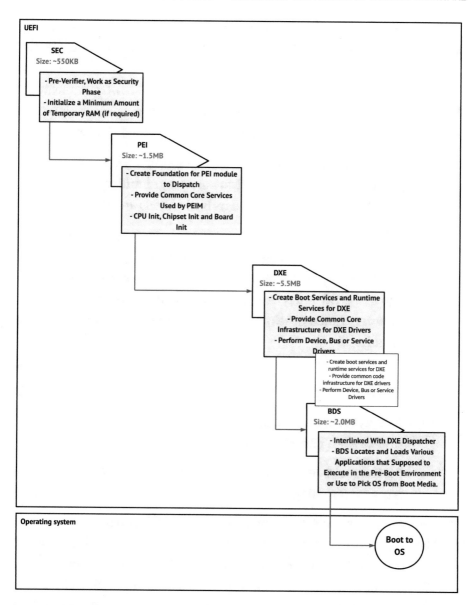

Figure 6-2. *Typical UEFI flow with size of each boot stage*

The takeaway from these figures is that ramstage as an individual stage is consuming around 80 percent of the total coreboot volume, and DXE is similar in the case of UEFI.

Today both firmware and the OS have an equal share of complexity in their domains. As we are interested in open source firmware development, let's discuss coreboot and the possibilities for designing LITE firmware.

- Ramstage has grown over time from a simple PCI configurator to a complex firmware programming block that does something beyond its basic needs and thus creates redundancy.

- Operating systems have also grown in capacity over the years. Hence, the things that were not possible decades ago in the OS and relied on the system firmware are now very much possible to perform using the kernel layer itself.

- The OS for sure can handle more than what ramstage does.

- Hence, we are now at an "intersection point" of the ramstage and operating systems.

- So, the real question is, do we really need a ramstage-like programming block?

The answer is simple: no, we can adopt a "LITE" model.

The system firmware needs to explore the possibility of being LITE where the proposal is to have a minimum functional firmware block with an original boot firmware methodology to boot to the operating OS. The basic agenda of a LITE system firmware would be removing the redundant firmware initialization and making as much use of the operating system as possible.

Over the years ramstage in coreboot and DXE in UEFI have grown beyond their boundaries, and system firmware space has been a bit of a dumping ground to put more OS-like services and applications.

Many features provided by ramstage are not required to be explicitly added into ramstage and don't have a real product need. For example:

- *SMM*: The limited usage model should depend on CPU vendors and product design requirements.

- *Support S3/Sleep*: Modern computing systems have support for connected standby, lucid sleep, or runtime suspend where such underlying legacy Sleep/S3 support can be moved from being mandatory to optional based on the platform design.

- *Runtime services*: This depends on the targeted operating system; hence, there is no point in publishing more runtime services than the OS is actually able to consume.

Using the LITE model, the system firmware can perform the limited initialization of chipsets components that are getting used "only" in firmware space to reduce the firmware boundary.

Mandatory PCI device enumeration and resource allocation: Figure 6-3 illustrates the current PCI device enumeration and resource allocation flow, where ramstage for example in the case of coreboot is responsible for picking all PCI devices from the available PCI tree and performing the predevice initialization and early chipset initialization, specifically to compute and assign the bus resources, enable devices on the bus, and finally initialize the devices on the bus. This iterative process of the PCI tree parsing and resource assignment and finally device initialization can take a significant amount of time in the boot process. This scenario is also the same with UEFI and Slimboot, being responsible for doing the entire PCI tree enumeration irrespective of being used in the firmware space or not.

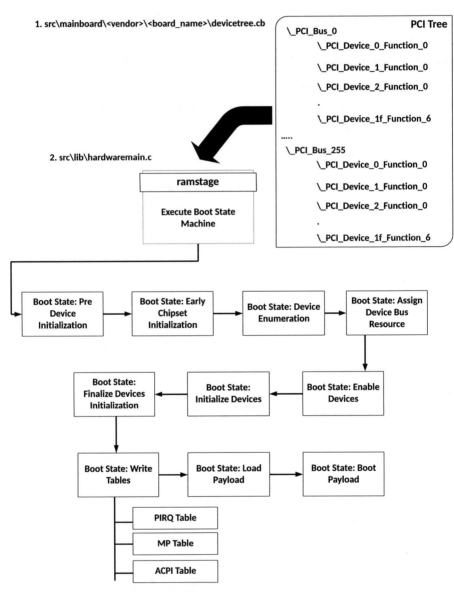

Figure 6-3. *Typical coreboot PCI enumeration process in ramstage*

In the LITE firmware design principle, the system firmware only needs to initialize and enable PCI devices that are getting used in the firmware space and perform the minimum operations prior to transferring the control to the payload or OS.

To adhere to the LITE firmware development strategy on coreboot, a new tag of "mandatory" was added into the PCI tree generation process to skip all the unnecessary device initialization in the firmware space and save a significant amount of system firmware boot time.

During static parsing of the PCI tree structure in coreboot in the LITE firmware model, all PCI device initialization will be skipped unless the "mandatory" keyword is tagged with that PCI device.

The following is the pseudocode from a coreboot reference where a minimum PCI enumeration can be achieved by adding the additional "mandatory" keyword checks to save on boot time. CONFIG_LITE_FIRMWARE is the token being used in the coreboot open source firmware to identify the platform using the LITE system firmware development model.

```
/*
 * Probe all devices/functions on this bus with some
   optimization for
 * non-existence and single function devices.
 */
for (devfn = min_devfn; devfn <= max_devfn; devfn++) {
        if (CONFIG(LITE_FIRMWARE)) {
            dev = pcidev_path_behind(bus, devfn);
            if (!dev || !dev->mandatory)
                    continue;
        }
        /* First thing, set up the device structure. */
        dev = pci_scan_get_dev(bus, devfn);
        ....
        ....
}
```

The following example from the X86-based QEMU emulation shows the reduction in PCI enumeration effort significantly in coreboot by performing only the mandatory PCI device initialization (host bridge and LPC in the following example), which is the minimum system firmware requirement to boot to the payload and further to the OS. The mandatory PCI device list might differ between platform designs, hence making it flexible for platform owners to add the minimum device initialization list as required.

Figure 6-4 explains the proposed LITE firmware-based PCI enumeration to avoid complexity and further reduce the firmware footprint and improve system boot time.

In the following example, the system firmware will perform the initialization and resource allocation for two devices alone (the devices are tagged with the "mandatory" keyword), compared to all possible devices in the existing model.

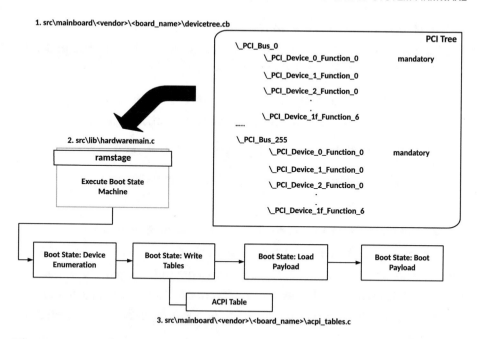

Figure 6-4. *Adopted LITE firmware model in coreboot for PCI enumeration*

Minimum CPU initialization: In a multiprocessor environment, the system firmware brings up only a single bootstrap processor after the power-on reset. Later in the boot process, the system firmware also needs to bring up all the applicable logical processors to perform simultaneous operations in parallel. Because of the limited knowledge in previous generation operating systems for bringing up all of the logical processors, it needs to rely on the system firmware. Typically, ramstage (in coreboot), like an advanced stage, is responsible for performing this multiprocessor (MP) initialization operation. It's also a fact to consider that each operation to bring up the other logical processor into action has its own latency as per CPU vendor design guide. Hence, the possible solutions to ensure minimum CPU initialization are as follows:

- Based on the real needs, design the system firmware to perform operations in a multithreaded environment.

- Early initialization of the processors during boot.

- Deferring initialization of all of the processors in the kernel.

Reduced ACPI table creation: ACPI stands for Advanced Configuration and Power Interface. The purpose of ACPI is to describe the underlying hardware and its interface to the operating system to let you understand that the hardware is present and how to configure it. It controls hardware actions such as the power button behavior, system sleep states, etc.

In the existing model, the creation of ACPI tables have been tied to the PCI enumeration using the dynamic ASL generation method; hence, the BIOS may perform any of the two possible operations as follows:

Option 1: Attach the required ACPI dynamic generation process to the PCI tree device marked as mandatory as follows, where ChromeOS needs an ACPI device for the embedded controller and hence attaches the device to the LPC interface:

```
device domain 0 mandatory
     device pci 1f.0 mandatory
          chip ec/google/chromeec
               device pnp 0c09.0 mandatory   end
          end
     end # LPC Interface
end
```

Option 2: Let the system firmware completely get rid of the ACPI creation process and try to utilize the kernel driver rather than relying on the underlying runtime firmware services. There is a kernel command-line parameter named `acpi`.

acpi: Many hardware platforms ship with buggy or out-of-specification ACPI firmware, which may cause unspecified problems. If the platform is randomly powering off or failing to boot due to potential ACPI-related issues, disabling ACPI is recommended in such scenarios. To potentially get rid of the additional complexity of pulling the required ACPI infrastructure into the prior boot stage, one could also explore this `acpi=off` kernel command to skip ACPI creation in the system firmware. The downside of this approach is that the system loses its capabilities to communicate with the system firmware, and the user space application or driver needs to create direct access to the underlying hardware to retrieve some key information like battery status, power-off, shutdown, etc.

Figure 6-5 illustrates the modified coreboot boot flow using the LITE firmware development model.

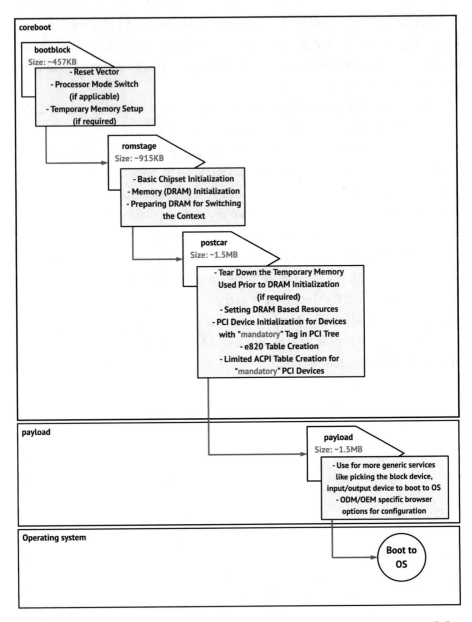

Figure 6-5. *coreboot boot flow with adapted LITE firmware model*

Figure 6-5 shows how this LITE model benefits the open source system firmware development approach. This approach to LITE system firmware development on coreboot could be applied to UEFI firmware development as well. In the case of UEFI, it would reduce the DXE stage by keeping only the required DXE modules to boot to the BDS stage.

Conclusion

- A reduction of ramstage (in coreboot) eventually reduces the code by 50 percent.

- Improved boot performance is able to reduce the boot time by an additional ~500ms.

- This effort might help the OEM/ODM to reduce the SPI Flash size and eventually optimize the platform bill of material cost.

- Given that operating systems are more sophisticated and feature-rich, this approach of moving more of the traditional firmware flows into the OS kernel will provide a more balanced approach long term.

- From a platform engineering team perspective, there will be very minimal firmware support required if this proposal is implemented successfully. There is a good amount of resource savings.

- People do not have to learn a specific boot state machine/PCI enumeration process/payload or complex protocol/services-oriented firmware development tricks. Instead, they can focus on the early kernel boot process.

Designing a Feature Kernel

The payload is an additional firmware entity used in system firmware to boot to the operating system. Boot firmware can be used with various payloads to provide a complete system firmware solution where ideally a payload's job is to find the required boot services like console input, console output, and block device or network device to boot to the OS. In addition, there could be some ODM/OEM-specific customization like a pre-boot environment to launch an application to certify the bootloader or diagnose the underlying hardware.

But the problem is that all payloads are different in nature from each other, and they have their own expectations from the boot firmware. Hence, there is no unification possible to boot to the operating system, although the targeted OS might be the same in all these cases.

Having a different payload for the same boot firmware creates various problems while developing system firmware:

- The underlying boot firmware needs to provide various interfaces as expected by different payloads, resulting in interfaces that are unused without any consumer of any service on the payloader side, resulting in higher development and validation time.

- The storage device is required to boot the OS from firmware therefore, the payload is likely to have such hardware support. For example: next generation block device support like UFS and NVME been added recently. Often this support is backported from the equivalent upstream kernel driver into the more limited firmware environment.

- There is a need to custom hardware initialization flows in the payload prior to the OS due to the lack of full OS system services and features. For example, the payload requires a boot beep for error reporting in case of faulty hardware. To implement the requirement either a dedicated hardware circuit or an audio driver in payload is required to generate an audio tone.

- The maintenance of the payload infrastructure is also difficult due to limited open source community support.

- The typical payload size is from 1.5MB (compressed) to about 6MB, which is eventually sitting in SPINOR and will result in additional BoM cost.

Figure 6-6 provides the overview of modern system firmware with different payloads, booting to the OS.

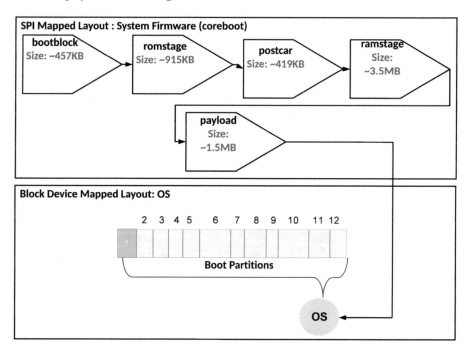

Figure 6-6. *coreboot boot flow in a current scenario*

Look at the "Boot Partitions" block 1, highlighted in Figure 6-6: it is the initial kernel block, typically sized about 4MB. During the platform boot, the payload tries to locate the initial kernel block from the boot media (NVME, eMMC, SATA, UFS, etc.) and then verifies it prior to loading it into the main memory. The initial kernel block is then run over memory to perform the root file system mount, followed by the boot kernel picking up the runtime kernel block to complete the boot sequence.

Design Principle

The idea of a "feature kernel" is to avoid having a dedicated payload attached to the BIOS to boot to the OS and possibly simplify the system firmware boot flow by using the LITE firmware model plus the feature kernel to further reduce the firmware boundary and improve the system booting time.

Figure 6-7 illustrates the proposed "feature kernel" boot flow with an open source firmware model, where the initial kernel block (about 4MB) would be part of SPI Flash, and the bootloader would load the boot kernel from SPINOR and run over the memory to perform the root filesystem mount, followed by the boot kernel to pick the runtime kernel from the bootable media. In that process, the payload dependencies can be removed as well.

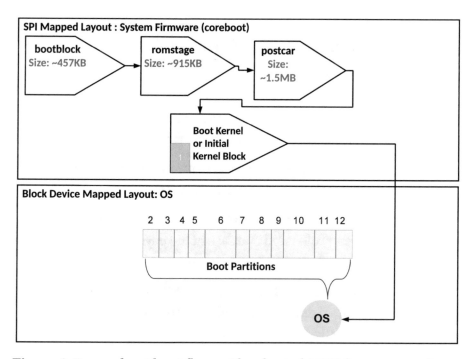

Figure 6-7. *coreboot boot flow with adapted LITE firmware and feature kernel*

Conclusion

The key benefits of this idea are as follows:

- In the past, the system firmware booting from SPINOR was considered as the Trusted Computing Boundary (TCB) and the OS partitions stored into block devices were always outside of this computing boundary. But this approach would bring the kernel within TCB, which means

    - The firmware update implementation using the power of the boot kernel could be more efficient than ever in this model.

- It is more scalable for future usages (i.e., support for advance boot devices/specs is native).

- There is no need to create a special hardware interface or driver support in the payload/ bootloader to bypass the audio codec to implement special solutions like boot beep, etc.

- There is a reduction in system firmware complexity to create dedicated interfaces for various payloads.

- We can avoid the additional porting effort of any new controller and interface in the payload from the kernel as and when required.

- There is a possible reduction of SPINOR size and dedicated development effort to create support for a newer SoC in the payload.

Design Multithreaded System Firmware

In the modern-day world, where usage of IoT devices (like automotive and navigation devices and home appliance devices) and client devices are rapidly increasing, performance is key. Users are expecting to see the device operational as soon as they press the power button or hold the device.

The increase in the complexity of compute, software updates, and the I/O subsystem has created new challenges to meet customer expectations, such as a better user experience with a faster boot to the OS, providing an instant-on experience.

As part of the enhanced user experience (UX), many applications using advanced computer systems now demand an instant system bootup time. A faster system response time is a key performance indicator (KPI) used by OEMs/ODMs for their product requirements for almost all computing sectors today, such as personal devices like modern smartphone/tablet/ laptop, healthcare equipment (ultrasound, defibrillators, and patient monitor devices), industrial devices (robots change arms) and MAG systems (firing a missile, fail-safe redundancy on airplanes, or similar single function devices), and office/home automation devices.

Figure 6-8 shows the typical client platform (x86 architecture based) boot path where the entire boot process is in sequential order. The average system boot time is expected to be less than 500ms from the G3 system state (no power applied) until the operating system (OS) hand-off, which includes the pre-power (All rails and clock stabilization), prereset (power sequencing), and post CPU reset (boot firmware and payload) boot path components. But in reality the system boot time is way beyond 500ms today (average ~2sec).

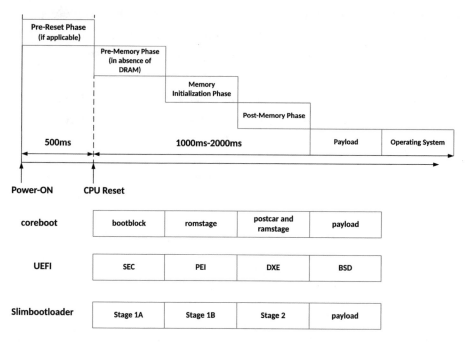

Figure 6-8. *Typical x86 based client platform reset flow with all BIOS*

It is important to note that the most time-consuming phase of the total boot path is the execution of the system firmware as mentioned in Figure 6-8, hence making it a critical phase to optimize to provide a fast boot experience.

Another point to consider is that an increased number of I/O subsystems attached to the motherboard, and every subsystem having its own device firmware, poses increasing challenges for product manufacturers to ensure periodic firmware updates with an instant system power-on experience.

Figure 6-9 shows a typical OEM platform design that more than 15 independent IP/device FW updates take place when the OS initiates the FW update. As the FW update takes place during the boot path where the entire boot process is in a sequential order, it's impossible to meet the expectation that the system firmware would be able to complete all device (SoC and Platform) firmware updates (measuring FW components, verifying FW components, loading FW into device, reading firmware version back to ensure successful FW update) within the regular time window, which is expected to be less than 500ms to 1sec from the G3 system state (no power applied) to the operating system (OS), hands off.

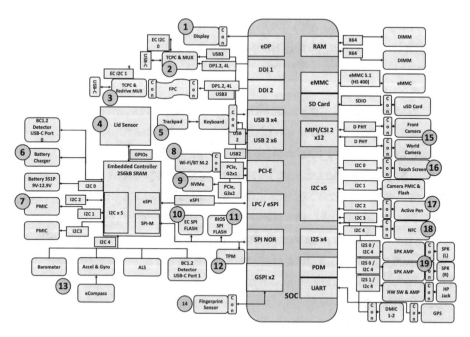

Figure 6-9. *Typical OEM client platform design with possible firmware update requirement*

As the entire BIOS boot takes place in a single-threaded environment, running only over the Boot Strap Processor (BSP) (even after multicores are available typically at ~650ms since CPU reset), it results in an indolent wait time on the BIOS side. Eventually this results in discrete and serial platform initialization where each independent IP/device initialization/ update is waiting for its execution time or turn. This entire process makes the platform slower while operating firmware updates and creates a bad user experience. Subsequently, this makes users afraid of accepting firmware updates, meaning the users will push out firmware updates without knowing the criticality of the update that might potentially fix some platform security issues.

Another use case is Windows 10X where the OS is moving to an AB servicing model and the operating system will update itself while running (i.e., while running OS version A, it will provision a new version B), versus today's scenario with the blue screen and percent countdown. Microsoft is now constraining the preboot time for doing BIOS/capsule updates, so having a speedier reboot is necessary to meet these emergent UX requirements.

All device manufacturers are looking toward an instant platform boot, without bothering whether the platform has mundane or bulky devices attached to it, whether the boot process is going through a firmware update initiated by the OS, etc. But the legacy boot process always runs in a single core, irrespective of modern-day CPUs being multicore processors in nature, where two or more cores are capable of running in parallel to execute tasks. This in turn forces the firmware code to run sequentially, leading to a slower boot time and ineffective usage of processor power and system resources to initiate SoC components, and/or platform devices update/initialization process, and thereby resulting in a higher platform boot time and ultimately a bad user experience.

Design Principles

The proposal is to enhance the boot process by adding concurrency to it by isolating boot functions and platform configurations, which will be executed with the boot firmware as the context master. Additionally, the method proposes configuring the platform components with additional cores for running concurrent processes. Finally, this method will also be applied in the process of firmware updates during the boot phase.

This section will explain the necessary changes in system firmware flow to create a multithreaded system firmware boot solution that overcomes the limitations mentioned in the previous sections.

Multithreading is the ability of a CPU to execute multiple processes concurrently. In the multicore platform, it is the responsibility of the BSP to perform multiprocessor initialization to bring application processors (APs) out from reset. In a multiprocessor (MP) environment, each processor can perform independent execution of assigned tasks.

The design principle is to provide an option to ensure a multithreaded environment where the BIOS can perform its tasks concurrently. To design a multicore environment, there might be some potential hardware or CPU/SoC architecture changes also required; the details can be found in the section "Innovation in Hardware Design."

The assumption is that the platform has made some hardware changes to support this system firmware design change proposal.

- This method decouples unidirectional communication flow in the boot firmware to allow independent BIOS tasks to perform over parallel threads.

- This method provides options for boot firmware to execute its tasks in a parallel thread-safe mechanism (without worrying about core synchronization between multiple firmware back-and-forth calls).

- This method provides flexibility to perform multiprocessor initialization early in the boot flow to maximize CPU resource utilization by the BIOS.

- The hardware design change proposal provides significantly larger temporary memory at the prememory phase in terms of the SRAM or LLC cache to execute independent tasks over dedicated cores in parallel in absence of physical memory or prior to DRAM initialization.

- This method implements a high-level synchronization construct as a "monitor" type inside system firmware to ensure tasks are getting performed in multiple cores and remain in sync to avoid any duplicate access. The "monitor" construct ensures that only one processor at a time can be given access to a task.

- Using the MONITOR/MWAIT instruction inside system firmware reduces latency between the core operations and wake time from idle.

- Use a semaphore to access potential shared resources inside the bootloader in normal mode.

Figure 6-10 illustrates the modified firmware boot flow of a system to leverage the new design proposal.

In the existing design, no tasks are getting executed over cores other than the BSP, although Aps are available and active later in the boot flow. In this proposed model, the BIOS is designed to work in a multithreaded environment, where all possible cores are available and active right at the reset break or within a very short time after reset.

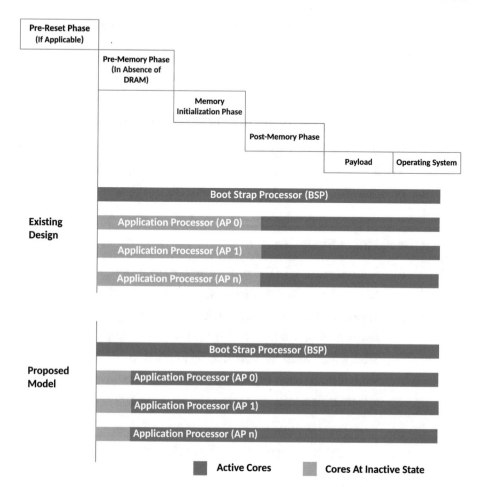

Figure 6-10. *Existing versus proposed system firmware flow with multicore environment*

To run multiple operations concurrently using the available hardware and CPU capacity, first the system firmware needs to split all the possible tasks required to boot to the OS into multiple subtasks and assign them over multiple cores to run in parallel. Hence, it needs a semaphore for providing a convenient and effective mechanism for core synchronization.

Here are the design principles to build this multithreaded system firmware logic:

- Implement monitor/mwait logic inside the system firmware to avoid idle time while resting the core, upon completion of a task and prior to assigning a new task.

- A single task is attempted by a single core at a time, and a task is assigned to the core if both the task and the core are available and free, respectively.

- To implement this solution, some data variables are needed, as shown here:

  a. *Shared region*: In the multicore environment, to avoid synchronization issues, a shared data region is needed where the interprocessor communication (IPC) variables will be stored. Task state variables will also be located in such shared data regions for allowing core synchronization.

  b. *Task state variable*: A "task" and "state" data structure is created with "n" number of planned tasks in it.

     i. Each task has its state tag to notify it if a task is waiting for the actual core to get assigned, if the task is in progress, or if the task is completed.

  c. *Initialization code*: Prior to entering into the critical region where each core will perform the independent hardware controller initialization task, the initialization code assigns all those tasks to its default state.

d. *Scheduler*: Create a scheduler inside the system firmware to assign the waiting tasks to the available cores, where "mwait" initially treated as "nop" and "monitor" would assign the next task instruction and immediately change the task state to "in progress." Once a core is done with its assigned task, it will mark the task state as "done" and wait an "mwait" for the next available task assignment.

   i. Respective cores would execute those assigned tasks and update the shared data variable. This step continues until all tasks are migrated to "done" states.

e. *Task assignment*: The idea here is to perform only the independent boot tasks to perform over a multithreaded environment, whereas the BSP would still continue to perform the typical hardware controller interdependent tasks.

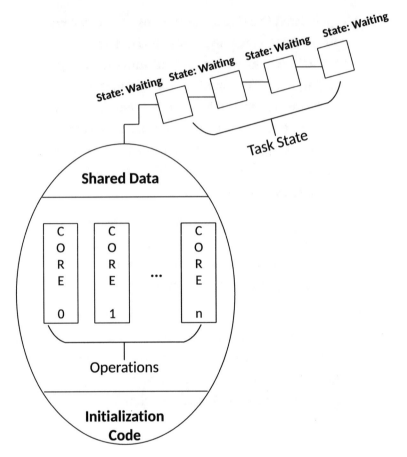

Figure 6-11. *Schematic view of a monitor*

- Prior to booting to the payload or operating system, all the available cores would need to reach a synchronization point, where the BSP would monitor the shared data region to check the state of the assigned tasks and the current condition of the cores. Ideally, all the tasks should get tagged with "done," and all the available cores should park into the "mwait" state and remain in active state.

The book *System Firmware: An Essential Guide to Open Source and Embedded Solutions* demonstrates a case study done on an x86 platform using this multithreaded system firmware design principle to perform the dynamic optimization of the system boot time without any additional hardware modification.

Conclusion

The following are the key benefits of this idea:

- This innovation helps to nullify legacy system firmware assumptions of a serialized boot or even static multithread boot to optimize the boot time. Rather, this method proposes an opportunistic platform boot by predicting when to initiate a multithreaded boot to optimize the boot time.

- This proposed solution might be useful for running the entire system firmware update shown in Figures 6-9 and 6-10 using all the available core's capacity. This will significantly improve the firmware update latency problems and ensure that the system never goes out of service.

- A proof-of-concept trial of informed multicore boot has been produced. It demonstrates the boot performance savings compared to the normal firmware boot method. (refer to the book *System Firmware: An Essential Guide to Open Source and Embedded Solutions* for more details)

Innovation in Hardware Design

Today system firmware is more complicated because of the underlying SoC and/or hardware design. Ideally the system firmware should just be responsible for performing the basic CPU and chipset initialization and then handing over control to the operating system. But because of several factors, like not having enough memory to access hardware resources early in the boot process and the need to set up temporary memory to continue the hardware access, such cyclic dependency in hardware design limits the innovation in firmware and tries to make the system firmware act like legacy firmware.

This section discusses such possible hardware limitations in the existing CPU and platform design and identifies the possible solution to design a simplified version of the system firmware to either reduce the boot boundary or optimize the platform BoM cost with a more complex hardware design.

Refer to Figure 6-12 to understand that the existing system firmware boot flow on any architecture has a significant dependency on the physical memory available during the early boot phase.

Take for example the x86 platform, where the legacy CPU design or the modern SoC design doesn't have a dedicated pre-initialization memory controller such as static RAM (SRAM), which is available in other CPU architectures like ARM. But as per the system firmware design, it needs memory after reset to perform chipset initialization using advanced firmware programming logic, which needs a basic programming infrastructure like a stack, heap, and functions to make the firmware development more modular. Rather, on the x86 platform, to mitigate the problem of not having ample memory at reset, the SoC architecture proposes using a shared cache between the various underlying hardware blocks inside CPU/SoC, as per Figure 6-12.

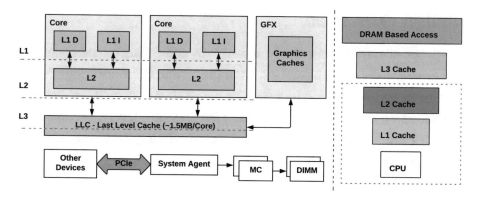

Figure 6-12. *Cache architecture on x86 architecture*

Because LLC is bigger in size than other available caches, it should be used in the absence of real physical memory or SRAM on x86 platforms. The process of cache being used as temporary memory is known as *cache as RAM* (CAR). This has its own complexity with several model-specific registers (MSR) that need to be programmed. Also, this programming recommendation might evolve generation after generation due to improved the cache architecture. Because CAR or temporary memory is quite limited, the entire chipset initialization can't really rely on this memory; rather, this limited memory is being served as the minimum memory required to set up the stack and initial programming requirement, until the time physical memory is initialized. Typically in the system firmware boot process on the x86 platform, early stages like bootblock and romstage in coreboot, SEC and PEI phases in UEFI, Stage 1A and Stage 1B in Slim Bootloader, are just for the preparatory work being done to mitigate the design limitation. Eventually this limitation also results in delaying the initialization of the security controller that is sitting deep into the SoC/ CPU hardware layer and unable to communicate with the host CPU in the absence of a good amount of physical memory.

Design Principles

The proposal is to create a platform design by combining the hardware and firmware-centric innovations. A simple system firmware design has a bottleneck on the platform hardware design. This section will highlight a futuristic system firmware design where the firmware-level complexities are being nullified by the hardware design to make a system firmware that is more generic, simpler, and robust.

Hardware Design Principles

Ideally, having a simplified SoC design will also reflect the simple system firmware design, without added complexity and so much preparatory work needed to perform basic chipset initialization even using the LITE firmware design principle.

This section will provide several hardware modification proposals for a simplified boot process.

Scenario 1:

Figure 6-13 provides a SoC design with an on-chip SRAM controller and reasonable numbers of SRAM attached for initializing CPU and I/O components and allocating resources without really depending on the DRAM initialization sequence.

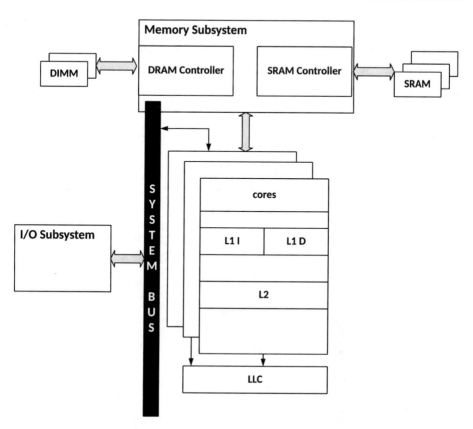

Figure 6-13. *Proposed SoC design with on-chip SRAM*

These kinds of SoC designs are costly compared to a DRAM-based hardware design, and at the same time the available SRAM memory is supposed to be limited. On a typical x86-based client and IoT platform, to complete the entire static device initialization (without off-board graphics or a network card), the system firmware requires about 32MB of memory, which is possible to accommodate using such hardware design. SRAM has a lower access time, so it's faster compared to DRAM; hence, it's efficient to meet the low-level access latency requirement on the boot firmware.

Scenario 2

Figure 6-14 provides an alternative proposal, where there is no need to increase the BoM cost by introducing SRAM like costly and dedicated hardware components into the SoC design, instead utilizing the existing SoC design and providing an additional interface to access the DRAM controller by an auxiliary processor sitting in the SoC.

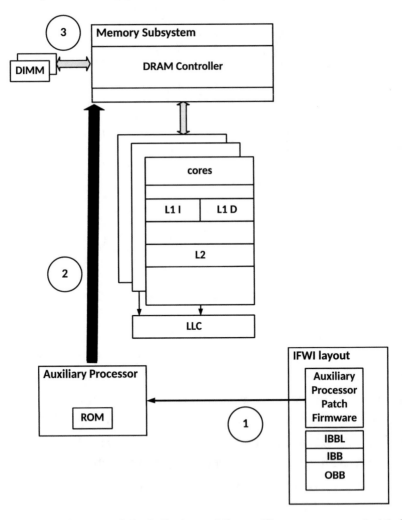

Figure 6-14. *Proposed SoC design with auxiliary processor initialize DRAM at prereset*

The auxiliary processor at the prereset stage would utilize its boot ROM to perform self-initialization and fetch the auxiliary patch firmware from the IFWI layout (present inside the SPINOR or block device) to initialize the DRAM controller and train the memory prior to the x86 cores hitting reset. After the CPU reset, the system firmware running on the host CPU won't necessarily perform that temporary memory setup; rather, it's able to perform flat access to physical memory.

Firmware Design Principle

The proposed hardware design changes described earlier in scenarios 1 and 2 would help to simplify the job of system firmware and also help to nullify the legacy requirement where the system firmware has to perform a few additional steps just to mitigate the problems described.

The following sections will provide the modified system firmware design to accommodate either of the hardware change proposals.

Figure 6-15 provides a high-level boot flow of the system firmware where either SRAM is available or an auxiliary processor like PSP in the AMD SoC reset architecture can be used to perform memory controller initialization.

1. Upon powering on the system, the auxiliary processor present inside the SoC will start execution immediately from its ROM. This is followed by fetching the updatable patch from the IFWI layout. The reason for having such an updatable patch into IFWI is so that it's easy to provide bug fixes if required and send new patches over firmware updates during system use in the field.

2. The auxiliary processor patch firmware has the required foundation code to initialize the DRAM memory controller and train the memory device.

3.   After DRAM controller initialization, memory is
     available at pre-CPU reset. The auxiliary processor
     will pass the available memory base and limit to
     the bootloader. Upon CPU release, the bootloader
     will use that memory range to create the system
     memory layout.

4.   At CPU reset, it breaks those legacy assumptions
     about x86 boot flow where the setting of temporary
     memory is no longer required. Hence, several boot
     phases can be removed with these assumptions:

     a. *On the coreboot side*: There is no need to have a
         dedicated bootblock, romstage, and postcar because
         all these stages are just meant to do the preparatory
         work prior to or during DRAM initialization.

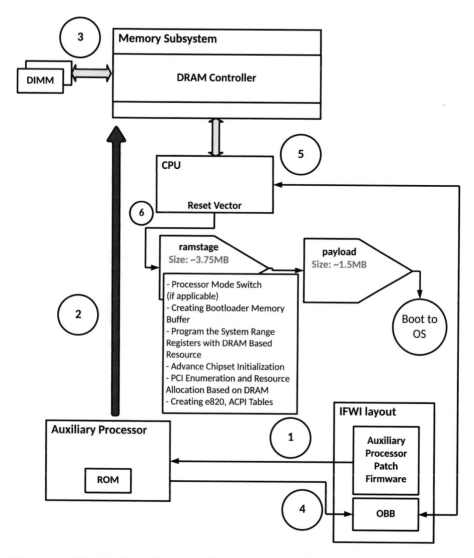

Figure 6-15. *Reduced system firmware boot flow with pre-initialized DRAM at reset*

b. *On the UEFI side*: The SEC and PEI phases can be eliminated as memory can be default initialized. All the necessary pre-work can be done in the DXE phase directly.

With memory available at reset, the reset vector can now be patched at DRAM mapped memory, rather than SPI mapped memory. The auxiliary processor loads the OBB image from SPINOR into DRAM prior to hitting CPU reset. The system firmware will start executing the code from the ramstage in coreboot (as per Figure 6-15) or DXE (as per Figure 6-16).

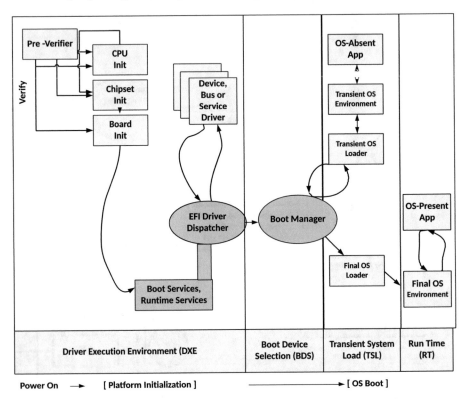

Figure 6-16. *Reduced UEFI boot flow with pre-initialized DRAM at reset*

5.   This process will help to reduce the firmware
     boundary, and the system firmware is now
     responsible for doing only the recommended
     chipset and CPU initialization. The BIOS will create
     its own system memory map as shown Figure 6-17
     and break the barrier between different boot stages
     with the only goal to perform the minimum and
     mandatory operations to boot to payload.

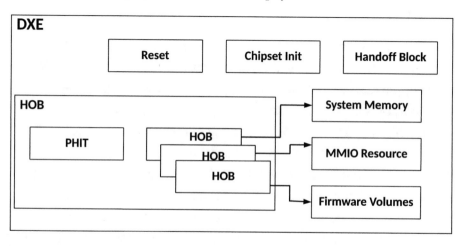

Figure 6-17. *UEFI DXE being the first stage after CPU reset*

Conclusion

The key benefits in this idea are as follows:

- Provide flexibility in system firmware design and don't
  really focus on implementing all the boot phases.

- Reduce the system firmware boundary by one-third,
  which eventually results in high optimization of system
  boot time and reduction of the SPINOR footprint.

- Having an auxiliary processor doing DRAM initialization prior to CPU reset and copying the OBB BIOS region into DRAM would provide a better opportunity to enforce the hardware assistant security rather than building security blocks using the system firmware.

Summary

This chapter provided an overview of the futuristic aspects of system firmware. It also explained several examples of its possible usages and all the opportunities to design better system firmware considering simplicity, performance, security, and open source philosophy. After reading this chapter, you should have a general understanding of the uniqueness of system firmware and hardware design. The idea here is to make sure you understand where the industry might be heading in the future. System firmware design in the future might expect to have such requirements as a minimum for any boot firmware working on any SoC/CPU architecture. The common traits across all these application examples of future system firmware design is the need for instant platform boot with reduced functionality and effective use of system resources without any additional cost of platform hardware. This chapter may also be useful to break the assumption about any BIOS or system firmware design where application engineers or designers might consider all the boot phases to be mandatory, rather to make it clear that those stages are flexible. Firmware designers could choose to pick the correct boot flow as per their platform design and hardware needs, to do meaningful and minimum tasks in the system firmware design to make life simple during the product development life cycle and after-life support as well.

Correction to: Firmware Development

Correction to:

Subrata Banik and Vincent Zimmer, Firmware Development,
https://doi.org/10.1007/978-1-4842-7974-8

In page 5 of Chapter 1, the content "x26" was published inadvertently, which has now been updated as "x86".

In page 173 of Chapter 2, the content "FlashTom" was published inadvertently, which has now been updated as "Flashrom".

The updated original version of these chapter can be found at
https://doi.org/10.1007/978-1-4842-7974-8_1
https://doi.org/10.1007/978-1-4842-7974-8_2

APPENDIX A

The Evolution of System Programming Languages

A system programming language is a programming language that is used to create system software. In the context of this book, we will refer to this type of language while developing firmware. Firmware development requires you to understand the underlying hardware and CPU architecture. Firmware development techniques should focus on the optimal usage of system resources while performing critical operations such as using memory or system power.

Here are some characteristics of system programming languages:

- System programming languages have a great deal of knowledge about the underlying CPU architecture. It is intended to create a machine-level language that will execute on the target hardware.

- The programming languages created by a system programming language can operate in a memory-constrained manner.

- A system programming language can directly use the system memory, CPU registers, and I/O components without any access restriction.

- In a firmware development project, more than one type of system programming language may be used. For example, a coreboot project is a combination of C, C++, assembly language, ASL, etc.

- Typically, these system programming languages are intended to create their own libraries that allow access to different hardware components such as input/ output and even to specific CPU architecture.

This appendix will walk you through the journey of system programming language where applicable to system firmware development. It will underline the need for a modernized approach in the future.

The History of System Programming Languages

Originally, system firmware was developed using assembly language. Assembly language is used for one-to-one resemblance of the mnemonics and machine language. The mnemonics are specific to CPU architecture; hence, assembly language needs another system program, named Assembler, to translate the assembly language statements into the machine language as per the target CPU architecture.

Assembly language was first developed in the 1950s. It eliminated the need for programmers to use a first-generation programming language and remember numeric codes and how to calculate addresses. Here are some advantages of assembly languages:

- Typically, the majority of CPUs are powered on with a memory-constrained environment; hence, running early programming using an assembly language doesn't require any specific infrastructure like other high-level system programming language demands. For example, running a C program makes use of the stack, which is set by the low-level assembly program.

- Assembly language, being a lower-level programming language, allows direct access to the hardware depending on the nature of the operations.

By the 1970s, assembly language was starting to be replaced with the evolution of high-level system programming languages that reduced the need for handwritten assembly codes with compiler-generated code. The knowledge of low-level hardware instructions no longer was essential as the high-level programming language introduced an abstraction that could remove the barrier of writing CPU architecture-specific code while performing an operation. For example, writing memcpy is much simpler in a high-level system programming language rather than implementing it in assembly.

Today, the scope of assembly language is limited only to early bootblock code that was intended to set the infrastructure to high-level programming execution or to execute specific processor instructions.

Although the scope of assembly language is limited in modern firmware projects, there are enormous benefits of understanding assembly language. In fact, it can be useful to understand any CPU architecture such as its register sets, memory and I/O operational model, specific CPU features, etc. Most high-level languages also provide an option to include assembly programming to perform some operations that are not possible without using inline assembly.

System Programming Languages Today

The most widely used modern system programming language, C, has been used for firmware development for the last 30 years. In parallel to the early development of the Unix operating system, the journey of C started in the years 1969–1973 by Dennis M. Ritchie. It was derived from the typeless language BCPL (grandparent) and the language B (parent), and it evolved as a type-based structural programming language that is suitable for both system software and application software. With *compilers* becoming available on every machine architecture, it omits the need for writing assembly code and generating efficient object programs. Therefore, C became a popular programming language for personal computers.

Finally, in the 1980s, the language was officially standardized by the ANSI X3J11 committee. Since the early 1980s, its use has spread much more widely so that it is clearly efficient enough to replace assembly language, sufficient enough to abstract the hardware as a high-level language, and provides specific implementation to access hardware like any low-level language. Undoubtedly, Unix's use of C was important for its success.

Here are some unique features of C that make it popular today:

- C remains a simple and small language, translatable with simple and small compilers.

- The language is sufficiently abstract from the machine details; hence, a program that is written for one architecture can be easily migrated with minimal changes in the tools.

- C provides a lot of built-in functions as part of the central library.

- It supports the feature of dynamic memory allocation where a program is able to allocate or free the previously allocated memory.

- Perhaps the most significant feature of C is pointers. It can directly interact with the memory by using pointers.

Table A-1 provides the steps for C program execution. For easy understanding, a programmer can remember the mnemonic *EPCALL*.

Table A-1. *C Program Execution*

Execution Step	Details
Editor	The programmer writes the source code using an integrated development environment (IDE), and the entire execution flow starts to ensure the written program can generate a binary that is loaded into memory for execution.
Preprocessor	The preprocessor is responsible for converting preprocessor directives to create an expanded source code.
Compilation	The expanded source code is sent to compiler, which converts the source code into the assembly code.
Assembler	The assembler is responsible for converting the assembly code into machine language. This is typically referred to as *object code* (.obj files).
Linker	The object code is sent to a linker, which links it to the included libraries. It converts it into executable code (.exe). Depending on the type of program, the executable format is converted into binary (.bin).
Loader	The loader is responsible for loading the executable code into memory, and then it gets executed. Based on the nature of the program, it accesses the system resources (either software or hardware).

Now let's take a look at the third step in the C execution flow, which is *compilation* (see Table A-2). This signifies why a programming language with the caliber of C was needed to replace assembly language from system programming. Table A-2 is a simple C program that performs the addition of two numbers. Attempts to write such a program in assembly language would need a specific low-level knowledge of instruction set architecture (ISA) across different CPU architectures. The introduction of C diminished the need for such handwritten assembly, and programmers can be less bothered about understanding such low-level machine architecture differences.

Table A-2. *C Program Compilation*

Code Written in C	x86 Assembler	ARM Assembler
```void main()```	```mov ax, a```	```mov r0, a```
```{```	```mov bx, b```	```mov r1, b```
``` int a = 10;```	```add ax, bx```	```add r2, r1, r0```
``` int b = 20;```	```mov c, ax```	```mov c, r2```
``` c = a + b;```		
```}```		

The Future of System Programming Languages

The 21st century hardware devices are more concerned about the safety and security of the platform and firmware being the closest entity of the hardware; it's important to ensure the system programming language that is being used for firmware development is *safe* enough. As per Common Vulnerabilities and Exposures (CVE) reports, in the last decade 70 percent of all security bugs being reported are due to memory safety issues. Tools and guidance are not able to prevent this class of vulnerabilities. At a recent conference, Microsoft and Chrome security experts acknowledged that the predominant system programming languages used by both companies are C and C++, which are *unsafe* languages in nature. An unsafe language allows full control to the developer to directly access any memory address using pointers and doesn't restrict or warn or alert developers when they are making basic memory management errors. Later, the attackers try to find those vulnerabilities and exploit them. Memory safety is a property of system programming languages that defines the mechanism for the firmware/software when dealing with memory access. It's basically a protection methodology maintained by the system programming language. Building the firmware/software (OS kernels, networking stack etc.), which allows easier access to the hardware using a memory-safe language, will help to mitigate such problems.

System programming languages are used in modern hardware, which was created several decades ago when security exploitation and attacks were not in consideration while developing system programs. The industry has started exploring other opportunities for low-level system program development using safe system programming languages. In the 2010s, Graydon Hoare at Mozilla Research designed a language called Rust for performance and safety, especially for safe concurrency. Since then it has gained use in the industry, and Microsoft has also started experimenting with it. As part of Project Verona, Microsoft's goal is to create a Rust-like safe system programming language that can help to create a safer platform for memory management.

The Rust programming language is designed for modern and future platforms where security and reliability are major concerns. It's a multimodel system programming language that provides the comfort of a high-level programming language and still is able to provide the low-level control. Here are some unique features of Rust that are the reasons behind its continuous popularity:

- *Memory safety*: Typically, being vulnerable to software bugs is caused due by coding errors such as buffer overflows, no provision for boundary checks, dangling pointers, etc. Tools like Coverity allow static memory analysis for C to ensure the program is free of memory errors. The Rust programming language implements a *borrow checker* for ensuring memory safety. It follows these principles:

- All variables are initiated before they are used.

- Movement of a variable value is not allowed while it is borrowed.

- When a variable goes out of scope, Rust automatically calls the drop function and cleans up the heap memory for that variable.

Table A-C is an example that shows both data pointers pointing to the same location using the C and Rust programming languages to highlight what the memory safety signifies and how Rust ensures safety at compile time rather than running into the undefined behavior error at runtime.

Table A-C. *Example*

Implementing Code in C

```
#include <stdio.h>

void main()
{
    char *src = "Hello";
    char *dst = src;

    printf("%s World!\n", src);
    printf("Writing %s World Program.\n", dst);
}
```

Output

```
Hello World!
Writing Hello World Program.
```

(*continued*)

Table A-C. (*continued*)

Implementing Code in Rust

```
1| fn main() {
2|     let src = String::from("Hello");
3|     let dst = src;
4|
5|     println!("{} World!", src);
6|     println!("Writing {} World Program", dst);
7| }
```

Output

```
error[E0382]: borrow of moved value: `src`
 --> main.rs:5:27
  |
2 |      let src = String::from("Hello");
5 |             --- move occurs because `src` has type
                    `std::string::String`, which does not
                    implement the `Copy` trait
3 |      let dst = src;
5 |                     --- value moved here
4 |
5 |      println!("{} World!", src);
5 |                                 ^^^ value borrowed
                                    here after move
error: aborting due to previous error

For more information about this error, try `rustc --explain E0382`.
```

- *Executable size*: Rust uses static linking to compile its programs, meaning all different types of libraries required by the Rust program will be compiled and be part of the executable. Typically, when a C executable runs, it actually makes a system call that transfers control to the operating systems to perform the required operation. For example, when the C executable wants to printf a message such as "Hello World!" it just makes the write system call to the standard output. But for the Rust programming language, it bundles all the required standard libraries so that it doesn't need to rely on OSs.

- *Better access to hardware registers*: Memory-mapped hardware registers are numerous in the firmware programming space, and unknowingly or unintentionally modifying a bit might be sufficient to change the behavior of the hardware. Hence, it's important to ensure that the compiler is able to detect any such scenarios where the given value is within the prescribed register boundary. Using a type-level programming to get more advanced checking on the memory-mapped register at compile time would help to make a safer system program.

- *Namespaces*: For any language, the names are the way to uniquely identify an entity and can be labels, variables, functions, etc. In Rust, a *namespace* is a logical grouping of declared names. It allows the occurrence of the same name in different namespaces without any conflict. For example, to maintain the semantics in function names in a system firmware project that involves cross-architectures, you need to maintain different techniques in the C programming language such as weak symbols and NULL pointer checks to ensure only one instance of the function call is getting included. Also, it's hard to debug and figure out which function is actually in use. In Rust, within a namespace, names are organized in a hierarchy, where each level of the hierarchy has its own name. The double colon (::) is an operator that is used to define the namespace. In Rust, calling `arch::halt()` is enough from the mainboard directory to resolve the symbol issues without any additional overhead.

The mainboard directory calls these functions:

```
src/mainboard/sifive/hifive/src/main.rs:154:    arch::halt()
src/mainboard/aaeon/upsquared/src/main.rs:39:    arch::halt()
```

The SoC directory implements the `halt()` function:

```
src/arch/riscv/rv32/src/lib.rs:9:pub fn halt() -> ! {
src/arch/x86/x86_64/src/lib.rs:13:pub fn halt() -> ! {
```

In the previous example, HiFive, a mainboard built around RISC-V SoC and upsquared, is a x86-based platform.

- *Replacement of the makefile*: A makefile is the set of instructions that you use to tell how to build your program. Typically, a handwritten makefile is too error-prone as you need to instruct the machine to include a set of files during compilation. Many high-level system programming languages are trying to remove the handwritten makefile dependency from programmers. In Rust, the `cargo-make` task runner is able to define and configure sets of tasks via `Cargo.toml` files and run them as a flow.

- *Hygienic macros*: For safe system programming, hygienic macros ensure there are no accidental captures of identifiers. Macros are getting preprocessed and expand the scope of the code prior passing the expanded source code to the compiler. A programming language embedded with a non-hygienic macro system has a problem where an existent variable may get hidden during the macro creation or even during its expansion, which finally would result in incorrect output. A system programming language that supports hygienic macros prevents macros from interfering with variables that are declared outside of the macro.

Demonstrate the Nonhygienic Macro Problem Using C

```
#include <stdio.h>
#define f(a,b) a*z

int main()
{
    int a = 2, b = 5, z = 3;
    printf("Multiplication Macro in `C` = %d\n", f(a, b));

    return 0;
}
```

Output:

```
Multiplication Macro in `C` = 6
```

In this example, after preprocessing the input variable, b is getting replaced by the local variable z, which results in unexpected output from this multiplication function.

Let's rerun the same multiplication operation in Rust that supports hygienic macros.

Demonstrate the Hygienic Macro Using Rust

```
macro_rules! f{
    ($a:expr,$b:expr)=>{
        {
            $a*$z
        }
    }
}
fn main() {
    let (a, b, z) = (2, 5, 3);
    println!("Multiplication Macro in Rust = {}", f!(a, b));
}
```

Output

```
error: expected expression, found `$`
  --> main.rs:12:16
   |
12 |            $a*$z
   |               ^^ expected expression
...
19 |     println!("Multiplication Macro in Rust = {}", f!(a, b));
   |                                           -------- in this macro invocation
   |
   = note: this error originates in the macro `f` (in Nightly
builds, run with -Z macro-backtrace for more info)

error: aborting due to previous error
```

The hygienic macro in Rust allows metaprogramming. Unlike macros in C languages, Rust macros are expanded into abstract syntax trees, rather than just string preprocessing, so programmers won't run into unexpected problems as illustrated earlier with the usage of nonhygienic macros.

In summary, a safe system programming language like Rust has the potential to perform low-level operations when needed with efficient access to the hardware register, has easy memory management, and also provides rich libraries that makes a programmer's job easier. In addition to platform security, another key area that all future firmware projects are continuously focusing on is system boot time. System boot time is critical, and there are several ways to reduce the boot time such as doing more operations in parallel even during the scope of system firmware. Today, performing parallel operations using C code might be a little risky due to its lack of memory safety techniques; otherwise, one of the key advantages of Rust as a system programming language for the future is its fearlessness during concurrency.

APPENDIX B

initramfs: A Call for Type-Safe Languages

Boot time is a *key performance indicator* (KPI) for modern computing devices, and development cost is an indispensable factor for calculating firmware development projects. Firmware is the first piece of the code that runs after a processor reset, and due to its privileged operation model, any exploits in the firmware are extremely difficult to detect. The majority of modern firmware development is based on the C system programming language, where the most skilled programmers even make simple mistakes that remain hidden from the compiler. These mistakes make firmware an ideal place for advanced persistent threats, and the system may become fatal to the attackers. To overcome these performance, development cost, and security issues in the firmware space over the past several years, the industry has started looking into the possibility of bringing the maturity of the Linux-like kernel (which is widely used and tested) to the proprietary firmware to establish trust in the computing system. Firmware projects have started accommodating embedded kernels as part of SPI Flash as a replacement for complex firmware drivers. This technique of embedding the kernels into the firmware's trusted computing boundary could help to improve boot time performance and allow platform configuration. Almost all new firmware stacks include a multiprocessing operating system with drivers, various protocol stacks, and a file system. Having an embedded

© Subrata Banik and Vincent Zimmer 2022
S. Banik and V. Zimmer, *Firmware Development*,
https://doi.org/10.1007/978-1-4842-7974-8

kernel is not enough, as it needs a root file system known as *initramfs* (which stands for "initial RAM file system"). initramfs is a root file system that is embedded into the kernel, and when the kernel starts, it checks for the presence of initramfs. If it's available then the kernel sets up a RAM file system and extracts initramfs into the RAM file system, so that the kernel can execute '/init'. The init program is typically a script-based implementation such as Perl Linux. In most cases, the kernel SPI Flash is used to boot to another kernel from the bootable media. These embedded root file systems contain a set of standard Unix-style programs written in C. Over a period of time, there have been several successful attacks against the C-based firmware, such as a buffer overflow issue named GHOST (GetHOST) in 2015 and a stack buffer overflow vulnerability allowed the remote attackers to induce a denial of service (crash). The more details can be found in the CVE-2021-3382 vulnerability report.

U-root is an embeddable root file system that is packed as an LZMA-compressed initramfs in cpio format, contained in a Linux compressed kernel image (bzImage), and placed in an SPI Flash device as part of the payload for a boot firmware image. The goal of u-root as a root file system is to provide minimal binary support, unlike most root file systems, which embed only binaries. Typically, u-root has only five essential programs: an init program (that contains minimal lines of code) and four Go-compiled binaries. The rest of the root file system contains the source, which can be compiled on demand as libraries and a set of u-root source files for basic commands. Currently, u-root packed into the firmware space is no longer a support source to binary generation. All these u-root utilities correspond to standard Unix utilities and are written in the Go language.

Go (often referred to as Golang) is a programming language created in 2009 by Google. Go is a modern programming language that provides memory safety, garbage collection, type-safe support, concurrency features, and interprocess communication. Here are some of the key benefits of the Go programming language:

- *Fast*: Go is a compiled language, which means it needs a compiler that converts the written code into a machine-level language. Brad Fitzpatrick highlighted at the GoCon conference in 2014 that Go in terms of performance is still comparable with the C language (although C is most efficient) but easier for developers to learn. Go, being a modern programming language, can utilize the multiprocessing nature of the modern computing system, which makes it performance efficient compared to the others, easy to learn, and more user friendly. Go manages to maintain a unique position because of its fast operation and easy-to-learn nature.

- *Concurrency*: Modern computing systems demand parallelized operations, and the Go language has built-in concurrency features. Go offers a light-weight process that has been implemented using a native goroutine; a function call prefixed with the go keyword starts a function in a new goroutine. Implementing multithreading with other languages like C is not that straightforward. For example, coreboot (built using the C programming language) has been unable to meet the expectation of concurrency for several decades.

- *Garbage collection*: Go has a strong commitment to garbage collection, and different Go releases have tried to improve the garbage collector logic.

- *Mixed language*: The Go language blurs the line between a high-level and low-level language; it is a high-level language, but it can be used to perform operations as a low-level programming language as needed. Having such a type-safe, high-level language that can be used for low-level embedded firmware might make the firmware security stronger than the user programs because an efficient static compiler might nullify all possible firmware-level exploits.

- *Open source*: Go is an open source programming language that makes it easy to build reliable and efficient software. Developers can get many useful libraries readily available at `https://golang.org/pkg/` for use.

In response to increasing security concerns on embedded devices, u-root was developed using the Go language, a modern language that provides memory safety, that was developed with minimal binaries and that delivers fast operations (the response time is about a millisecond while compiling the source to binary). The initial layout of a u-root file system is described as follows: the `/src` directory contains a set of u-root source files for basic commands such as `cat`, `cmp`, `date`, etc. The `/go/bin` directory is for any Go tools built after boot; the `/go/src/` for source package and toolchains is needed for these programs; the `/go/pkg/tool/` directory contains binaries for supporting the target OS and architecture, and one *init* binary. When a Linux kernel starts, it locates initramfs, sets up a RAM file system, and extracts initramfs into the RAM file system. Finally, the kernel starts the `/init` process, and the `init` binary as part of u-root sets up some basic directories, symlinks, and files and builds a command installer. u-root can create an initramfs file system in two different modes.

- *Busybox mode*: One busybox-like binary comprises all the Go tools that users are asked to include. In this mode, u-root copies and rewrites the source of the tools that the user was asked to include to be able to compile everything into one busybox-like binary. This is the only supported mode for the firmware.

- *Binary mode*: Each specified binary is compiled separately, and all binaries are added to initramfs.

u-root is the initramfs file system for the LinuxBoot project. The user can then boot to the kernel using kexec from a block device or over a network. u-root contains boot policy tools, also written in the Go language that supports fbnetboot and localboot.

The benefits of the Go language are that it is simple, fast, secure, type-safe, and concurrent. Additionally, when developing initramfs using u-root over traditional scripts, compared to a fixed set of commands being available, this approach of having source code as part of a binary while doing a firmware project provides more flexibility to create new commands using on-demand compilation. Further, init could build a special shell at boot time that pulls in built-ins to extend the shell without modifying the whole binary.

Glossary

ACPI   Advanced Configuration and Power Interface

AHB   Advanced High-performance Bus

AMBA   Advanced Microcontroller Bus Architecture

APB   AMBA Advanced Peripheral Bus

APCB   AMD PSP Control Block

AXI-AP   AMBA AXI Access Port

BBS   BIOS Boot Specification

BCT   Binary Configuration Tool

Blobs   Binary Large Objects

BMC   Baseboard Management Controller

BSP   BootStrap Processor

CBI   CrOS Board Info

CCD   Closed Case Debug

CoC   Code of Conduct

CodeXL   A comprehensive tool suite used on AMD-based platforms to access the CPU, GPU, and APUs with a single program

CPU   Central Processing Unit

CrOS   Chrome/Chromium OS

CSP   Cloud Service Providers

© Subrata Banik and Vincent Zimmer 2022
S. Banik and V. Zimmer, *Firmware Development*,
https://doi.org/10.1007/978-1-4842-7974-8

DCI	Intel Direct Connect Interface
DTB	Device Tree Blob
DTC	Device Tree Compiler
DTFS	Device Tree File System
EC	Embedded Controller
EDKII	A modern, feature-rich, cross-platform firmware development environment for the UEFI and UEFI Platform Initialization (PI) specifications
ELF	Executable and Linking Format
FD	Firmware Device
FRU	Field Replaceable Unit
FSP	Firmware Support Package; a specification designed with a standard API interface to perform silicon initialization and provide information to the boot firmware
FV	Firmware Volume
GCC	GNU Compiler Collection
GDB	GNU Debugger
GDT	Global Descriptor Table
Gerrit	A code review and project management tool for Git-based projects
Git	An open source version control system
GitHub	A web-based version control repository hosting service for Git
GOP	Graphics Output Protocol
HII	Human Interface Infrastructure

ICMB	Intelligent Chassis Management Bus; provides a standardized interface for connecting satellite controllers and/or BMC in another chassis
IDE	An integrated development environment used for software development
IFR	Internal Forms Representation
IPMI	Intelligent Platform Management Interface
JTAG	Joint Test Action Group, an industry standard for verifying the hardware design
KVM	Keyboard-Video-Mouse
MP	Multi-Processor
MTRR	Memory Type Range Register
OpenTitan	An open source project for building a transparent, high-quality reference design and integration guidelines for creating silicon root of trust (RoT) chips
OpROM	Option ROM
OS	Operating System
PEI	Pre-EFI Initialization
PI	Platform Initialization
PIC	Position Independent Code
PPI	PEIM to PEIM Interface

Rings	Used to define the criticality or privilege level that different system components use to operate on the host system; On IA architecture Ring 0 is considered the most privileged operation and typically the kernel is operating in that ring, whereas on the ARM platform, Ring 3 is considered the most secure and involves running secured firmware from SoC vendors, Secure Monitor, and Trusted ROM firmware
RunBMC	A smarter, simpler, open approach to out-of-band management for servers
Rust	A modern system programming language designed for performance and safety, especially safe concurrency
SCM	Source Control Management
SDK	Software Development Kit
SFF	Small Form Factor
SMBUS	System Management Bus
SoC	System on Chip
SSH	Secure Shell
SVN	Subversion
SW-DP	Serial Wire Debug Port
SWD	Serial Wire Debug
SWJ-DP	Serial Wire/JTAG Debug Port
TTM	Time-To-Market
TXT	Trusted eXecution Technology
u-bmc	An open source firmware for baseboard management controllers
UEFI	Unified Extensible Firmware Interface

UPD   Updatable Product Data; a data structure that holds configuration regions that are part of the FSP binary

VBE   VESA BIOS Extensions

VBIOS   Video BIOS; used to program either onboard graphics or discrete graphics card and is specific to the device manufacturer

VCS   Version Control System

VESA   Video Electronics Standards Association

VFR   Visual Forms Representation

VNC   Virtual Network Computing

WinDbg   Windows Debugger

XDP   eXtended Debug Port

XIP   eXecute-In-Place

ZBL   Zeroth Stage Boot Loader; an SoC bootloader for RISC-V that loads an ODM/OEM bootloader from the SPI Flash

Reference

Websites

Coredna. *What is Open Source Software?,* Comparing open source software and closed source software (introduction): `https://www.coredna.com/blogs/comparing-open-closed-source-software`

GCFGlobal. *Open source vs. closed source software,* Understanding different types of computer software (Chapter 1): `https://edu.gcfglobal.org/en/basic-computer-skills/open-source-vs-closed-source-software/1/`

Wikipedia. *Comparison of open-source and closed-source software,* Understanding different types of computer software (Chapter 1): `https://en.wikipedia.org/wiki/Comparison_of_open-source_and_closed-source_software`

Wikipedia. *Intelligent Platform Management Interface,* Understanding IPMI interface specifications that provide management and monitoring capabilities independently of the host system software (Chapter 1): `https://en.wikipedia.org/wiki/Intelligent_Platform_Management_Interface`

OpenBMC: A Linux Foundation Project. *OpenBMC Github,* Steps to access OpenBMC code repository (Chapter 1): `https://github.com/openbmc/openbmc`

Intel Corporation. *EC FW application modules,* Zephyr-based embedded controller firmware documentation (Chapter 1): `https://intel.github.io/ecfw-zephyr/reference/modules.html`

© Subrata Banik and Vincent Zimmer 2022
S. Banik and V. Zimmer, *Firmware Development,*
https://doi.org/10.1007/978-1-4842-7974-8

REFERENCE

Intel Corporation. *Microchip MEC15xx modular embedded control card (MECC),* The reference hardware used to showcase EC FW open source (Chapter 1): `https://intel.github.io/ecfw-zephyr/reference/supported_hw.html`

Jessie Frazelle. *Open-source Firmware,* Open-source firmware step into the world behind the kernel (Chapter 1): `https://queue.acm.org/detail.cfm?id=3349301`

UEFI org. *Embedded Controller Interface Description,* ACPI_Embedded_Controller_Interface_Specification (Chapter 1): `https://uefi.org/specs/ACPI/6.4/12_ACPI_Embedded_Controller_Interface_Specification/embedded-controller-interface-description.html`

Weibeld net. *Smartphone Modem Access with AT Commands,* Explaining what AT commands are and how they can be used to issue direct commands to the baseband processor of a smartphone (Chapter 1): `https://weibeld.net/mobcom/at-commands.html`

Aspeed. *AST2500,* ASPEED's sixth-generation server management processor (Chapter 1): `https://www.aspeedtech.com/server_ast2500/`

Jordan Mulcare. *Baseboard management controller solution is cost-effective,* Understanding the cost effective solution of BMC (Chapter 1): `https://www.electronicspecifier.com/products/boards-and-backplanes/baseboard-management-controller-solution-is-cost-effective`

Inspur Electronic Information Industry Co., Ltd. *NF5280M5 Product Technical White Paper,* The Inspur Yingxin NF5280M5 server is dedicated toward meeting Internet, Internet Data Center (IDC), cloud computing, enterprise markets, and telecommunications application requirements (Chapter 1): `https://www.inspur.com/eportal/fileDir/defaultCurSite/resource/cms/2020/04/2020040211224398612.pdf`

Matthew Lee, Intel Corporation. *White Paper: Embedded Controller Usage in Low Power Embedded Designs,* This white paper is intended to give readers an overview of embedded controller usage (Chapter 1):

https://www.intel.com/content/dam/www/public/us/en/documents/white-papers/controller-usage-low-power-designs-paper.pdf

NXP. *Zephyr™ OS for Edge Connected Devices,* The Zephyr Project strives to deliver the best-in-class RTOS for connected resource-constrained devices, built to be secure and safe (Chapter 1): https://www.nxp.com/design/software/embedded-software/zephyr-os-for-edge-connected-devices:ZEPHYR-OS-EDGE

Mazen Gedeon and Anas Nashif, Intel Corporation. *Zephyr™ OS on Embedded Controller,* open source embedded controller firmware development with the Zephyr OS (Chapter 1): https://zephyrproject.org/open-source-embedded-controller-firmware-development-with-the-zephyr-os/

Maurice Ma, Intel Corporation. *Python Setup Browser for UEFI VFR,* Demonstrate how to convert the UEFI VFR setup into YAML format and browse setup options on target or host (Chapter 2): https://github.com/mauricema/uefi_vfr_cfg

Slim Bootloader. *SBL Configuration,* Slim Bootloader Open Source Project (version 1.0) documentation (Chapter 2): https://slimbootloader.github.io/developer-guides/configuration.html

Susan Potter. *Gerrit vs. Github,* Highlighting code review and codebase management differences between Gerrit and GitHub (Chapter 3): https://gist.github.com/mbbx6spp/70fd2d6bf113b87c2719

OpenGenus Foundation. *Gerrit vs. GitHub vs. GitLab,* Understanding the advantages of Gerrit as compared to GitHub and GitLab (Chapter 3): https://iq.opengenus.org/gerrit-vs-github-vs-gitlab/

Atlassian. *Git Tutorials,* Learn Git with Bitbucket Cloud (Chapter 3): https://www.atlassian.com/git/tutorials/learn-git-with-bitbucket-cloud

Atlassian. *Version Control for Beginners,* Explaining what version control is (Chapter 3): https://www.atlassian.com/git/tutorials/what-is-version-control

REFERENCE

Beepsend. *Understanding Gerrit,* Abandoning Gitflow and GitHub in favor of Gerrit (Chapter 3): `https://www.beepsend.com/2016/04/05/abandoning-gitflow-github-favour-gerrit/`

GeeksforGeeks. *Open-Source Version Control Tools,* Top five free and open source version control tools (Chapter 3): `https://www.geeksforgeeks.org/top-5-free-and-open-source-version-control-tools-in-2020/`

DevMountain. *Git vs. GitHub*, Understanding the difference between Git and GitHub (Chapter 3): `https://blog.devmountain.com/git-vs-github-whats-the-difference/`

Intel Corporation. *Power Management Controller Debugging,* Debug methodology for low-power platform state using power management controller (PMC) core driver and telemetry driver (Chapter 4): `https://01.org/blogs/2019/using-power-management-controller-drivers-debug-low-power-platform-states`

Maxim Goryachy, Mark Ermolov, HITBSecConf 2017 CommSec, Amsterdam. *Intel DCI Secrets*, x86 hardware debugging (Chapter 4): `https://conference.hitb.org/hitbsecconf2017ams/materials/D2T4%20-%20Maxim%20Goryachy%20and%20Mark%20Ermalov%20-%20Intel%20DCI%20Secrets.pdf`

ARM Limited. *Debugger usage on Armv8-A,* Learn the architecture: debugger usage on Armv8-A (Chapter 4, System Debugging): `https://developer.arm.com/documentation/102140/latest/Program-load`

Asmita Jha. *IoT Security,* hardware attack surface: JTAG, SWD (Chapter 4): `https://payatu.com/blog/asmita-jha/hardware-attack-surface-jtag-swd`

Kudelski Security Research, *SWD – ARM'S ALTERNATIVE TO JTAG,* Understanding the ARM Debug Interface (Chapter 4): `https://research.kudelskisecurity.com/2019/05/16/swd-arms-alternative-to-jtag/`

Universal Scalable Firmware. *Linux Payload,* To build a basic Linux payload conforming to universal payload standard (Chapter 6): `https://github.com/UniversalScalableFirmware/linuxpayload`

Coreboot GitHub. *Starting from scratch,* A document for how to build coreboot (Chapter 6): `https://doc.coreboot.org/tutorial/part1.html`

References for Chapter 5

UEFI. *Getting a Handle on Firmware Security,* A document to explain why Firmware is an easy target for attacker: `https://uefi.org/sites/default/files/resources/Getting%20a%20Handle%20on%20Firmware%20Security%2011.11.17%20Final.pdf`

Cybersecurity Dive. *A security expert's guide to the top-exploited vulnerabilities,* The biggest and baddest ransomware groups love an easy vulnerability: `https://www.cybersecuritydive.com/news/CISA-CVE-most-common-vulnerability-2020-2021-ransomware/604426/`

Kim Zetter. *Inside the Cunning, Unprecedented Hack of Ukraine's Power Grid,* The hack on Ukraine's power grid was a first-of-its-kind attack that sets an ominous precedent for the security of power grids everywhere: `https://www.wired.com/2016/03/inside-cunning-unprecedented-hack-ukraines-power-grid/`

Naked Security. *HP LaserJet printers at risk of fiery hacker attack,* A study discovered a security vulnerability in "tens of millions" of HP LaserJet printers that could allow a remote hacker to install malicious firmware: `https://nakedsecurity.sophos.com/2011/11/29/hp-laserjet-printers-at-risk-of-fiery-hacker-attack/`

Books, Conferences, Journals, and Papers

- M. Howard and S. Lipner, *The Security Development Lifecycle,* Redmond, WA, USA: Microsoft Press, 2006.

REFERENCE

- S. Myagmar, A. J. Lee, and W. Yurcik, "Threat modeling as a basis for security requirements," in Symposium on Requirements Engineering for Information Security, 2005, pp. 1–8.

- Varghese and A. K. Bose, "Threat modeling of industrial controllers: A firmware security perspective," *2014 International Conference on Anti-Counterfeiting, Security and Identification (ASID)*, 2014, pp. 1–4, doi: 10.1109/ ICASID.2014.7064951.

Index

A

B

© Subrata Banik and Vincent Zimmer 2022
S. Banik and V. Zimmer, *Firmware Development*,
https://doi.org/10.1007/978-1-4842-7974-8

H

Printed in the United States
by Baker & Taylor Publisher Services